BETWEEN
RISING
POWERS

The **Institute of Southeast Asian Studies (ISEAS)** was established as an autonomous organization in 1968. It is a regional research centre dedicated to the study of socio-political, security and economic trends and developments in Southeast Asia and its wider geostrategic and economic environment.

The Institute's research programmes are the Regional Economic Studies (RES, including ASEAN and APEC), Regional Strategic and Political Studies (RSPS), and Regional Social and Cultural Studies (RSCS).

ISEAS Publishing, an established academic press, has issued more than 2,000 books and journals. It is the largest scholarly publisher of research about Southeast Asia from within the region. ISEAS Publishing works with many other academic and trade publishers and distributors to disseminate important research and analyses from and about Southeast Asia to the rest of the world.

BETWEEN RISING POWERS

China, Singapore and India

ASAD-UL IQBAL LATIF

LSEAS

INSTITUTE OF SOUTHEAST ASIAN STUDIES

Singapore

First published in Singapore in 2007 by
ISEAS Publishing
Institute of Southeast Asian Studies
30 Heng Mui Keng Terrace
Pasir Panjang
Singapore 119614

E-mail: publish@iseas.edu.sg
Website: <http://bookshop.iseas.edu.sg>

The responsibility for facts and opinions in this publication rests exclusively with the author and his interpretations do not necessarily reflect the views or the policies of ISEAS or its supporters.

ISEAS Library Cataloguing-in-Publication Data

Latif, Asad-ul Iqbal.
   Between rising powers : China, Singapore and India.
   1. Singapore—Foreign relations—China.
   2. China—Foreign relations—Singapore.
   3. Singapore—Foreign relations—India.
   4. India—Foreign relations—Singapore.
   5. Singapore—Foreign relations
   6. China—Foreign relations— Southeast Asia.
   7. Southeast Asia—Foreign relations—China.
   8. India—Foreign relations— Southeast Asia.
   9. Southeast Asia—Foreign relations—India.
   I. Title
DS610.47 C5L35   2007

ISBN 978-981-230-413-1 (soft cover)
ISBN 978-981-230-414-8 (hard cover)
ISBN 978-981-230-517-8 (PDF)

Typeset by Superskill Graphics Pte Ltd
Printed in Singapore by Photoplates Pte Ltd

For
DR CHARLES LESLIE WAYPER
1912–2006
My Supervisor at Cambridge
and
MRS HILDA MARGARET WAYPER
1913–1983

Contents

Contents

Foreword

The rise of China and India has become an issue of global significance as we enter the 21st century. Concerns about Malthusian dilemmas, economic stagnation and weak governance of these countries clearly seem to have given way to debates on what the future holds for international politics involving China and India as responsible "stakeholders" of the international system. Singapore, with its pragmatic foreign policy driven by an unsentimental balance of power realism, is one of the most active players in the region trying to engage both powers. Singapore's important role in building stronger ties between the two countries and ASEAN has attracted considerable attention, especially as Singapore has played a major role in promoting preferential trading arrangements (free trade agreements) between ASEAN and both China and India. Singapore's vital role in ASEAN also means that both China and India are striving to have closer working relations with Singapore. This book is therefore an important and timely contribution to the debate on Singapore's emerging relationship with China and India.

Reflecting the title of the book, this work captures the essence of how Singapore is positioning itself between China and India. While Asad notes that Singapore's engagement of China is deeper, longer and more substantial, both New Delhi and Singapore are trying to enhance their relations with each other. The book provides a penetrating analysis of India's attempt to be a major player in the Southeast Asian region. While most academic writings on Singapore's relations with India and China tend to focus on the economic rationale of these relations, this book is one of the first attempts to outline both the political and military/defence aspects of their relations. Asad argues convincingly that these aspects are equally significant, if not more important than the economic relationship as Southeast Asia could be a theatre of competition between China and India as these two emerging powers expand their spheres of influence. He also predicts that the region could be a theatre for India to evolve new partnerships with China, thereby moving from the post-1962 policy of containment to co-engagement with China. Asad predicts that Singapore's relations with these two emerging powers will have important implications not only for the country but also for the larger ASEAN region.

Asad's work is an extremely important study that is filling a dearth in scholarship about Singapore's efforts to facilitate China and India's engagements with Southeast Asia. As such, it is a must read for scholars and policy-makers interested in the international politics of Southeast Asia, China and India. This important contribution will go a long way in providing new insights into the region's international politics. It is only with this enhanced understanding that we will be able to formulate new strategies of engagement and appropriate policies in dealing with the two rising Asian giants.

Barry Desker
Dean, S. Rajaratnam School of International Studies
Director, Singapore Institute of Defence and Strategic Studies
Singapore

Preface

Singapore is located at the southern end of the Straits of Malacca, the shortest sea route between China and India. Geography has moulded Singapore's self-definition much as it has shaped the contours of the rest of Southeast Asia: south of China, east of India. Placed within overlapping Sinic and Indic zones, Singapore's *entrepôt* role has served both. Today, as China and India emerge as rising powers, a port city is going beyond its trading role to engage them in political and security terms. This study examines how Singapore is positioning itself between China and India, two ancient entities rising simultaneously today. Singapore's engagement of China — like Beijing's contemporary engagement of Southeast Asia — is deeper, longer and more substantial than India's reach into the region. However, New Delhi is trying vigorously to make up for lost time. Its ties with Singapore are patently a part of that effort. The structure of this book, which treats Singapore's relations with China far more extensively than its relations with India, reflects the inherent asymmetry of the two Asian giants' contemporary interaction with the city-state and the region. However, this book examines how New Delhi is shaping up into a Southeast Asian player by extending its already preponderant influence in South Asia.

Much scholarly work now is focused on the economic rationale for the upswing in relations between a liberalizing India and a regionalizing Singapore, a development that replicates Singapore's economic *rapprochement* with China in the 1970s. However, the political and security aspects of the city-state's relations with the two regional powers are no less important because Southeast Asia is a part of the theatre of engagement between Beijing and New Delhi, a theatre that offers India a potential role as a counterweight to China. Singapore's pivotal position at the intersection of the two powers' emerging influence gives it an importance larger than would be suggested by its miniscule size. Singapore is important, too, to Japan and Russia, but these two existing great powers are outside the scope of this study, which focuses on the new gravitational orbit created by rising powers China and India. Singapore's relations with the two countries have implications not only for itself but for the region. This is a study of the evolution of those relations.

This work essentially is an essay in diplomatic history premised on the idea that Singapore's foreign policy outlook reflects an unsentimental balance-of-power realism nuanced by an emphasis on liberal internationalism in its pursuit of economic security. This study of Singapore's efforts to facilitate China's and India's engagement of Southeast Asia shows how a city-state is responding to the emergence of the two great powers.

Asad-ul Iqbal Latif
Institute of Southeast Asian Studies
Singapore
31 December 2006

Acknowledgements

This book is the outcome of a research project at the Institute of Southeast Asian Studies (ISEAS), where I work as a Visiting Research Fellow. I am indebted to Mr K. Kesavapany, the Director of ISEAS, and Dr Chin Kin Wah, the Deputy Director, for supporting this project. Dr David Koh, Coordinator of the Regional Strategic and Political Studies Programme under which the project falls, helped me with advice on the importance of structure in a book's value and appeal. Mr Verghese Mathews, Mr Mark Hong and Mr Sudhir Devare, three of my colleagues at ISEAS, shared with me their insights into how international relations are conducted and how the great issues of war and peace are decided for generations to come. Another person from whom I learnt a great deal is Mr Lee Khoon Choy, the veteran politician, diplomat and former Senior Minister of State who organized the groundbreaking trips made by the Republic's leaders to China from 1975 to 1980. Mrs Y.L. Lee, ISEAS' Head of Administration, and Mrs Christina Goh, the Personal Assistant to the Director, were unfailing sources of help in matters administrative and more. Mrs Triena Ong, Managing Editor of ISEAS' Publications Unit, ensured the manuscript's smooth and speedy transition to a book, which has benefited from the Production Editor, Ms Fatanah Sarmani's unerring eye for detail. I am grateful to all of them.

Outside ISEAS, I benefited from the intellectual climate created by the presence of distinguished scholars in the universities, think-tanks and research institutes: Dean Barry Desker of the S. Rajaratnam School of International Studies, who kindly has contributed this book's Foreword; Professor Wang Gungwu and Professor John Wong of the East Asian Institute; Dean Kishore Mahbubani of the Lee Kuan Yew School of Public Policy; Professor Tommy Koh and Mr Arun Mahizhnan of the Institute of Policy Studies; Mr Gopinath Pillai and Professor Tan Tai Yong of the Institute of South Asian Studies; and Professor Simon S.C. Tay of the Singapore Institute of International Affairs. I also wish to thank the anonymous reviewers who read the manuscript and reverted with their criticism, praise and suggestions for change. I have incorporated their recommendations wherever possible, as a result of which this book is much better than the manuscript that it began life as. However, I solely am responsible for any errors or faults that might remain.

Dr Charles Leslie Wayper, who supervised both my M.Phil. and my M. Litt. theses at Cambridge University, passed away in early 2006. He always had more concern for his students' books than for his own. To him, and to his wife, Mrs Hilda Margaret Wayper, this book is dedicated in gratitude and remembrance.

About the Author

Asad-ul Iqbal Latif is a Visiting Research Fellow at the Institute of Southeast Asian Studies. His areas of research include Singapore's political and strategic relations with China, India and the United States. He graduated with Honours in English from Presidency College, Calcutta, and received his Master of Letters degree in History at Cambridge University, where he was Raffles (Chevening) and S. Rajaratnam Scholar. He was a member of the president's committee of the Cambridge Union Society, the university debating club, and a member of the editorial committee of the *Cambridge Review of International Affairs*. He was a Fulbright Visiting Scholar at Harvard University's Weatherhead Center for International Affairs in 2006. A journalist before joining ISEAS, he worked at *The Statesman* in Calcutta, *Asiaweek* in Hongkong, and *The Business Times* and *The Straits Times* in Singapore. He was a Jefferson Fellow at the East-West Center in Hawaii in Spring 2001.

CHAPTER I

INTRODUCTION
Soundings from History

An extraordinary display of discord erupted between China and Singapore in July 2004, when Lee Hsien Loong paid a private visit to Taiwan shortly before becoming the city-state's Prime Minister. Beijing responded with almost visceral asperity to the visit, saying that it had violated Singapore's commitment to the one-China policy and had hurt China's core interests. China followed up its words with punitive action, cancelling bilateral visits and exchanges and threatening to delay talks on a bilateral free trade agreement. Beijing was mollified only after Singapore emphasized its support for the one-China policy and its opposition to Taiwanese independence.[1] What was astonishing about the dispute was China's vehement denunciation of a Taiwan visit by the leader-designate of a sovereign nation whose troops actually trained in Taiwan. The Chinese response prompted Eric Teo Chu

Cheow to place the pique in historical perspective.[2] According to him, Beijing's ire went beyond the Taiwan visit and expressed its frustration over what it saw as Singapore's increasing tilt towards the United States at a time when China was wary of America's intentions. Among the signs of the apparent tilt were Singapore's "eagerness" to sign a free trade agreement with Washington in the midst of the American invasion and occupation of Iraq, "for which Singapore pledged support for the US-led coalition in Iraq"; and Singapore's support for an American proposal to send its troops to help patrol the Malacca Straits, which "shocked" the Chinese. Certain quarters in Beijing saw Singapore as participating in a pro-US and anti-Chinese coalition of countries such as Japan, Taiwan, and South Korea that were forming a *de facto* arc of containment against China. The "mentality behind China's ancient tributary system seems to be bearing out on certain recent geo-political trends emanating from China", Teo argues, mentioning Beijing's desire to reduce America's influence in the Asia-Pacific and advance its own vision of Asian regionalism by excluding the United States from the region, which "Beijing may once again consider its own 'backyard' ". Teo views Beijing's "charm offensive" towards Singapore's neighbours as being among its moves to "pacify" China's immediate region, "as in the old days of China's imperial tributary system under the Ming and Qing Emperors". Teo's use of an historical analogy suggests that China's imperial past remains a framework by which current events might be judged. He is not alone. Positing an intriguing historical analogy, another scholar argues that the evocative image of China's desire for a free trade agreement with the Association of Southeast Asian Nations (ASEAN) being a modern-day tributary system may be an exaggeration, but seeing in it the economic statecraft of China's strategy of peaceful ascendancy is historically apt.[3]

Does history have a message?

PAX SINICA?

That history helps in the analysis of contemporary international behaviour hardly is a novel idea. As Adda B. Bozeman notes in *Politics and Culture in International History*, knowledge of the meanings which a nation traditionally has attached to keywords such as peace, war and freedom, or what other values and institutions it has prized, helps to assess "the authenticity and worth of presently existing international arrangements and assumptions".[4] In that spirit have appeared attempts to apply a study of China's past to international relations. Notable among them is Alastair Iain Johnston's theoretical work, *Cultural Realism: Strategic Culture and Grand Strategy in Chinese History*.[5] Focusing on the Ming dynasty's grand strategy against the Mongols (1368–1644), Johnston reads ancient military texts as sources of Chinese strategic culture to ask whether they speak of a single strategic culture. He goes on to study the effect of the strategic culture on Ming decision-making, and shows what effect strategic preferences had on Ming policies towards the Mongols. One conclusion that can be drawn from his work is that the realist strand running through the classics helps to explain why the Chinese have been no less apt to use force than any other civilization. More recently, Martin Stuart-Fox has made a case for treating seriously patterns of Chinese behaviour in the past in assessing its likely actions now. Drawing on the constructivist concepts of "regimes" and "strategic culture", which acknowledge the role that ideas, norms and expectations play in international relations, he uses two conceptual tools to underscore the importance of worldviews in determining how states act. The first tool is "foreign relations culture", which refers to "the assumptions embodied in worldview in relation to which polities (today nation-states) understand and conduct their relations with other polities"; and the second tool is the "bilateral relations regime", which refers to "the compromise set of (often implicit) norms, understandings and procedures which two polities come to accept in conducting relations with each other".[6] These two conceptual tools enable scholars to understand why relations between China and Southeast Asia historically took the form that they did.[7] To another scholar, the return of traditional culture as an explanation of the Chinese theory and practice of international relations lies in the gradual erosion of Marxism as a source of action.[8]

References to the tributary system in the context of China's expanding economic links with Southeast Asia are particularly sensitive given the controversial system's role in China's relations with pre-colonial Southeast Asia and, by implication, its putative role today. Martin Stuart-Fox's conceptualization of the tributary system suggests that it was more a ritualized mechanism of trade than a reflection of China's colonial designs on Southeast Asia. Tribute, for the Chinese, entailed not the transfer of wealth but "symbolic submission", it being well known that the tributary states received gifts that were more valuable than the tribute they offered. The tributary system allowed China to uphold the fiction that it could do without the support of anything material from the barbarians, all it sought being the symbolic acknowledgement of the Middle

Kingdom's status in a Sino-centric world order.[9] Southeast Asian rulers, on their part, saw the tribute as an exchange of gifts, a polite formality that accompanied lucrative trade relations.[10]

However, the tributary system, whose majestic sweep was dramatized by the Ming dynasty voyages of Admiral Zheng He into the South China Sea and across the Indian Ocean to the shores of East Africa, has come under the scrutiny of scholars whose work is becoming a part of the international debate, now more than three decades old, over the implications of China's rise for the world, particularly Asia. A paper by Geoff Wade, "Ming China and Southeast Asia in the 15th Century", sharpens the edges of that debate by characterizing the maritime expedition, which is celebrated in Chinese scholarship today as voyages of friendship, as having acted in reality "mainly as a military force in an attempt to impose a *pax Ming* on what we now know as Southeast Asia and the Indian Ocean".[11] Emphasizing the military nature of the voyages, Wade notes that the large force "would have played a major threatening role, useful in encouraging recalcitrant foreign rulers to travel to the Ming court".[12] When military threat proved insufficient, violence followed.[13] Wade cites other uncomfortable aspects of Ming policy by examining the "colonial processes" which turned formerly non-Chinese polities into Chinese regions during that era;[14] Ming China's strategy of divide-and-rule to break down major polities into smaller units whose rivalry would reduce their threat to China;[15] the "economic exploitation" of frontier polities;[16] and Ming encouragement of the movement of Chinese people into newly-conquered areas.[17] In another paper, Wade employs a close reading of the *Ming Shi-lu* annals to assert powerfully that "most of the rhetoric centring on China's 'civilising' role and most of the actions taken on this basis, were intended to validate and assist Chinese political expansion and assimilation".[18] In yet another paper, Wade characterizes Ming hegemony as having produced "proto maritime colonialism", not full-fledged control of territory but political and economic control of ports and trade routes along the major East-West maritime trade network along with the seas between.[19] This approach was a prelude to what the Portuguese did in the 16th century.[20]

Wade's thesis has been attacked by Tan Ta Sen, President of the International Zheng He Society in Singapore, who disagrees with the notion that the admiral was a colonist whose foray into Southeast Asia foreshadowed the Western incursion into the region a century later. Apart from challenging some of Wade's specific assertions, such as the nature and degree of military action that accompanied the voyages, Tan contends that with such a large fleet, Zheng He could have embarked on conquest, but he did not do so, instead helping small states to defeat invasion and crush rebellion.[21] The reason for the absence of a colonial mindset in China, Tan avers, is that unlike the commercial and industrialized West, the Ming Dynasty was an agrarian economy that had no need to seize others' natural resources, markets and manpower and turn countries into colonies. As for vassal states, they indeed were obliged to pay tributes "but *nothing* would happen to them if they failed to send tributary missions".[22]

That China's relations with Southeast Asia were imperial, *qua* Wade, is undeniable. But whether they were proto-colonial, or colonial in their essence, is debatable. Here, particularly in assessing the implications of China's rise for Southeast Asia's future, it is important to remember the nuanced observations of Wang Gungwu,[23] whose contribution on Ming relations with Southeast Asia to *The Chinese World Order: Traditional China's Foreign Relations*[24] was an early intervention in a debate that is becoming increasingly acrimonious today. In one of his latest forays into the scholarly conflict over China's rise, he cautions against automatically attributing historical bad faith to Chinese aspirations today. Wang notes that after three decades of Zheng He's "exceptional" voyages, the Ming emperors returned to the control of traditional lands and forbade foreign adventures. "The Ming reaffirmed what had distinguished the Chinese historic empire for more than a thousand years: its self-centredness and its belief in its invulnerability and self-sufficiency."[25] The danger, Wang argues, lies not in China's worldview emanating from its own history but in a strand of modern Chinese historiography which, influenced by the study of modern Western history, has sought to reinterpret the notion of empire to draw comparisons with European empires in Asia. Wang writes: "One of the consequences of this reinterpretation was to cast the tributary system in an unhistorical frame, one that tended to match tributary states with European colonies even though the Chinese had not conquered or governed any of the states outside imperial borders."[26] A study of the tributary relationships reveals that "there was really no Chinese empire outside Chinese lands, and the self-perception of historic empire is misleading, if not actually false".[27] Wang declares that, today, there is no place for an historic empire or a tributary system. Placing fears expressed in the context of speculations about Greater China in comparative perspective, he recalls fears about the Japanese empire, which, "having failed to achieve its Greater Asian Co-Prosperity Sphere as a framework for its imperial ambitions, then used its economic power to bring it about. Is this what China might do?... If so, it would be a new phenomenon having little to do with the historic dynastic empires of the past".[28] Reiterating the point that it is not China's past that is worrying but how it might respond to what other countries are doing in the present, he writes: "What would be new and alarming to the region would be a modernized China finding that it has to behave like the modern great powers of the West."[29] Wang's point is that Europe's past does not have to be China's future.

But other scholars like David C. Kang go further — or backwards, depending on one's point of view — by seeking in China's past Asia's future. Kang's premise is that relations in East Asia historically have been more peaceful and stable than those in the West. Arguing that a strong and stable China preserved hierarchical order, he juxtaposes the "considerable informal equality" that prevailed in this order till the intrusion of the Western powers in the 19th century. Those powers represent a Western tradition of international relations consisting of formal equality among nation-states but informal hierarchy and nearly constant conflict among states.[30]

Drawing lessons from that Sino-centric Asian order, he notes that Southeast Asian countries are not forming a balance against China today.[31] "There is likely to be far more stability in Asia — and more bandwagoning with China — than balance of power theorists expect," he declares,[32] adding that Asian countries "may not make the choice that many Westerners assume they will" if forced to choose between the United States and China.[33] "Superficially" Westphalian Asian countries, which have not undergone the same process of development as the West and have historical and cultural traditions different from those of the West, do not necessarily function like Western states.[34]

In a robust response to Kang, Amitav Acharya argues that Asia has no need to revert to the hierarchy of a Chinese-ordered past to find its way out of the insecurities of a post-colonial order centred in the West. "Asia's future will not resemble its past. Instead of sliding into anarchy or organizing itself into a pre-Westphalian hierarchy, Asia is increasingly able to manage its insecurity through shared regional norms, rising economic interdependence, and growing institutional linkages."[35] Disputing Kang's suggestion of a benevolent China keeping the regional peace, Acharya argues that the Asian order did not depend on any "intrinsic Chinese tendency for peaceful management of its relations with neighbours" because Chinese policy was driven by *realpolitik*. Then, unlike the past when China was the "only available power that its neighbours could turn to if they had to seek security against their rivals", there are relatively powerful players in Asia today. There can be no bandwagoning in Asia, and hence no East Asian hierarchy, without China "usurping or balancing" U.S. power, in which case there would be greater competition and rivalry that would produce the instability that would undermine Kang's "optimism about Asia's security order",[36] Acharya declares, drawing attention to the balance of power choices that Asian countries, like others, can make. Importantly, Acharya notes, China itself does not speak about Sino-centric or tributary systems, preferring, instead, the language of Westphalia.[37] He warns against using scenarios based on cultural historicist arguments because important "structural and normative differences" between the past and the present obstruct Asia's return to a neo-Confucian order.[38] In fact, Acharya argues, Indian ideas were far more important "catalysts of cultural and political interaction and change" in Southeast Asia than ideas from classical China, whose ideational leadership of the region did not go beyond Vietnam.[39] In a pointed rejoinder to Kang's argument that no Asian power is trying to balance China, Acharya avers that India is balancing China and that ASEAN recognizes India's role as a potential counterweight to any threat from China down the road.[40]

This declaration draws attention to India's role in the region today — and the past that lies behind a revitalized role.

PAX INDICA?

The tributary system was the material expression of a Chinese cosmology in which the Mandate of Heaven made the Emperor the interface between Heaven and Earth, he being both the Son of Heaven and the ruler of the Middle Kingdom. For most of the two millennia of Chinese relations with Southeast Asia, until the 19th century, dealings between them were conducted on the basis of this Sino-centric world order.

India was different. In the classic formulation of G. Coedes in *The Indianized States of Southeast Asia*, Indians, unlike Chinese, "nowhere engaged in military conquest and annexation in the name of a state or mother country". The Indian kingdoms that emerged in "Farther India" enjoyed only ties of tradition with Indian dynasties; there was no political dependence.[41] One form which India's relationship with Southeast Asia took was the transmission of the notion of the *mandala*, a Sanskrit term featured in Indian manuals of governance that demarcated the power of kings in terms of circles forming around them. O.W. Wolters reads the map of early Southeast Asia as a patchwork of often overlapping *mandalas*. While, in theory, a king imbued with divine and universal authority claimed hegemony over other rulers in his *mandala* who were his allies and vassals, in practice, the *mandala* represented "an often unstable political situation in a vaguely defined geographical area without fixed boundaries". Smaller centres tended to look in all directions for security as the spheres expanded or contracted. Each *mandala* contained tributary rulers among whom some would repudiate their vassalage when opportunity arrived and embark on building up their own set of vassals. The *mandala* system did not stop war, but victories rarely obliterated local centres, whether by colonization or through the power of centralized institutions of government.[42]

Acharya makes a convincing case for treating the *mandala* system as one of the sources of contemporary Southeast Asia's regional state-system, two other sources being Stanley Tambiah's notion of a "galactic polity" and Clifford Geertz's "theatre state" in Bali.[43] "And just as the *mandala*, the galactic polity and the theatre state could be the basis of an imagined Southeast Asian community during the classical period, the 'ASEAN Way' has been at the core of efforts to build a Southeast Asian regional identity in the modern era," Achaya argues.[44]

Compelling as Acharya's argument is, India's peacefully relaxed pre-colonial relations with Southeast Asia need to be put in the context of how the country's own history has shaped its conception of national security and influenced its regional relations. Providing this perspective is the objective of a study on whether a rising India will follow the pattern of rising great powers by attempting hegemony in its region.[45] Manjeet Singh Pardesi conceptually bases his study on four questions whose answers reveal a state's grand strategy: What are the state's national objectives? What is the international system within which the state pursues these objectives? What are the available grand strategic means? What grand strategic ends does the state seek? He answers these questions for India by applying to his analysis the record of five pan-Indian powers: the Mauryas, the Guptas, the Mughals, British India and the Republic of India. Pardesi draws his idea of pan-Indian powers from Joseph W. Schwartzberg's analytical division of the subcontinent into five geographic regions: Northwest, North Centre, Northeast, West and South.[46] Schwartzberg defines as pan-Indian those powers whose reach extended over significant portions of at least four of the five regions, including areas lying both north and south of the Vindhya-Satpura Range. In this conceptual scheme, there were nine pan-Indian powers: the Mauryas, Guptas, Rashtrakutas, Khaljis, Tughluqs, Mughals, Marathas, British India and the Republic of India. Pardesi excludes from his study the Rashtrakutas, Khaljis, Tughluqs and the Marathas primarily because of the brevity of their rule.[47] In his analysis of his five chosen pan-Indian powers, he finds a remarkable degree of continuity in state behaviour. The continuity ranges from a realist drive to maximize power by using force when necessary "under the veneer of morality"; and an attempt to seek strategic autonomy by trying to establish hegemony in the subcontinent; to treating warfare as an intrinsic part of statecraft, but with a tendency to dominate, assimilate or accommodate opponents instead of destroying them. Then, the pan-

Indian powers displayed both a defensive strategic orientation against extra-regional powers and "offensive defence" in the subcontinent. Lastly, the pan-Indian powers adapted themselves gradually to changing political and military trends while behaving consistently in terms of the other trends.[48] Pardesi believes that a rising India will act in consonance with the "core features of the theory of offensive realism". It will seek hegemony in South Asia and the Indian Ocean, resist extra-regional influences there, and attempt to become an extra-regional power in the Middle East, Central Asia and Southeast Asia.[49]

What gives Pardesi's analysis its cutting edge is his reading of the behaviour of the Republic of India. Although, in dealing with its internal security problems, India's approach has been to seek political accommodation with restive groups within a secular and democratic framework, it has not been shy to use force, as in Punjab, Jammu and Kashmir and northeast India. These expressions of state policy follow on from other Indian actions, such as when, early into independence, India forcibly annexed the princely state of Hyderabad in 1948, and incorporated the state of Goa and the former Portuguese colonies of Daman and Diu through military means in 1960. Then, India practised "offensive defence" in the Bangladesh War of 1971 and in its military interventions in Sri Lanka and the Maldives in the 1980s (the latter two, though, by invitation from their governments). India "assimilated" Sikkim in 1975.[50] Apart from examples of "territorial expansion" and the use of force, Pardesi cities the presence of "protectorates" — India being the only Asian state that has underwritten the security of other states, these being Bhutan and Nepal — as evidence of Indian foreign and security policy upholding the main

tenets of offensive realism.[51] He also notes pointedly
that, after India's successful intervention in the East
Pakistan civil war that led to the dismemberment of
Pakistan and the emergence of Bangladesh in 1971,
India promulgated its own version of the Monroe
Doctrine. This "Indira Doctrine" asserted that South
Asian states facing domestic political problems should
first seek help within the subcontinent. Also, the
presence of an extra-regional power in the subcontinent
and/or the Indian Ocean region would be considered
adverse to India's security interests unless that power
recognized India's predominance.[52]

Pardesi's thesis is thought-provoking, but he pays
insufficient attention to transitions in Indian self-
perceptions, not least the Gujral Doctrine. In a bold
break with the Indira Doctrine, I.K. Gujral formulated,
first as Foreign Minister and then as Prime Minister,
five points premised on non-interference in the affairs
of India's neighbours and respect for their sovereignty.
Gujral declared in 1997: "The 'Gujral Doctrine', if I may
call it so, states that, first, with its neighbours like
Bangladesh, Bhutan, Maldives, Nepal and Sri Lanka,
India does not ask for reciprocity, but gives and
accommodates what it can in good faith and trust.
Second, we believe that no South Asian country should
allow its territory to be used against the interests of
another country of the region. Third, that none should
interfere in the internal affairs of another. Fourth, all
South Asian countries must respect each other's
territorial integrity and sovereignty. And finally, they
should settle all their disputes through peaceful bilateral
negotiations."[53] Taking into account the asymmetry
between India and its smaller neighbours, Gujral's
"accommodating bilateralism" endeavoured to meet
the "apprehensions and demands of its neighbours

without insisting on any reciprocity on their part, even if such reciprocity was required to meet India's interests".[54] Whether the Indira Doctrine or the Gujral Doctrine has had greater impact on Indian foreign policy-making is open to debate, but the point is that "offensive realism" is not the only strain in Indian diplomatic thinking that is relevant to its expected posture in Southeast Asia.

As with China, history provides a necessary backdrop to some of the latest developments on the foreign policy horizons of rising India. The United States has decided to help India become a major world power in the 21st century. Initiatives such as the Next Steps in Strategic Partnership, the U.S.-India Global Democratic Initiative, and the New Framework for the U.S.-India Defence Relationship attest to the comprehensive range of issues over which Washington and New Delhi are finding it possible to accommodate each other's interests. These are overarching issues as well: defeating terrorism, stopping nuclear proliferation, promoting democracy, and preserving a stable Asian balance of power. In assisting in the growth of India's global power, officials in the Administration of George W. Bush have said that they understand fully the military implications of their stance.[55] Indeed, Washington has agreed to supply New Delhi defence equipment that it refused to do in the past (although it is not immediately apparent how the supply would alter the existing balance of power), and it has set up a series of high-level strategic dialogues. The Indo-U.S. nuclear deal became law in the United States in December 2006.

Outside the Administration, former U.S. Secretary of State Henry Kissinger has declared as being compatible with American interests India's avowed desire to prevent another dominant power from emerging between Singapore and Aden.[56] In framing his remarks against the legacy of Britain's East of Suez policy, Kissinger has provided a fillip to Indian neo-Curzonians who see their strategic neighbourhood as stretching from West Asia to Southeast Asia.[57] Kissinger also expects India to conduct its strategic Aden-to-Singapore policy in China's neighbourhood.[58] East of Suez means precisely what it says.

Tempting as the prospects of this apparent outsourcing of America's hegemonic presence in southern Asia might be to some Indians, others believe that a replay of British India's imperial role would be anachronistic today. K. Subrahmanyam, for example, writes that that kind of thinking belongs to the 19th century, when the Royal Navy and the British Indian Army needed only to contend with "autocratic kings and sheikhs with armies of little competence" whom they coerced into accepting the arc of British supremacy from Aden to Singapore. Subrahmanyam recalls that during the Vietnam War, Kissinger himself envied the 19th century British for having had at their disposal the British Indian army to police the area from Aden to Singapore. But that era came to an end with decolonization and the rise of nationalism. "Vietnam, Afghanistan and now Iraq prove that the kind of overlordship the Royal Navy and the British Indian Army exercised over the arc from Aden to Singapore cannot be repeated in the 21st century," Subrahmanyam argues, adding: "Presumably Kissinger has lost sight of the fact that Singapore is now at the heart of a ten nation grouping — the ASEAN — which is wisely cultivating a multifaceted security relationship with all the major powers of the world."[59] At a conceptual level, what Wang Gungwu says about the dangers of misusing historiography in China applies to India as well. References to "Greater India", "Farther India" or "Hindu colonies in the Far East" are a case in point. Benudhar Patra cites a critique of the Greater India theory by H. Kulke and D. Rothermund, who argue that it was a by-product of the Indian freedom movement. In Kulke's and Rothermund's view, Indian historians "struggling under the stigma of their own colonial subjection tried to compensate for this by establishing the fact that even India was strong enough to establish colonies in ancient times".[60] India's rise *per se* is not a threat to Southeast Asia; a powerful India behaving like imperial Western powers and seeking to replicate the colonial regional order would be a different story. The reason would be less Indian history — two centuries of them colonized — and more any valorization of colonial Indian history as the template for the foreign relations of independent India today.

It is important to acknowledge the cautionary note about China and India struck in such studies because they offer at least a partial framework for assessing the prospects of these countries' relations with Singapore and the broader Southeast Asian region within which Singapore operates. International relations have a past, and historical analogies make their greatest impact when they occur at what might be turning points on the road ahead. At the beginning of the 21st century, Singapore is engaging two Asian powers with ancient living pasts. The histories of nations cannot be held against them, but nations can be held to their histories. It is this truth that lends a degree of contemporary astringency to Singapore's relations with two nations that are also civilizations that can reshape the course of Asian affairs in this century.

SINGAPORE IN HISTORY

The rise of the two Asian giants places in relief the contours of an island-state carved out by the cutting edges of maritime cycles of trade and conflict. Singapore was known to mariners as early as the 3rd century. By the 7th century, the Srivijaya empire, the first of the maritime states in the Malay archipelago, linked ports and cities along the coasts of Sumatra, Java and the Malay peninsula. Singapore was probably one of the outposts of Srivijaya, an *entrepôt* and supply point for Chinese, Thai, Javanese, Malay, Indian and Arab traders. According to an early chronicle which names the island Temasek, the city of Singapura — Lion City — was established there in 1299. Over the following three centuries, Singapore came under the sway of several regional powers, including the empires of Srivijaya, Majapahit and Ayuthhaya, and the Malacca and Johore sultanates. Its fortunes touched their nadir in 1613, when the Portuguese burnt down a trading post at the mouth of the Singapore River "and the curtain came down on the tiny island for two centuries".[61] Kwa Chong Guan therefore positions Singapore within the cycles of Asia's trading world, which he visualizes as natural economic zones in the Straits of Malacca in which a number of emporia competed to establish supremacy and form a *mandala*, or circle of kings, to control trade in the Malacca Straits. Part of that economic network was the Malay world spanning the Johore River, the Riau islands down Lingga and Singapore, which formed a "natural economic zone" from the 16th to the 18th centuries. Political and economic power in this zone shaped itself around a series of *istanas*, or palaces, which "shifted up and down" the Johore River and Bintan before moving to

Singapore in the 19th century.[62] In another account, 14th century Singapore lay at the margins of the Tai and Javanese *mandalas*. "The most that either of them demanded from Singapore was tribute. No foreign governors ruled this island till Raffles arrived, but politically Singapore may simultaneously have belonged to a mainland and an insular *mandala* or sphere of influence."[63] The evolution of Singapore's maritime role in Asia, interrupted by the Portuguese, was restored in 1819, when Stamford Raffles set up an outpost on the island to service the East India Company's China trade. Raffles created the template of a new island-economy.

Following two world wars, the Japanese Occupation, decolonization, Merger with the Malayan hinterland, and Separation from Malaysia, Singapore on its independence in 1965 resumed its position within the cycles of Asia's trading world. In doing so, it became a beneficiary of a maritime world order that had prevailed over a territorial one. This conclusion is suggested by a book published in the 1980s, when Richard Rosecrance viewed the geopolitical landscape since 1945 as being poised between two historical legacies: one, a territorial system of power that went back to the world view of Louis XIV and was presided over in the late 20th century by the Soviet Union and to some extent the United States; and the other legacy, an oceanic or trading system of power left as a legacy by Britain in the 1850s that had shaped itself around the Atlantic and Pacific Basins.[64] Actually, the "San Francisco System" — the interwoven strands of political-military and economic commitments among the US and its Pacific allies that were catalyzed by the San Francisco Peace Treaty process of 1950–51[65] — made a crucial contribution to the Pacific order from which Singapore benefited. The system enmeshed defeated Japan in a network of Washington-centred relationships that both protected Tokyo from Moscow and Beijing, and protected smaller countries that had been victims of Japanese wartime aggression from the strategic consequences of Japan's post-War economic rise. In obtaining security through prosperity, the system provided a trading city-state like Singapore with an incomparable opportunity to rejoin the international system that World War II had interrupted.

On independence, then, Singapore recovered its position as an island-economy that had been made, unmade and revived by seaborne cycles of time, trade and war. It resumed its historical role, one that now was empowered by sovereignty but one that also was made more precarious by the need to protect that sovereignty. Trade remained its rationale, but in order to preserve that rationale, it would have to ensure that the powers that mattered would have enough of a stake in the nascent nation-state to desire its survival and success. Suffering, as a trading emporium, from the "chronic fragility" of not having an agrarian base or large internal market,[66] it therefore reinvented itself as a Global City whose economic choices, and the political freedom to make those choices, would not be under the exclusive control of its immediate neighbours. "We draw sustenance not only from the region but also from the international economic system to which we as a Global City belong and which will be the final arbiter of whether we prosper or decline," Foreign Minister Sinnathamby Rajaratnam declared in 1972.

Singapore's self-perception as a global city sharpened its sense of the roles played by commerce and power in the destiny of nations. Out of that sense emerged an unsentimental attitude to the great powers that defined the choices of an island-city and city-state.

NOTES

1 "Singapore says it opposes Taiwan independence", *China Daily*, 12 July 2004; Jiang Zhuqing, "China: Lee's Taiwan visit damages relations", *China Daily*, 14 July 2004; and other sources.

2 Eric Teo Chu Cheow, "Rising Sino-US Rivalry — A Case in Point following the Recent Sino-Singaporean Row over Taiwan", *Taiwan Perspective e-Paper*, Issue No. 41 (Institute for National Policy Research, Taipei, 30 September 2004).

3 Vincent Wei-cheng Wang, "The Logic of China-ASEAN FTA: Economic Statecraft of 'Peaceful Ascendancy' ", in Ho Khai Leong and Samuel C.Y. Ku, eds., *China and Southeast Asia: Global Changes and Regional Challenges* (Singapore and Kaohsiung: Institute of Southeast Asian Studies and Center for Southeast Asian Studies, National Sun Yat-sen University, Kaohsiung, Taiwan ROC, 2005), p. 37.

4 Adda B. Bozeman, *Politics and Culture in International History* (Princeton: Princeton University Press, 1960), pp. 9–10.

5 Alastair Iain Johnston, *Cultural Realism: Strategic Culture and Grand Strategy in Chinese History* (Princeton: Princeton University Press, 1998). Tiejun Zhang argues, however, that traditional Chinese strategic culture was characterized primarily by "cultural moralism" and its contemporary version is marked by "defensive realism" that emphasizes material strength more than it does cultural and ideational preferences. See, "Chinese Strategic Culture: Traditional and Present Features", *Comparative Strategy* 21 (2002): 73.

6 Martin Stuart-Fox, "Southeast Asia and China: The Role of History and Culture in Shaping Future Relations", *Contemporary Southeast Asia* 26, no. 1 (2004): 122.

7 Ibid.

8 Wang Jisi, "International Relations Theory and the Study of Chinese Foreign Policy: A Chinese Perspective", in Thomas W. Robinson and David Shambaugh, eds., *Chinese Foreign Policy: Theory and Practice* (Oxford: Clarendon Press, 1994) cited in Gerald Chan, *Chinese Perspectives on International*

Relations: A Framework for Analysis (Houndmills and New York: Macmillan Press and St. Martin's Press, 1999), p. 57.

9 Martin Stuart-Fox, *A Short History of China and Southeast Asia: Tribute, Trade and Influence* (Crows Nest, NSW: Allen & Unwin), p. 33.

10 Ibid., pp. 33–34.

11 Geoff Wade, "Ming China and Southeast Asia in the 15th Century: A Reappraisal", Asia Research Institute, National University of Singapore, Working Paper Series Number 28 (July 2004): 13.

12 Ibid., p. 11.

13 Ibid.

14 Ibid., p. 17.

15 Ibid., p. 24.

16 Ibid., p. 29.

17 Ibid.

18 "The *Ming Shi-Lu* as a source for Southeast Asian History", <http://epress.nus.edu.sg/msl>, p. 28.

19 "The Zheng He Voyages: A Reassessment", Asia Research Institute, Working Paper Series Number 31 (October 2004): 18–19.

20 See Terence Tan, "Admiral Zheng He 'Set out to Colonize Southeast Asia' ", *Straits Times*, 11 November 2004.

21 Tan Ta Sen, "Did Zheng He Set Out to Colonize Southeast Asia?", in *Admiral Zheng He & Southeast Asia*, edited by Leo Suryadinata (Singapore: Institute of Southeast Asian Studies and International Zheng He Society, 2005), p. 50.

22 Ibid., p. 53. Author's emphasis.

23 Among his seminal writings are "Early Ming Relations with Southeast Asia: A Background Essay", in Wang Gungwu, *Community and Nation: China, Southeast Asia and Australia* (St Leonards, NSW: Asian Studies Association of Australia in association with Allen & Unwin, 1992), pp. 77–107; and "China and Southeast Asia 1402–1424", in the same volume, pp. 108–30. See also his "Ming Foreign Relations: Southeast Asia", in Wang Gungwu, *China and the Chinese Overseas* (Singapore: Times Academic Press, 1991), pp. 41–78.

24 John King Fairbank, ed., *The Chinese World Order: Traditional China's Foreign Relations* (Cambridge: Harvard University Press, 1968). Wang's background essay on early Ming relations with Southeast Asia appeared in this volume as well.

25 Wang Gungwu, *The Chinese Way: China's Position in International Relations* (Oslo: Scandinavian University Press, Norwegian Nobel Institute Lecture Series, 1995), p. 54.
26 Ibid., p. 56.
27 Ibid., p. 58.
28 Ibid., pp. 58–59.
29 Ibid., p. 69.
30 David C. Kang, "Getting Asia Wrong: The Need for New Analytical Frameworks", *International Security* 27, no. 4 (Spring 2003): 66–67.
31 Ibid., p. 82.
32 Ibid.
33 Ibid., p. 83.
34 Ibid., p. 84. Kang's ideas are encapsulated also in "Hierarchy and Stability in Asian International Relations", in G. John Ikenberry and Michael Mastanduno, eds., *International Relations Theory and the Asia-Pacific* (New York: Columbia University Press, 2003), pp. 163–89.
35 Amitav Acharya, "Will Asia's Past Be Its Future?", *International Security* 28, no. 3 (Winter 2003/04): 150.
36 Ibid., pp. 154–55.
37 Ibid., p. 156.
38 Ibid., p. 163.
39 Ibid., p. 156.
40 Ibid., pp. 150–51. Kang's rejoinder to Acharya, in the same issue of *International Security* is that "the notion of hierarchy is well established in the international relations literature, and balancing should not be the default hypothesis in international relations theory" (p. 173). Kang reiterates that other states accommodated China in the past, and that hierarchy existed in Asian international relations historically (p. 174). On Acharya's point that India is a balance to China, Kang remarks that although India is an important factor in South Asia, "the fact that China extends into two regions does not mean that the two regions are the same" (p. 179).
41 G. Coedes, in Walter F. Vella, ed., *The Indianized States of Southeast Asia*, translated by Susan Brown Cowing (Honolulu: University Press of Hawaii, 1968), p. 34. Among the leading proponents of the "Greater India" thesis was the Indian historian R.C. Majumdar. He describes how India's land and sea trade with the region developed into "regular colonization,

and Ind*ians established political* authority in various parts of
the vast Asiatic continent that lay to the south of China proper
and to the east and south-east of India". See, R.C. Majumdar,
India and South East Asia, edited by K.S. Ramachandran and
S.P. Gupta (Delhi: B.R. Publishing Corporation, 1979), p. 16.
But even as he acknowledges the thrust of Majumdar's thesis
on how Indian culture spread to Southeast Asia, Benudhar
Patra notes that the Greater India theory is not free from a
"chauvinistic approach". See, "Kalinga in South East Asia",
Orissa Reference Annual 2004, p. 160.

42 O.W. Wolters, *History, Culture, and Region in Southeast Asian
Perspectives*, revised edition (Ithaca, New York: Cornell
University, Southeast Asia Program Publications, in cooperation
with the Institute of Southeast Asian Studies, Singapore, 1999),
pp. 27–28.

43 Amitav Acharya, *The Quest for Identity: International Relations
of Southeast Asia* (Singapore: Oxford University Press, 2000),
p. 20. Religion, trade, colonization and war are other factors,
of course. Ibid., pp. 26–37.

44 Ibid., p. 29.

45 Manjeet Singh Pardesi, "Deducing India's Grand Strategy of
Regional Hegemony from Historical and Conceptual
Perspectives", Institute of Defence and Strategic Studies,
Singapore, Working Paper No. 76, April 2005.

46 Joseph E. Schwartzberg, *A Historical Atlas of South Asia*, second
imprint (Oxford: Oxford University Press, 1992).

47 Pardesi, op. cit., pp. 10–11.

48 Ibid., p. ii.

49 Ibid.

50 Ibid., pp. 33–34.

51 Ibid., p. 50.

52 Ibid., p. 41, citing Stephen P. Cohen, *India: Emerging Power*
(Washington, D.C.: Brookings Institution Press, 2001),
pp. 137–38.

53 I.K. Gujral, "Aspects of India's Foreign Policy", a speech
delivered at the Bandaranaike Centre for International Studies,
Colombo, 20 January 1997, <www.stimson.org/southasia/
?sn=sa20020116302>.

54 J.N. Dixit, *Makers of India's Foreign Policy: Raja Ram Mohun Roy
to Yashwant Sinha* (New Delhi: HarperCollins Publishers India
and The India Today Group, 2004), p. 220.

55 Ashley J. Tellis, "Indo-US Relations Headed for a Grand Transformation?", *YaleGlobal Online*, 14 July 2005, <http://yaleglobal.yale.edu/article.print?id=5999>.

56 *Indian Express*, 16 November 2004.

57 George Curzon, *The Place of India in the Empire: Being an Address before the Philosophical Institute of Edinburgh on October 19, 1909* (Elibron Classics, 2003), replica of 1909 edition by John Murray, London. For a study of Curzon's influence on Indian foreign policy thinking, see C. Raja Mohan, "Rediscovering Lord Curzon", in *Crossing the Rubicon: The Shaping of India's New Foreign Policy* (New Delhi: Penguin Books, 2005), pp. 204–36.

58 *Indian Express*, 16 November 2004.

59 "The Aden-Singapore illusion", *Indian Express*, 11 December 2004.

60 Patra, op. cit., p. 157.

61 This account of Singapore's history is drawn from the United States' Library of Congress Country Studies, <http://lcweb2.loc.gov/cgi-bin/query/r?frd/cstdy:@field(DOCID+sg0012)>.

62 Kwa Chong Guan, "Remembering Ourselves", in Kwok Kian-Woon et al., eds., *Our Place in Time: Exploring Heritage and Memory in Singapore* (Singapore: Singapore Heritage Society, 1999), pp. 56–57.

63 John Miksic, "Between Two Mandalas: Singapore, Siam, and Java", Benjamin Batson Memorial Lecture 2005, Asia Research Institute, Working Paper Series No. 51, September 2005, p. 59.

64 Richard Rosecrance, *The Rise of the Trading State: Commerce and Conquest in the Modern World* (New York: BasicBooks, 1986), p. 16.

65 Kent E. Calder, "Securing security through prosperity: The San Francisco System in comparative perspective", *Pacific Review* 17, no. 1 (March 2004): 136.

66 Philippe Regnier, *Singapore: City-State in South-East Asia* (London and Honolulu: C. Hurst & Company and University of Hawaii Press, 1991), p. 239.

CHAPTER II

ENGAGING
THE POWERS

Hedley Bull's *The Anarchical Society: A Study of Order in World Politics* is premised on the idea that states form a society without government. In citing that apparent paradox, Bull upholds the position of Hugo Grotius on international reality against the traditions of both Thomas Hobbes and Immanuel Kant. In the Hobbesian or realist tradition, international relations are defined by conflict between states, peace being but "a period of recuperation from the last war and preparation for the next". In the Kantian or universalist tradition, by contrast, humans seek companionship in transnational relationships, with the horizontal conflict of ideology between liberators and oppressed cutting across the boundaries of states and possessing the potential to sweep the system of states away.

In between these two grand extremes stands the Groatian or internationalist tradition, which argues that sovereigns or states are limited in their conflicts by common rules and institutions, but that they do not thereby lose their character as the principal players in international politics.[1] Between the nightmare of perpetual war in the making, and the dream of perpetual peace, intervenes the imperative of commerce. "The particular international activity which, on the Groatian view, best typifies international activity as a whole is neither war between states, nor horizontal conflict cutting across the boundaries of states, but trade — or, more generally, economic and social intercourse between one country and another."[2] Grotius' emphasis on the freedom of the seas is an early indication of the importance of trade in the proper functioning of the international system,[3] a leitmotif of Singapore's worldview as well.

Indisputably, Singapore's foreign policy does not correspond to every element of the Groatian tradition that other authors have identified. Martin Wight, for example, emphasizes the primacy of domestic policy in the Groatian paradigm, contrasting it with both the realist approach — which declares the primacy of foreign policy — and the revolutionist promotion of international ideological bonds in Kantianism.[4] Clearly, the primacy of domestic policy over foreign imperatives does not apply to a trade-dependent city-state.[5]

That said, other elements of the Groatian tradition, such as its emphasis on the rights of peaceful trade in civilization, are reflected in Singapore's outlook. Indeed, so great is the salience of trade in Singapore's foreign relations that N. Ganesan, looking back on 40 years of independence, argues that "Singapore has outlived its archrealist outlook in foreign policy".[6] While the core values of its foreign policy output are territoriality, sovereignty, internal political order and economic growth, with both territoriality and sovereignty being embedded in a realist notion of international relations, the imperatives of trade and prosperity call for a liberal cooperative approach.[7] Noting that, as a rule, the city-state is prepared to trade with any country whatever be its ideological complexion, Ganesan goes so far as to claim that "the Singapore government has successfully established a trade policy that is effectively decoupled from its foreign policy". Unless trading relations with other states are explicitly subject to international sanctions, they are regarded as being "outside the bounds of foreign policy".[8] Ganesan overstates his case here: the notion of decoupling is problematic because it suggests that Singapore ostensibly would be prepared to put its trading interests ahead of the general interests of its foreign policy, an argument that is difficult to understand. Instead, what is true, as Ganesan himself notes elsewhere in his book, is that Singapore's economic initiatives, such as inviting investment from the advanced economies, are part of a broader attempt to achieve "national viability by twinning its interests with those of friendly great powers. The synergies achieved from such congruence were worth much more than its economic implications".[9] Far from trade policy being decoupled from foreign policy, the two are linked inextricably. Linda Y.C. Lim underscores this point in a contribution to *The Political Economy of Foreign Policy in Southeast Asia*, where she argues that Singapore's foreign policy-makers have used its success as a market-driven economy, opposed to centrally-planned models of Third World development, to argue that the city-state must not be allowed to fail. "The implication is that the West has an interest in ensuring Singapore's continued political survival as a sovereign nation (should that ever be threatened), which itself hinges on its economic viability."[10]

Trade, then, is an integral part of Singapore's sense of self, and the Groatian perspective on trade as constituting the characteristic activity of the society of states is consonant with Singapore's expectations of security in the anarchical society of states. But that selfhood is based on broader requirements of international stability and order. Here, as even the internationalist Grotius acknowledges, states and not supranational bodies remain the key players in international affairs. For international relations to be stable — a condition that is a prerequisite for trade to play the beneficial role which it does for countries like Singapore that depend on access to foreign markets and investment — what is required is a balance among the great powers which can keep the peace. The imperative of giving the great powers a stake in Singapore's survival and success led it to adopt a balance-of-power strategy anchored in a realist approach. As Bull readily acknowledges, states operate in an unequal world. Great powers, whether they engage in war or in trade, strive to lay down the rules of international engagement. How they behave defines the parameters of both opportunity and threat for the rest. Unlike the unfortunate Melians, who spurned the Athenian offer of achieving security through incorporation into their economic empire because they preferred the liberty which they enjoyed in the Spartan scheme of things, Singapore plays by the survivalist rules of the game: great powers do what they want and small powers do what they must in order to survive. In Thucydides' Melian Dialogue, the Melians turn down the Athenian offer, preferring to trust and to invoke, to

Athenian astonishment, sources of security such as signs and divinations.[11] Not so Singapore, which has taken Thucydides' salutary tale to heart. It thus has placed itself vicariously within a realist tradition of thinking about international relations stretching from Sun Tzu, Thucydides and Chanakya Kautilya through Niccolo Machiavelli and Thomas Hobbes to Hans Morgenthau and the reworking of realist theory into neorealism or structural realism in the work of Kenneth E. Waltz.[12]

Singapore's foreign policy reflects simultaneously, then, a marked Groatian emphasis on liberal internationalism in the pursuit of aspects of security, including the critical economic aspect, but with elements of a realist balance-of-power strategy on key issues such as physical survival. The fact that economic links with the rest of the world are as crucial as physical security to an island trading-state helps explain why these aspects of Singapore's foreign policy are so closely linked. The foreign policy of Singapore could be seen as an extended commentary on Bull's theoretical forays into international history. The anarchical society is leavened by the capacity of trade to act as an alternative to war, but that society is characterized ultimately by the capacity of states to use power to pursue their interests, to the point of using, or threatening to use, force to secure those interests. Great powers naturally have greater latitude to do this than do other powers. Singapore's interactions with powers, great, greater or rising, acknowledge this uncomfortable reality.

BALANCE OF POWER

The concept of a balance of power is a notoriously elusive one. If invoked in its classical European sense of rival, competing or smaller powers lining up to restore a balance disrupted or disturbed by the emergence of a hegemon, then contemporary Southeast Asia is a good example of the *absence* of a balance of power. Had such a principle operated in the region, countries from Thailand to the Philippines and Singapore in between would have closed ranks against the United States, the sole superpower and therefore the hegemon *par excellence* today, which they have palpably not done. Instead, they have preferred to line up with it. Yet, the notion of a balance of power has been a perennial theme in the pronouncements of Singapore's leaders, who have sought to utilize its lessons for the city-state's survival and security. They appear to reflect Leifer's English School approach to the concept and his application of it to Southeast Asia and Singapore. To Leifer, balance of power refers both to a situation — the distribution of power — and to a policy of preventing the undue dominance of one or more states that would monopolise the terms on which regional order was made and sustained.[13] Jurgen Haacke draws attention to the fact that Leifer distinguished between the adversarial balance of power tradition linked to realism and expressed in countervailing political-military strategy; and the associative, Groatian balance of power tradition. Leifer — and this might be said of Singapore's leaders, too — believed that where associative arrangements might not be sufficient to prevent a rise of a hegemonic power, countervailing arrangements might be called for.[14]

Singapore's leaders have articulated the principles of its foreign policy for many years now. Lee Kuan Yew encapsulated the realities of a small state's survival early into independence by noting that Singapore's foreign policy "must be one to encourage, first, the major powers in the world to find it — if not in their interests to help us — at least in their interests not to have us go worse" because, in the last resort, "it is power which decides what happens and, therefore, it behoves us to ensure that we always have overwhelming power on our side".[15] S. Rajaratnam fleshed out the regional elements of the outlook, noting that because Singapore was regarded by the world and by its neighbours as a "strategic key" in the area, "we shall ensure that our foreign policy and our defence policy do not increase tensions and fears among our neighbours". Southeast Asia was a battleground of great-power politics; if Singapore became a pawn, the chances of military conflict breaking out would be greater. By not falling into the hands of one power bloc, Singapore would ensure that an opposing power bloc did not panic into taking "desperate and dangerous counter-measures".[16] A decade later, Lee Khoon Choy made the same point when he remarked that Singapore's foreign policy had sought to ensure that it did not become a pawn of any single great power. Were this to happen, it would circumscribe Singapore's independence while increasing tensions and dangers of war in the area. He argued that "if one small state in this part of the world allows itself to become a pawn in this manner, there are likely to be reactions from other big powers; neighbouring states may also feel threatened and feel compelled to allow a similar role to another big power".[17]

Elaborating on by then an almost existential motif in Singapore's foreign policy thinking, Brigadier-General Lee Hsien Loong, then Political Secretary (Defence), gave a comprehensive account of the security options of small states in a speech to the Singapore Institute of International Affairs on 16 October 1984.

Though he did not speak about Singapore in particular, it was obvious that he was drawing on the Republic's security perceptions and assessments. He mentioned four classes of strategy — development, diplomacy, deterrence and defence — as many of which as possible a small state needed to apply to survive. On diplomacy, he noted that it encompasses the traditional strategies of alliance, non-alignment, neutrality and balance of power. The problem with alliances is that they fail when they cease to be in the interest of the dominant partner; also, they can impinge on the independence of the weaker partner. Non-alignment is more of a slogan than a policy prescription. Neutrality, as Cambodia proves, means that a small state's refusal to pick quarrels with others does not necessarily mean that others will refuse to pick a quarrel with it. "Innocence is no protection against crime." A balance of power policy, therefore, can be more productive in certain circumstances. For a small state, the policy "depends on the competing interests of several big powers in the region, rather than on linking the nation's fortunes to one overbearing partner. The big powers can keep one another in check, and will prevent any one of them from dominating the entire region, and so allow small states to survive in the interstices between them". True, the equilibrium can be upset by a power changing course or withdrawing from the contest; also, a small state cannot "manipulate the big powers with impunity". Hence, for states situated "fortuitously at one of these points of balance, it is wiser to keep to the balance as long as possible, rather than to tilt for one power, or to seek to exclude all of them". Also, a small state should try to strengthen ties with its neighbours by refraining from provocative behaviour, paying regard to their sensitivities in the management of its domestic policies, and creating a network of symbiotic relationships.[18]

Underpinning Singapore's view of international relations is the reality that it neither has, nor has it pretended to possess, the ability to create or even to contribute decisively to a balance of the great powers.[19] Nevertheless, it has benefited from an evolving balance because of its significance to that balance, and because of its policies towards it. As for significance, Singapore needed to fulfil three conditions, Yuan-li Wu argues in *Strategic Significance of Singapore: A Study in Balance of Power*. First, the great powers must be convinced that the city-state is of considerable strategic and/or economic importance to each of them; secondly, that the "direct interests of each big power can be adequately served without bringing Singapore under its sole domination to the exclusion of other big powers"; and thirdly that "the interests of each can be served only by preventing the sole domination of Singapore by others".[20]

It did fulfil those conditions during the formative phase of its international relations, which occurred during the Cold War. First, Singapore's strategic significance made it of great importance to the great powers, especially the superpowers. Lying at the conjunction of sea routes from Europe and India in the west, from China, Japan, Indochina and Thailand in the north, from Borneo and the Moluccas in the east, and from Java and Australasia in the south, Singapore is one of the many islands that can allow a naval power to dominate the Straits of Malacca as it leads out to the South China Sea. However, unlike the other islands, as far-flung as the Andamans and Sri Lanka, which dominate the 300-mile northern approaches to the South China Sea, Singapore lies on the Straits of Malacca, which are only 40-mile wide.[21] Were a great power to control the city-state, its capacity to influence navigation in the economically and strategically important Straits would be considerable. Thus, in the early years of Singapore's independence, both the United States and the Soviet Union might have been willing to "fill the vacuum left by Britain's military pull-out", providing Singapore with an easy choice at the very start of a difficult independence. However, the Republic decided "not to bargain her vast strategic assets to the superpowers in return for protection".[22] That choice led to the second condition. The two superpowers were willing to permit Singapore this independence of action because their interests did not require them to act otherwise, particularly since maritime Southeast Asia was not as intense an arena of Cold War confrontation as was mainland Southeast Asia. Indeed, it was one of Singapore's nightmares that the Malay Right in post-1965 Kuala Lumpur might encourage American intervention in the deteriorating communal situation in Malaysia, turning the country into "another fire-storm like Vietnam". That would pose a terrible choice for Singapore, but Lee Kuan Yew was adamant that, no matter what happened across the Causeway, the Americans would not be allowed to turn Singapore into another Santo Domingo, intervening to install a government to their liking.[23] While it is unclear whether the United States would have intervened in Malaysia given its liabilities in Vietnam, it was that fear which had made Lee declare soon after independence: "It is fundamental. If the British bases go, there will be no American bases in Singapore."[24] Thirdly, however, though neither superpower tried to bring Singapore under its exclusive influence, each was convinced sufficiently of the city-state's importance to be against its domination by the other superpower.

These conditions have held through the Cold War and its aftermath, marked by the rise of China and India. What also has held, therefore, is Singapore's strategy of encouraging the presence of all great powers in Southeast Asia.[25]

CHINA AND INDIA

The entry of China and India into the global economy in the last two decades of the 20th century marked a major shift in human affairs. China was not just another contemporary player but "the biggest player in the history of man".[26] China's transition at the end of the 1970s towards what it characterized as a socialist market economy — but what a commentator described astutely as China's replacement of Marxism-Leninism with Market-Leninism[27] — heralded a radical change in the direction of international relations. Then, when India decided to join the global economy in the 1990s after its stymied attempt to do so in the mid-1980s, it entrenched Asia's claim to a prominent place in the economic and political scheme of things.

This was not the first time that China and India had been ascendant economically. As late as in 1700, their shares of world income had been comparable to Europe's. But colonialism and the emergence of the United States had disrupted the balance of economic power in the 18th century. The disruption had continued well into the 20th century. Eric Hobsbawm's periodization of modern history — the Age of Revolution (1789–1848), the Age of Capital (1848–75), the Age of Empire (1875–1914) and the Age of Extremes (1914–91) — draws attention to a Eurocentric world order that did not disappear completely with formal decolonization after World War II. The Cold War struggle for supremacy was waged between two superpowers, one a European offshoot and the other a Eurasian power whose political culture was anchored in its Russian inheritance as a European great power. Even as they had supplanted the players of a Europe-centred colonial order, they had to work with its legacy as managers and guarantors of international security. Their contest — with its Marshall Plan, NATO, Warsaw Pact and its COMECON — had demarcated the outer possibilities of world order. But when the Cold War ended and China, which had embarked on reform during that conflict, saw its reforms take off, what it unleashed was nothing less than the collective memory of a billion able people hungry for success after a century of humiliation at Western hands; the depredations of war waged by an imperial Japan that had replicated the colonial European quest for exclusive spheres of influence; civil war, revolutionary independence, early euphoria, and then autarchy and the domestically-inflicted disasters of the Great Leap Forward and the Cultural Revolution. It is that energy undeterred by the cruelties of history that the existing great powers would have to incorporate into the evolution of a new international order.

India, with another billion people, was also bringing its collective memory into contemporary play. Colonialism may well have delivered India from the Asiatic mode of production into a capitalist global economy, as Karl Marx argued, but it had done so on terms not Indian. Among other indicators, Indian per capita income had fallen under East India Company rule from 1757 to 1857 while British gains had been substantial, and the free trade imperialism imposed on India and other British colonies had favoured British exports.[28] The loss of autonomy under colonial rule had driven the early leaders of independent India to protect the country's fledgling economic autonomy from foreign capital and multilateral financial organizations that they did not trust because they could not control them. However, the planning system in independent India had led to the country basically excluding itself from the world trading system. In 1991, the costs of this policy became clear when India faced a parlous foreign exchange situation. The problem prompted its leaders to embark on the need for reform by exploring export markets instead of protecting domestic markets through import substitution. Their strategy entailed making Indian products competitive by liberalizing the domestic economy. Also, as China's entry into the global economy delivered dramatic results without eroding palpably the country's freedom of action on the domestic and foreign fronts; and as India saw that instead of looking at a constrained China it would have to deal with an increasingly prosperous China that would also be an increasingly powerful China, it took the plunge into contemporary history.

It was against this background that Minister Mentor Lee Kuan Yew delivered the keynote speech at the official opening of the eponymous School of Public Policy in Singapore in April 2005. Interestingly, the country's founding Prime Minister and architect of its foreign policy chose to speak on China and India. Beginning on a personal note, he said that he had taken a deep interest in both China and India ever since he had begun his political life in 1950. "Like all democratic socialists of the 1950s, I have tried to analyse and forecast which giant would make the grade. I had hoped it would be democratic India, not communist China." Comparing the two countries, Lee went on to examine the record of their public and private sectors; the priority they placed on education in their development; their ability to attract foreign investment; the challenges they face; and the role of intangible factors such as ethnicity and national ethos in the performance of the two nations. His conclusion was open-ended: "Whether China or India will prove to be the better model for other developing countries we will know by the middle of this century."[29] Although Lee was speaking of China and India as competing models for developing nations and not developed Singapore, it was clear from the thrust of his remarks that he saw the two powers as helping to set the tone for the rest of Asia in the coming decades. Other countries would have to ponder possible outcomes and navigate their course accordingly.

Singapore had begun to do so already. The current phase of its engagement with China goes back to the 1970s. It welcomed the possibilities of the *rapprochement* between the United States and China in 1971 that led to a reordering of Asian affairs during the Cold War. Singapore's engagement with China gathered steam when Deng Xiaoping launched his definitive reforms in 1978. Indeed, Deng saw the possible contours of post-communist China during his 1978 visit to Singapore, which had succeeded in combining remarkable economic progress with an authoritarian stability that was familiar in the Leninist idiom of Chinese politics. Singapore and China drew closer as Asia's most populous power embraced market reforms and opened its borders to foreign trade and investment. Singapore became a vocal advocate of the need for other countries to engage China, facilitate its inclusion in the world order, and hence give it a stake in the preservation of a prosperous, peaceful and stable international order. Other powers were urged to give post-revolutionary China a place in the *status quo* commensurate with its status so that Beijing would have reason to be a *status quo* power and not revert, rebuffed, to revisionism.

Lee's speech in 2005 did not detract from that fundamental approach to China, but it did draw attention to the other Asian power that Singapore was also courting: India. Socialist China's self-imposed quarantine from the global economy had survived less than three decades of revolutionary fervour after independence in 1949, the demise of Marxism-Leninism as the state's legitimizing ideology following swiftly from the death of Chairman Mao Zedong in 1976. In democratic India, what was at stake four decades after independence in 1947 was the future of a bureaucratic planning system that empowered the state but bred inertia and inefficiency in the economy, a system that critics mockingly labelled the Licence Raj after the expired mandate of the British Raj. As India returned to the global economy, haltingly at first in the mid-1980s, Singapore seized that transitional moment, encouraging the reform process and pursuing closer relations with the subcontinental giant. Singapore's efforts did not bear fruit immediately, one reason being that India's closely-contested politics and the presence of powerful domestic interests threatened by a foreign economic presence precluded the creation of a quick political consensus on reforms. But that consensus did take shape sufficiently to permit India to sign the Comprehensive Economic Cooperation Agreement (CECA) with Singapore in 2005. Singapore could take some satisfaction from its success in having read India correctly enough to persevere through the apparent anarchy of its politics.

ENGAGING RISING POWERS

There is a critical difference between Singapore's engagement of United States and other powers during the Cold War, and its policy towards China and India now. The earlier set of powers was mature; was established in the international order; and collectively exercised preponderant power in the international system, which they sought to legitimize by supplying international values, norms and institutions consonant with their own interests. China and India are, by contrast, rising great powers. They are entering the turf; they are not guarding it. They can be expected to play by the rules, but also test the rules of play. Muthiah Alagappa goes so far as to declare that nearly every major power — China, Japan, Russia and India — except the United States "is dissatisfied with the present distribution of power, and its status and role in the Asian international system".[30] Hence, engaging rising great powers, which bring their growing expectations and untested intentions to the international system, is not the same as living with existing great powers.

This point is made powerfully by Randall L. Schweller in a seminal essay, "Managing the rise of great powers: history and theory".[31] After assessing why rising powers are dangerous — because they are tempted to expand — and why they need to expand — because the requirements of national growth generate lateral pressure to expand their activities for a range of reasons from the need for raw materials and living space to the need for religious converts, military bases or adventurism — Schweller argues that emerging powers find it easier to join the league of great powers under multipolarity than under any other type of system.[32] Significantly, China and India are rising, not in a relatively comfortable multipolar system but in a U.S.-led, basically unipolar, and potentionally transitional moment in history. Theoretically, what are the expected responses in such a situation? According to Schweller, state responses to rising powers resolve themselves into six basic policy options: preventive war, an option that appeals to states, which historically have been unlikely to accept their national decline peacefully; balancing/containment, or opposing the stronger or more threatening side in a conflict by allying with the weaker side; bandwagoning, or joining the stronger coalition; binding, a policy under which states do not form a counter-alliance against a threatening state because they fear greater conflict and even war, and choose to ally with the rival to manage the threat through an agreement of restraint; engagement, or the use of non-coercive means to blunt the non-*status quo* aspects of a rising power's behaviour so that the growing power is employed in ways that are consistent with peaceful change; and buckpassing/distancing, when a state seeks to get a free ride on the balancing efforts of others or hide rather than meet the challenge from a rising, dissatisfied power by aligning itself with other threatened states. Schweller notes that states are not obliged to choose a single strategy but may combine several strategies.[33]

In assessing the likelihood of which strategy or strategies states may choose, he asks the essential question of whether the rising power's essential values can be protected and promoted within the *status quo*. Revisionist states with limited aims call for an engagement strategy. Meeting their legitimate demands through reasonable concessions converts disgruntled states into defenders of a new settlement that upholds the fundamental features of the existing order.[34] Commending the engagement strategy, he argues that when the established power is confronted by a limited-aims revisionist state and seeks to end the rivalry with the challenger, "the appropriate strategy is neither purely cooperative nor purely competitive but instead a mixture of both carrots and sticks".[35] The established power tries to satisfy the rising power's limited revisionist goals and to "modify its behavior through economic and political rewards as well as the threat of force".[36]

This realization is writ large in Singapore's engagement of China as world capitals led by Washington try to bring Beijing into the international order. India is too recent an addition to the realm of emerging great powers to feature on the canvas of existing great powers' strategies of engagement or containment, but what happens on the Chinese front of international relations may have intimations for India's entry to the ranks of great powerhood.

Singapore's economic ties with China and, increasingly, its trade and investment links with India, are well-documented.[37] This study adopts a different approach. It seeks to place developments bringing Singapore, China and India closer within a geopolitical framework. Weaving history into contemporary international relations, it asks how well the city-state is positioning itself between the two ancient Asian powers as they reinvent themselves in the new millennium. It begins by looking at Singapore's early relations with China and India.

NOTES

1 Hedley Bull, *The Anarchical Society: A Study of Order in World Politics* (Houndmills and London: Macmillan, 1977), pp. 24–26.

2 Ibid., p. 27.

3 Hugo Grotius, *Mare Liberum*, translated with a revision of the Latin text of 1633 by Ralph Van Deman Magoffin, *The Freedom of the Seas, or the Right Which Belongs to the Dutch to Take Part in the East Indian Trade* (New York: Oxford University Press, 1916). The theme of freedom of the seas is present also in Grotius' seminal work, *De Jure Belli ac Pacis*, 1625, translated as *On the Law of War and Peace*, available on <http://www.geocities.com/Athens/Thebes/8098/?200524>. For a study of Grotius' influence on Dutch trade policy towards Southeast Asia, see Peter Borschberg, "Hugo Grotius, East India Trade and the King of Johor", *Journal of Southeast Asian Studies* 30, no. 2 (September 1999): 225–48.

4 Martin Wight, in *International Theory: The Three Traditions*, compiled and edited by Gabriele Wight and Brian Porter, 1996 reprint (London: Leicester University Press, for the Royal Institute of International Affairs, London, 1991), p. 274.

5 Ibid., p. 275.

6 N. Ganesan, *Realism and Interdependence in Singapore's Foreign Policy* (London and New York: Routledge, 2005), p. 11.

7 Ibid., pp. 15–16.

8 Ibid., p. 17.

9 Ibid., pp. 44–45. See also Narayanan Ganesan, "Singapore: Realist cum Trading State", in Muthiah Alagappa, ed., *Asian Security Practice: Material and Ideational Influences* (Stanford: Stanford University Press, 1998), pp. 579–607.

10 Linda Y.C. Lim, "The Foreign Policy of Singapore", in David Wurfel and Bruce Burton, eds., *The Political Economy of Foreign Policy in Southeast Asia* (Houndmills and London: Macmillan, 1990), pp. 129–30.

11 For an intense account of realism *versus* idealism in the Melian Dialogue, see W. Julian Korab-Karpowicz, *How Can International Relations Theorists Benefit from Reading Thucydides?* <www.da-vienna.ac.at/userfiles/KorabKarpowicz.pdf>.

12 Ganesan, *Realism and Interdependence in Singapore's Foreign Policy*, pp. 4–7, comments on the state of play in international relations theories and small states.

13 Michael Leifer, "Truth about the Balance of Power", in Chin Kin Wah and Leo Suryadinata, compilers and editors, *Michael Leifer: Selected Works on Southeast Asia* (Singapore: Institute of Southeast Asian Studies, 2005), p. 153.

14 Jurgen Haacke, "Michael Leifer and the balance of power", *Pacific Review* 18, no. 1 (March 2005): 54.

15 "We Want To Be Ourselves", speech to the University of Singapore, 9 October 1965.

16 *Republic of Singapore Parliamentary Debates: Official Report*, Vol. 24, 16 December 1965, cols. 257–58.

17 Lee Khoon Choy, "Foreign Policy", in C.V. Devan Nair, ed., *Socialism that Works ... The Singapore Way* (Singapore: Federal Publications, 1976), p. 109.

18 *Straits Times*, Singapore, 6 November 1984.

19 Obaid Ul Haq, "Foreign Policy", in Jon S.T. Quah et al., eds., *Government and Politics of Singapore*, revised edition (Singapore: Oxford University Press, 1987), p. 285.

20 Yuan-li Wu, *Strategic Significance of Singapore: A Study in Balance of Power* (Washington, D.C.: American Enterprise Institute for Public Policy Research, 1972), p. 4.

21 Wong Lin Ken, "The Strategic Significance of Singapore", in Ernest C.T. Chew and Edwin Lee, eds., *A History of Singapore* (Singapore, Oxford and New York: Oxford University Press, 1991), p. 18.

22 Eric Charles Paul, "The Viability of Singapore: An Aspect of Modern Political Geography", unpublished Ph.D. dissertation submitted to the University of California (Berkeley, 1973), p. 312.

23 K.G. Tregonning, "Lee Kuan Yew and the Americans", *The Bulletin*, 25 September 1965.

24 Singapore Government Press Release, 30 August 1965, p. 6.

25 The foregoing analysis of Singapore's balance of power strategy draws on Asad-ul Iqbal Latif, "The Security of New States, Pakistan and Singapore: A Study in Contrast and Compulsions", a thesis submitted to the University of Cambridge for the degree of Master of Letters in History, 1993, pp. 102–4. For a comprehensive study of the later phase of Singapore's engagement of the United States, the Soviet Union and other powers, see Bilveer Singh, *The Vulnerability of Small States Revisited: A Study of Singapore's Post-Cold War Foreign Policy* (Yogyakarta: Gadjah Mada University Press, 1999).

26 Lee Kuan Yew, cited in Daniel Burstein and Arne De Keijzer, *Big Dragon China's Future: What It Means for Business, the Economy, and the Global Order* (New York: Simon & Schuster, 1998), p. 97.

27 Nicholas D. Kristof, "China Sees 'Market-Leninism' as Way to Future", *New York Times*, 6 September 1993.

28 Angus Maddison, *The World Economy: A Millennial Perspective* (Paris: Development Centre of the Organisation for Economic Co-operation and Development, 2001), p. 21.

29 Lee Kuan Yew, "Managing Globalization: Lessons from China and India", Keynote Speech at the official opening of the Lee Kuan Yew School of Public Policy, 4 April 2005 at Shangri-la Hotel.

30 "Constructing Security Order in Asia: Conceptions and Issues", in Muthiah Alagappa, ed., *Asian Security Order: Instrumental and Normative Features* (Stanford: Stanford University Press, 2003), p. 92.

31 Randall L. Schweller, "Managing the Rise of Great Powers: History and Theory", in Alastair Iain Johnston and Robert S. Ross, eds., *Engaging China: The Management of an Emerging Power* (New York: Routledge, 1999), pp. 1–31.

32 Schweller, ibid., pp. 2–6.

33 Ibid., pp. 7–17.

34 Ibid., pp. 19–20.

35 Ibid., p. 24.

36 Ibid.

37 One recent volume that studies the economic dimension in detail is K. Kesavapany, *India's Tryst with Asia* (New Delhi: Asian Institute of Transport Development, 2006). For the business aspects, see Alain Vandenborre, *The Little Door to the New World: China-Singapore-India* (Singapore: SNP Editions, 2005).

CHAPTER III

TENTATIVE ENCOUNTERS
China, India and Indochina

Lee Kuan Yew's choice of democratic India over communist China in the 1950s underscored the political logic of Singapore's relations with Beijing, which were far less warm than its ties with New Delhi on Singapore's independence in 1965. Other factors supporting the Singapore view were that communist China was helping insurgencies in Southeast Asia, and that Beijing was an ethnic source of attraction to Chinese in the region. Lee's People's Action Party (PAP), democratic socialist and anti-communist in orientation, had to contend with the dual pulls of ideology and ethnicity that China exercised on the Chinese majority in Singapore, where the PAP was pledged to the principle of multiracialism and not nationalism predicated on Chinese supremacy.[1] India, by contrast with China, identified itself with the ideals of democracy, socialism and non-alignment, these values being consonant with the PAP's self-definition and worldview as well.

Yet, in the decade and a half after Singapore's independence, several trends redrew the Asian security landscape that Singapore inhabited. The Sino-Indian War of 1962 rebuffed hopes of Third World internationalism inaugurated by the Bandung Conference of 1955, in whose spirit of Afro-Asian solidarity had originated the Non-Aligned Movement that was established in 1961. Dawn in Bandung was overtaken by the high noon of colonial retrenchments, superpower initiatives, and consequent alignments that marked Asia's trajectory from the mid-1960s onwards. Britain announced in 1967 that it would withdraw its forces in Malaysia and Singapore by the mid-1970s, a date that was subsequently brought forward to 1971. The Sino-Soviet split, which had begun in the late 1950s, peaked in 1969. The Soviet Union's Asian collective security proposal, first advanced by Nikita Khruschev in 1956, was taken up by Leonid Brezhnev in 1969 as a means of containing China, whose domestic and foreign policies by then were convulsed by a Cultural Revolution that revived fears of Beijing as an unpredictable and destabilizing force in Asian politics. The Soviet security proposal came on the heels of the Brezhnev Doctrine of 1968, which asserted Moscow's control over Warsaw Pact countries and its right to define "socialism" and "capitalism" in its relations with socialist countries, which would not be allowed to deviate from Soviet leadership in their conduct of domestic politics and international relations. This doctrine provided the justification for the Soviet invasion of Czechoslovakia in 1968 and the invasion of Afghanistan far down the road in 1979, although Kabul was not a Warsaw Pact capital.

Even as Moscow tightened its international grip in the late 1960s, America escalated its involvement in the Vietnam War, but in 1969 there appeared the Nixon Doctrine, which set the stage for "Vietnamization", or the policy groundwork that culminated in the eventual U.S. withdrawal from Vietnam. As part of this doctrine, Richard Nixon declared that the United States would honour its treaty commitments and provide a shield if a nuclear power threatened a nation allied to Washington or one whose survival it considered vital to its security; in cases involving other types of aggression, the United States would furnish military or economic assistance when this was asked for in accordance with its treaty commitments, but the nation that was threatened directly would have to bear the primary responsibility of providing the manpower for its defence. The doctrine was seen as a declaration of America's unwillingness to send its troops into Asian conflicts — and a message to Asian nations to redraw their security parameters accordingly, particularly as the durability of American engagement in Asia was placed in sharp relief by the Soviet Union's strategic advances into Asia. The India-Pakistan War at the end of 1971, which occurred after the signing of the Indo-Soviet Treaty of Peace, Friendship and Cooperation in August that year, led to the independence of Bangladesh from a Pakistan supported by America and China.

However, that war was preceded by perhaps the most significant development for Asia as a whole: the Sino-U.S. *rapprochement,* whose early stirrings included Henry Kissinger's secret trip to Beijing in July 1971 and which was formalized during Richard Nixon's February 1972 visit to China. By the time that *rapprochement* had matured into the establishment of diplomatic relations in 1979, it had overshadowed for Asia the course of the U.S.-Soviet *détente* that had begun in the first half of the 1970s and petered out in the second half. The conclusion of the Vietnam War with the dramatic American departure from Saigon in 1975 marked a grave deterioration in Washington's contribution to the security of non-communist Southeast Asia. That development was rebalanced only somewhat by the formation of the Association of Southeast Asian Nations (ASEAN) in 1967. As China and the United States drew closer, so did independent Vietnam to the Soviet Union. The signing of the Soviet-Vietnamese Treaty of Friendship and Cooperation in 1978 was followed by Hanoi's invasion of Cambodia the same year and by Beijing's punitive action against Vietnam soon after in 1979. In the Indochina conflict of the closing years of the decade was coalesced the latest confluence of Cold War forces that had changed Asia's security trajectory in the decade-and-a-half since Singapore became independent. Amidst this flurry of world affairs, Singapore made its security calculations as China benefited because of its posture towards the United States and India palpably drew close to the Soviet Union. This chapter will examine the role of the Indochina conflict in the evolution of Singapore's relations with the two Asian powers, after sketching the city-state's initial relations with Beijing and New Delhi.

CHINA

China had an economic presence in colonial Singapore. The Bank of China set up a branch there in 1936 to channel the diaspora's financial support to the Chinese mainland in its struggle against Japanese imperialism. After China's independence in 1949, the bank served as a point of unofficial diplomatic contact with Beijing. Much later, when Singapore was a part of Malaysia, the bank came close to being shut down but was saved by Separation, leading Michael Leifer to believe that its existence well might have featured in the degree of political tolerance that Beijing extended to independent Singapore. As an *entrepôt*, Singapore was naturally drawn to trade with China, and Chinese emporia selling cheap products helped to keep down the cost of living. However, Leifer notes that at issue in the development of Singapore's relations with China is "the need to separate out economics from politics. In that respect, Singapore's flag did not follow trade." The nascent government not only sought to register its distinct political identity but promoted economic and military ties with Taiwan while adhering to a one-China policy.[2]

There were several reasons for Singapore's reservations about China. Beijing, which had shared Sukarnoist Indonesia's condemnation of Malaysia's formation as a neo-colonialist plot, did not recognize Singapore's independence till 1970, preferring to refer to the city-state as a part of Malaya. Colouring Singapore's perceptions of China were the early political battles that that the PAP fought with pro-communist and pro-Chinese forces. During the Cultural Revolution, Prime Minister Lee Kuan Yew was branded a "running dog" of American and British imperialism. It was only in late 1970 that Beijing quietly changed its attitude to

Singapore because it wanted as many countries as possible to check the expansion of the Soviet Union's influence into Southeast Asia.[3] Moscow had signed a trade deal with Singapore in 1966, set up a trade mission there in 1967, and established diplomatic relations with the city-state in 1968.[4] It was with an eye to these developments that Beijing embarked on its overtures to the region, including Singapore. Some movement occurred in bilateral relations when Singapore allowed a ping-pong team to play in Beijing in 1971, and accepted a Chinese offer to send a ping-pong team to Singapore the following year. Singapore also voted at the United Nations in support of an Albanian resolution transferring China's seat from the Republic of China to the People's Republic of China. Even as these tentative steps in Sino-Singapore relations were being taken, Beijing was changing its position on the overseas Chinese, many of whom had taken up citizenship in the countries where they lived, by discouraging them from returning to China. This helped smoothen the prospects of ties between Beijing and Singapore, whose caution was based on a firm desire not to be seen as a Third China (after the Chinese mainland and Taiwan) either by Beijing or by Singapore's neighbours. Singapore had to "cope regionally with the recurrent charge that ethnic affinity would make the island, at the very least, an agent of influence for China".[5] The change in China's stance towards Southeast Asian Chinese was helpful here. However, there was another issue that remained unresolved: China's ties with the Malayan Communist Party (MCP), a source of friction between Beijing, and Malaysia and Singapore. Beijing budged little on this issue, placing it in the context of its support for liberation movements against colonialism. That said, since only support from within the country and not from Beijing could cause a movement to succeed, if Southeast Asian countries and China had a "forward-looking view", their relations could improve and they could have diplomatic relations.[6] China was not so much giving up its ideological stake in liberation movements in Southeast Asia — for to do so would be to weaken its leadership of those movements and invite the Soviet Union to replace it in that role — as it was finessing a dual strategy of party-to-party ties with communist movements contingent on their domestic performance, and state-to-state ties that depended on how amicable governments were towards Beijing.[7] The formula was sufficiently ambivalent to permit China to retain its revolutionary credentials while tackling pragmatically the challenge from the Soviet Union.

Intimations of a breakthrough in Singapore's relations with Beijing appeared in two stages. The first was in March 1975, when Foreign Minister S. Rajaratnam visited Beijing. He assured his hosts that the city-state would not allow Moscow, whose ships were repaired in Singapore, to use that access for subversive activities against its neighbours, including China. Rajaratnam also explained that, given regional sensitivities about Singapore being a Chinese-majority country, it would establish diplomatic relations with China only after Indonesia had done so. (This occurred, finally, in 1990.) Rajaratnam's trip was followed by Lee's visit in May 1976. Lee's memoirs capture vividly the interplay of factors that came to the fore. To ensure that Beijing did not treat the visit as one by kinsmen Chinese, the Singapore delegation included the Jaffna Tamil Rajaratnam and Malay parliamentary secretary Ahmad Mattar; moreover, all meetings would be conducted in English. At Beijing airport, Lee and his delegation were received by chanting schoolgirls and a banner that proclaimed support for the people, but not the government, of Singapore — a pointed reminder of how the communists in Beijing viewed the PAP. In his meetings with Chinese leaders, Lee made it clear that Singapore would not be pro-China merely because it had a Chinese majority, and declared that his government would prevent pro-communist Chinese at home from harming Singapore, but added that Singapore would not be anti-China. The stronger China became, the better and more equal would be the balance between the United States, the Soviet Union and China, Lee declared. An impromptu meeting with an ailing Mao Zedong took place, too. At a meeting, Huo Guofeng, the Chinese Premier, fudged on the issue of why Beijing was supporting the MCP, a Malaysian party that sought to liberate a foreign country, Singapore. Lee defended Singapore's decision to train its troops in Taiwan. He pointed out again that the city-state's neighbours would have greater suspicions the more China embraced it as a kinsman country. Hua reiterated China's disapproval of dual nationality for people of Chinese descent living abroad but reiterated the traditional and kinsman-like relations between the peoples of Singapore and China, which were beneficial to the development of relations.[8] There was clearly an impasse over both ethnic and ideological issues. It continued into the late 1980s, when Singapore viewed with unease China's tendency to play up ethnic ties with Chinese from time to time, "whether for remittances, investments, commercial gain or even psychological 'patronage' ".[9]

That said, however, Lee's 1976 visit marked for Singapore the high point of a process reaching beyond it that had begun with the Sino-U.S. *rapprochement* of

1971 and the signing of the Shanghai *communiqué* in 1972. China's decision to turn towards the United States announced the second phase of the Cold War, the first having been capitalist America's conflict with a putatively united socialist bloc that included the Soviet Union and China. In the second phase, China, hitherto an "ideological missionary state", found a different focus for its regional interests, these being to prevent Vietnam from acting as the regional agent of Soviet expansionism.[10] Lee, who had advised Richard Nixon as far back as in 1967 to engage China, could take some heart from the way in which Washington and Beijing were drawing closer and thereby holding out the possibility of turning China into a *status quo* power in Southeast Asia. A truer congruence of Sino-American interests would have to await Soviet-backed Vietnam's invasion of Cambodia in 1978, but the emerging patterns of Asian realignment were visible already.

Before getting to 1978, the turning point in Singapore's political relations with pre-reform China, let us examine how the city-state's initially warm relations with India had deteriorated markedly by around the same year, 1978.

INDIA

Singapore-India relations got off to a good start in 1965 because no political baggage weighed down economic relations between the two Commonwealth countries. Economic relations between them in the following decade took the form of trade, technical assistance and joint ventures. "India's admiration for Singapore's success was comparable to the same feeling it had for Japan's acheievement," Somkiat Onwimon writes. Singapore was India's best export market in ASEAN.

India enjoyed a favourable trade balance with the city-state of about US$200 million, India's best performance with any ASEAN country. Indian exports to the city-state consisted mainly of industrial machinery and other engineering products such as transport equipment, vehicles and parts, and iron and steel. Food items, textiles and popular Indian films were other exports. Singapore's exports consisted of crude rubber, copper, tin and natural gums, natural gum resins, balsam, lacs, spices and books. Indian investments, however, were not as extensive as the Western investments that were driving Singapore's economic transition from an *entrepôt* to an industrial centre.[11]

These economic ties were part of a larger meeting of minds in Singapore and India notwithstanding New Delhi's refusal to provide the island-state with a military adviser to help it build up five battalions. "I had half expected the Indian government might not want to take sides against Malaysia," Lee writes.[12] New Delhi and Singapore enjoyed close political relations, with the city-state supporting India during its conflicts with Pakistan, and the Tashkent Declaration.[13] Several bilateral visits took place, and Singapore's leaders were keen on involving India in Southeast Asian security arrangements following the departure of Western powers in the late 1960s. Lee emphasized the need for an Indian presence in the region either through a multilateral security arrangement "or by the enunciation of an 'Asian Monroe Doctrine' to dissuade possible 'poaching' in Asia".[14] Kripa Sridharan sees in Singapore's attitude a reflection of several factors: the vulnerability of a small state in a region becoming a cockpit of major-power-rivalries, the challenges of adjusting to a proximate power such as communist China, and Singapore's not very friendly relations with its neighbours. "Given these, it did seem useful to cultivate India as a possible counterweight."[15]

That counterweight did not materialize. Although China's expansionist potential linked ASEAN states and India in a common concern, and although New Delhi did not want Southeast Asia to become a Chinese sphere of influence, India was unwilling to contemplate forming a defensive anti-Beijing bloc with countries situated on China's periphery because of New Delhi's opposition to entering into any defence pacts.[16] During her trip to Southeast Asia in 1968, Indian Prime Minister Indira Gandhi did suggest a three-tier programme encompassing economic cooperation; the free exchange of ideas, resources and know-how among developing and developed countries; and, most interesting, "an international guarantee by the big powers that [the] neutrality and independence of aspiring nations would be preserved to help them develop their nationalism through popular governments".[17] The third proposal drew much interest. Indira Gandhi clarified later that India wanted to see all the powers that mattered in the area to be guarantors. Sridharan notes the difficulties with the proposal, such as whether China would agree to be a guarantor and whether the superpowers would be willing to take on additional responsibilities. But even before the idea could be refined, Gandhi "confounded everybody by saying that her suggestion of (an) international guarantee was restricted to Indochina and that she was merely thinking aloud".[18] India missed an opportunity to insert itself into the nascent security equations of Southeast Asia. The reason was India's aversion to the formation of pacts and bases, which grew from an innate dismissal of the idea that power vacuums could result from the absence of such security arrangements. India therefore was not convinced when Lee, during his 1970 visit there, expressed fears that a British withdrawal from Southeast Asia would create a vacuum, and New Delhi did not make any specific security proposal for the region.[19]

It was in the following year, 1971, that the geopolitical realities in which Singapore and India operated came into sharp focus. India found itself entangled in the civil war in East Pakistan, where the Pakistani military had cracked down on Bengali separatists and caused an outflow of refugees to India.[20] In the midst of the crisis, Henry Kissinger's secret trip to Beijing through Rawalpindi in July, and the possibility of a Sino-U.S. *rapprochement*, led to a new unanimity of Soviet and Indian interests. Moscow was confronted with a new global balance of power of which it would be the principal loser. The regional implications of that new balance of power could be disastrous as well for Indian strategy on East Pakistan. New Delhi took up a two-year-old offer from the Soviet Union to conclude a Treaty of Peace, Friendship and Cooperation. The Russians were hesitant initially: They wanted to know what exactly India expected, especially since it wanted the draft offer of 1969 expanded to include a "consultation" clause. When India made it clear that it was not seeking a formal — or secret — commitment of Soviet military assistance in case China intervened in an India-Pakistan war, Moscow agreed, and the treaty was signed on 9 August.[21] However, Article 9 stipulates that, in the case of an attack or the threat of an attack, the signatories would enter into consultations directed at removing the threat. Thus, while the treaty did not commit the Soviet Union to protecting India, the phrasing of Article 9 was broad enough to leave open that possibility — and certainly broad enough for China to take a Soviet response very seriously. In the event, the India-Pakistan war of 1971 took place without any determining military intervention by the external powers. It led to the defeat and break-up of Pakistan, reiterated India's role as the dominant power in South Asia, and cemented Indo-Soviet ties as Bangladesh emerged as an independent state in the teeth of Chinese and American misgivings over the disintegration of Pakistan.

Lee visited India in November 1971, just before the outbreak of the war. He praised India's patience in dealing with the situation in its neighbourhood, but "he did not seem entirely sanguine about India's strategic partnership with the Soviet Union".[22] It is not difficult to discern why. In 1971, what was taking shape was Singapore's belief in the value of a Sino-U.S. *rapprochement*, a belief predicated on the fact that a China drawn firmly into the orbit of *status quo* powers would be beneficial for Southeast Asian states at the receiving end of Beijing's support for insurrectionary movements in the region. India, by contrast, had embraced the Soviet Union, entrenching the superpower's influence in South Asia and giving it one more card to play in the Cold War. New Delhi's suspicion of Washington and its distrust of Beijing had finally taken the form of a treaty with a Moscow hostile to both Washington and Beijing. The Indo-Soviet Treaty, although modest in scope compared to the Sino-U.S. *rapprochement*, was a direct response to the constellation of forces bringing America and China together. It would have been difficult for a country supporting a breakthrough in Sino-U.S. relations to welcome the possibility of an Indo-Soviet *entente*.

If 1971 revealed the distance between Singapore and India as the great powers realigned themselves in Asia, the Vietnamese invasion of Cambodia in

December 1978 and their occupation of that country in January 1979, and the Sino-Vietnamese war of February 1979 placed New Delhi and Singapore in two intensely distinct geopolitical blocs. The Indochinese conflict therefore is examined here in some detail, fleshing out China's role in, and the responses of Singapore and India to, the last convulsion to grip Southeast Asia before the Cold War ended.

THE INDOCHINA CONFLICT

The origins of Vietnam's invasion of Cambodia in 1978 were many. One was Vietnam's historical self-perception of its role in Indochina, drawn from the Chinese strategic concept of heartland and periphery that had provided the rationale for China's rule, invasion and Sinicization of Vietnam itself. The Vietnamese saw Indochina as part of their sphere of influence much as China had viewed Southeast Asia.[23] There were material factors as well. The need for rice and cultivable land had led to the annexation of Kampuchea Krom, later known as the French colony of Cochinchina, by Vietnam (Annam) in the 17th and 18th centuries; this is cited as the starting point of the conflict between Cambodia and Vietnam.[24] French colonial policy added to the potential for conflict.[25] Pre-colonial and colonial legacies fused into the ideological impulse for a Hanoi-led Indochinese Federation that was formulated in 1935.[26] The federation appeared achievable following Vietnam's victory against the United States in 1975. Vietnamese armed forces installed a client regime in Laos, but they were unable to do so in Cambodia because of Cambodian nationalism, the desire of the external powers at Geneva in 1954 to ensure Cambodia's sovereignty, and the political skills of Prince Norodom Sihanouk; and the rise to power in 1975 of the Khmer Rouge, a fellow-communist movement that, however, was not under Vietnamese control.[27] When the Khmer Rouge launched military attacks on Vietnam, it provided Hanoi with the rationale to counter-attack, but this response need not have involved a full-scale invasion and occupation. It took the form it did because it satisfied Vietnam's long-standing imperial ambition to dominate its weaker neighbour.[28]

That ambition was given a fillip by the role of the Soviet Union. Moscow had offered Hanoi a friendship and cooperation treaty in 1975. That treaty was signed, after the two sides had smoothened out differences over the Vietnamese draft, on 3 November 1978. Article 6 of the Treaty of Friendship and Cooperation between the Socialist Republic of Vietnam and the Union of Soviet Socialist Republics addressed security concerns. It said: "In case either Party is attacked or threatened with attack, the two Parties signatory to the Treaty shall immediately consult each other with a view to eliminating that threat and taking appropriate and effective measures to ensure the peace and security of the two countries."[29] The Vietnamese attack on Cambodia on 25 December 1978 suggested that the two events were coordinated, but the reality is that Hanoi had not informed Moscow of its plan to invade Cambodia until after the event. Nevertheless, Stephen J. Morris notes, the Soviet factor aided in the realization of Hanoi's plans in Indochina because Vietnam would not have tried to challenge China without the political, military and economic support of the Soviet Union and its East European allies. The Soviet Union, estranged from both China and the United States, saw its Vietnam policy as an opportunity to curb Chinese influence and

undercut American power. By the time the Soviet-
Vietnamese alliance was formalized in 1978, it was
clearly aimed at China, and subsequent to the 1978
invasion of Cambodia, Moscow's willingness to help
Hanoi amounted to the attempted creation of a regional
hegemonic order under Soviet auspices, and accelerated
the pace of the Sino-U.S. *rapprochement*.[30]

China's Role

China was the key factor in these developments. In the
Vietnamese view, it was guilty of several transgressions.
A book published by the Vietnamese Foreign Ministry
in 1979 said that Beijing had favoured the recognition
of two Vietnams with two separate governments at
Geneva in 1954, had wanted a protracted war for the
Vietnamese communists instead of a quick solution,
and had tried to isolate Hanoi in certain ways. During
the Cultural Revolution, China had interfered with
Soviet arms shipments to North Vietnam, had organized
Chinese residents in Vietnam, and had sabotaged
Hanoi-Washington negotiations during the Johnson
Administration so that Vietnam would bear the brunt
of fighting the Americans. Then, the Chinese desire for
rapprochement with the Nixon Administration had
undermined the Vietnamese negotiating position by
urging Hanoi to make a compromise in exchange for
American accommodation on the Taiwan issue; also,
Beijing had pressed Hanoi at the end of the Paris
Agreement between Le Duc Tho and Henry Kissinger
to postpone Vietnam's drive for reunification, holding
out as a carrot the promise to maintain China's 1973
aid level for five years. (Vietnam was reunited on
2 July 1976.) The book accused China of harbouring
hegemonic ambitions towards Indochina and a desire

to dominate Southeast Asia because, among other reasons, it had claimed sovereignty over most of the Gulf of Tonkin while oil speculation was on near the offshore islands in 1974; it had seized the Hoang Sa (Paracel) islands from Saigon's troops in January 1974; and it had asked Hanoi to supply the Khmer Rouge during its final offensives in 1975, thereby carrying out China's obligations towards the Cambodian communists while avoiding a breach of tacit Sino-American agreements not to supply communist Indochinese forces. This approach had put Hanoi in a difficult position.[31] The close interplay of ideological and material factors in this indictment attests to the depth of Vietnamese bitterness towards China, an historical rival with which relations had been sabotaged by the bad faith of a supposedly fraternal communist party unable to rise above China's national interests. That was, in essence, the Vietnamese view. Cambodia was a sub-plot in the larger Sino-Vietnamese drama.

The Chinese view was equally bitter. Beijing, which had given Hanoi massive help — US$20 billion — during the Vietnam War, not only saw the Vietnamese as ingrates but felt doubly offended because they had aligned themselves with its arch-enemy, Moscow. The ethnic factor had come into play as well. In the early 1970s, the Vietnamese communist party purged ethnic Chinese and Chinese-trained cadres because it feared Chinese hostility over its tilt to Moscow. In 1976, Hanoi turned its attention to the ethnic Chinese population of Vietnam, and in 1978 it expelled hundreds of thousands of ethnic Chinese in the north to China. It was a combination of such factors that cemented a Beijing-Phnom Penh alliance, which had been ambivalent till then. China's fear of Soviet encirclement made it see the Vietnamese-Khmer Rouge clashes as a challenge from what it called Soviet social imperialist expansion.[32] Vietnam became a sub-plot in the Sino-Soviet drama.

China's position on Vietnam reflected three interests: to uphold the independent existence of the three Indochinese states all operating within the purview of China's regional and security interests, which meant getting Vietnam out of Cambodia and Laos; preventing the arrival of an "Asian Cuba" by getting Soviet influence out of Vietnam in particular and Indochina in general; and gaining control over the South China Sea so as to play a dominant role in the entire region.[33]

China's invasion of Vietnam bore out these themes. During a January 1979 visit to Washington, Deng Xiaoping prepared the Americans for the coming Chinese action against the "Cubans of the East", who were moving on to embrace an Asian collective security system that threatened both the United States and China. On a stopover in Tokyo, he informed the Japanese that the Americans had been told of the invasion plans. Back home, he discussed at the Central Military Commission in early February the range of possible Soviet responses, from verbal condemnations to a limited raid across the border to a full-scale invasion. The Chinese decided that the third possibility was unlikely.[34] They went ahead. China's 29-day incursion into Vietnam beginning on 17 February 1979 was a limited punitive action that involved ground forces only. Chinese casualties were heavy, but provincial capitals in the border region fell, including Lang Son, which could have led the way into the Red River Delta. Having signalled to Hanoi that Chinese troops could have moved into the heartland had they so wished, Beijing announced on 5 March that the Vietnamese had been sufficiently chastised and that the campaign was over. The Chinese withdrawal was complete by 16 March. While it is true that China failed to compel Vietnam to withdraw from Cambodia, what it did achieve in a limited punitive war was a diplomatic objective: to expose as unreliable Soviet assurances of military support to Vietnam. In that sense, Beijing "did achieve a clear strategic victory by breaking the Soviet encirclement and by eliminating Moscow's threat of a two-front war".[35] Moscow apparently took to heart Deng's warning that China was prepared for a full-scale war with the Soviet Union, a warning that had been accompanied with all Chinese troops along the Sino-Soviet border being put on emergency war alert, the setting up of a new military command in Xinjiang, and the evacuation of about 300,000 civilians from the Sino-Soviet border.[36] Moscow did deploy warships off the coast of Vietnam, perhaps to deter a Chinese naval attack on the Vietnamese mainland and disputed island chains, but the Americans countered that move by deciding to send two aircraft carriers to a position where they were a day's cruise away from Vietnam.[37] In the event, the practical limitations of the Soviet-Vietnamese treaty were laid bare. Even more important from the regional point of view, the Chinese move, unchallenged by any substantial intervention by Moscow in Hanoi's favour, deterred a Vietnamese attack on Thailand.[38] At a broader level, Beijing became convinced that Moscow "lacked the political will to resort to war in order to sustain the Soviet sphere of influence in Asia". This conviction led Beijing to inform Moscow on 3 April 1979 that it intended to terminate the 1950 Sino-Soviet Treaty of Friendship, Alliance, and Mutual Assistance when it reached the end of its 30-year term in 1980.[39] Chinese leaders said after the war that "a lesson for Vietnam is also a lesson for the Soviet Union".[40]

Singapore's Response

Singapore's response revolved on two issues. The first was sovereignty. As a small state, it was particularly concerned over the implications "for all small nations in condoning or approving the armed overthrow of even a hateful government by a foreign army".[41] The "hateful government" was a reference to the government of Democratic Kampuchea led by Pol Pot, whose genocidal treatment of Cambodians was being used by the Vietnamese to justify their invasion and occupation of Cambodia. Although Singapore had no kind words for Pol Pot, it did point out that, till shortly before their ouster, he and his murderous colleagues used to be favourites of the same Hanoi government that was now revealing the atrocities of the fallen regime. Singapore's stance was that Democratic Kampuchea deserved to keep its seat at the United Nations because it was the legal government of Cambodia. If this did not happen — or even if the country's UN seat was left vacant — this caving in would mean the world body lending legitimacy to a blatant act of aggression by one state against another. Commenting on the Heng Samrin government that the Vietnamese had installed in Phnom Penh, Singapore pointed out that in February 1979 it had signed a Treaty of Friendship and Cooperation with Vietnam containing a clause that allowed for Vietnamese troops to be invited in. Singapore noted the ominous implications of this arrangement: "First invade a country. Then set up a front organization which will sign a treaty requesting outside armed intervention after the invasion has taken place, and all would be perfectly legal."[42] The legal issue of sovereignty was the first aspect of Singapore's position, the basis on which it was determined to mobilize international forces to reverse the Vietnamese occupation of Cambodia.

The second issue was that of balance-of-power politics. The American withdrawal from Vietnam had created a vacuum that China and Vietnam were competing to fill. Singapore did not deny that Vietnam had apprehensions about China since, for "small nations all great powers are potential threats",[43] and it was against a policy of bleeding Vietnam white to punish it for its Cambodian adventure. The presence of a strong and peaceful Vietnam, which had fought off both the French and the Americans, was a source of stability in a Southeast Asia adjoining a vast country like China. However, Singapore insisted that Vietnam was using its apprehension about a China threat "as a pretext to realize its own imperialist ambitions", recalling that, not so long ago, Vietnam itself had rejected the American thesis of a China threat when "the Americans sent troops into Vietnam for precisely the same reason — to save the rest of Southeast Asia, including Vietnam, from the Chinese menace".[44]

The link between Vietnam's regional actions — which Singapore placed in the context of Hanoi's unfulfilled aspirations for an Indochinese Federation that possibly could be extended to the rest of Southeast Asia — and the Soviet Union's global role lay in the world "imperialist". *From Phnom Penh to Kabul* excoriated relentlessly Moscow's motives in supporting Vietnamese expansionism. Drawing parallels between the Vietnamese invasion of Cambodia and the Soviet invasion of Afghanistan a year later, it said that the two related events attested to "the struggle for the establishment of a Communist world order".[45] Both were wars for a Soviet Empire, fought in one case through direct invasion and in the other through a proxy.[46] The bottom line: the "vacuum" created by the collapse of Western empires in the Third World "must be filled in the name of international proletarianism". The last of "Western imperialist wars" was fought in Vietnam. Within just three years of that war ending, "Vietnam, which had fought a war for national independence continuously for 30 years has now been harnessed to the cause of a socialist universal empire".[47] Vietnam's reinvention as part of a fresh empire, in the wake of a drawing down of American forces in Southeast Asia, threatened to create a new balance of power in the region inimical to Singapore's interests.

On the basis of these two issues, Singapore developed a "minimum" and a "maximum" objective regarding the resolution of the Cambodian crisis. The minimum objective was that the *status quo ante* should be restored by Cambodia withdrawing from the sphere of Soviet and Vietnamese influence to become again a buffer between Hanoi and Bangkok. This objective differed from Indonesia's and Malaysia's desire to see the Vietnamese-installed Heng Samrin regime consolidate itself. Singapore's position was closest to that of Thailand, which saw a direct threat to itself from the Vietnamese occupation of Cambodia. Indeed, Hanoi's troops had attacked Cambodian refugee camps in Thailand. The proximity of Hanoi's invading troops in Cambodia and uncertainty over Vietnamese intentions had driven Thailand into a quasi-alliance with China, which shared Bangkok's interests in curbing Vietnamese expansionism and which possessed both the will and the power to protect Thailand from Vietnamese encroachment. Singapore's maximum objective was the re-establishment of a genuinely independent, neutral and non-communist Cambodia (which necessarily would include the routing of the

Khmer Rouge) and the emergence of a non-aligned Vietnam that could work with ASEAN; Singapore was even prepared to accept the emergence of an Indochinese Federation if this were to be decided on freely by Cambodians, Laotians and Vietnamese and if this were not to be the result of a drive for hegemony by Hanoi. That maximum goal was shared by the other ASEAN states.[48]

Singapore embarked on a highly vocal condemnation of Hanoi's designs at the United Nations and elsewhere. It played a major role in the formulation of a common Indochina policy for ASEAN, initiating, organizing and coordinating most of the grouping's activities[49] so that the situation in Cambodia did not become a *fait accompli* because of a lack of international interest. As the main architect of ASEAN's Indochina policy, Singapore mediated between Thailand, and Indonesia and Malaysia.[50] It pointed out repeatedly that the crux of the conflict lay, not in the human-rights excesses perpetrated by the Khmer Rouge, dreadful though these were and strong though Singapore's reservations about the Pol Pot regime always had been; nor in the humanitarian crisis caused by the outflow of the "boat people", largely ethnic Chinese refugees who were fleeing Vietnam by sea; but in Vietnam's action, backed by the Soviet Union, in invading a neighbour in gross violation of the United Nations Charter. It was the consequences of that invasion that needed to be reversed; to focus attention either on the Khmer Rouge's atrocities or on the plight of the Vietnamese refugees, real though these were in themselves, was to fall prey to Hanoi's attempt to divert attention from its own, central and unacceptable role in the crisis. Resistance to Vietnamese aggression was necessary also because, otherwise, Vietnam would be emboldened to behave similarly with other regional countries, principally Thailand. As for the "boat people", it was not insignificant that most of them were Vietnamese of Chinese origin. Could it not be, Singapore argued, that Hanoi's motives in creating conditions that led to their departure was to cause an outflow of ethnic Chinese refugees who, if they landed elsewhere in Southeast Asia in sufficient numbers, would exacerbate underlying tensions between non-Chinese and Chinese in the host states, complicating their governments' relations with China? If that was the Vietnamese strategy, what humanitarian purpose could be achieved by keeping the refugees at the forefront of the Indochina issue?

A comprehensive analysis of the course of the Cambodian crisis, and the diplomatic initiatives that accompanied it, is beyond the scope of this study.[51] However, it is true to say that the crisis created a degree of convergence between the views of China and Singapore notwithstanding the Republic's opposition to Beijing's continuing support for communist/Chinese insurgencies in Southeast Asia, a support that complicated Singapore's efforts to entrench a common ASEAN position on the Vietnamese invasion of Cambodia. The close congruence of views between Thailand, threatened by Vietnam, and China helped Singapore consolidate an ASEAN position on the conflict that overcame the early reservations of Indonesia and Malaysia.

Intimations of the convergence between Singapore's and China's approaches to Vietnam's intentions were evident in November 1978, the month preceding the invasion. Deng Xiaoping, on a visit to Singapore, said that if Hanoi succeeded in controlling Indochina, the Indochinese Federation would "expand its influence and serve the global strategy of the Soviet Union to move southwards into the Indian Ocean... Wherever the Soviet Union attacked, China would help to repel the attack. To have peace, Asean had to unite with China and repel the Soviet Union and its Cuba in Southeast Asia, Vietnam".[52] To Lee, the problem was that while China wanted Southeast Asian countries to join it in isolating the "Russian bear", Singapore's neighbours wanted it to unite and isolate the "Chinese dragon". The reason was that there were no "overseas Russians" in Southeast Asia leading communist insurgencies supported by Moscow, but there were "overseas Chinese" supported by the Chinese Communist Party and government who were posing threats to Thailand, Malaysia, the Philippines and, to a lesser degree, Indonesia.[53]

During Lee's visit to China in November 1980, Premier Zhao Ziyang told him that China would try to allay Malaysian and Indonesian suspicions towards it. "He said Malaysia and Indonesia could never win over Vietnam away from the Soviet Union unless either Vietnam renounced regional hegemony, in which case it would not need the Soviet Union, or the Soviet Union renounced global hegemony, in which case it would not need Vietnam."[54] In his talks with Deng, Lee conveyed the point that Thailand and Singapore were in danger of being viewed as China's "stooges" because of their support for the Democratic Kampuchea Government's seat at the United Nations. Lee noted that Malaysia and Indonesia must be satisfied that continued support of the Democratic Kampuchea Government would not result in the restoration of China's influence in Cambodia. Both countries, he declared, believed the Vietnamese argument that ASEAN's actions helped China to make Vietnam weaker and would allow Beijing to increase its influence in Southeast Asia. "Malaysia and Indonesia saw China as the supporter of communist forces that had troubled them for the last 30 years," Lee recalls.[55] When Deng asked him repeatedly to help promote an alliance between the Cambodian resistance groups, Lee got him to confirm that China would encourage the establishment of a non-communist front to resist the Vietnamese; and that Beijing would accept the emergence of an independent Cambodian government after a Vietnamese withdrawal, a government on which China would have no hold.[56]

These Chinese agreements helped Singapore to create a common ASEAN position on Cambodia. Singapore's strategy was to try and break the nexus between China as a communist state and China as a sponsor of ethnic-Chinese-cum-communist movements in Southeast Asia. Once this break was effected, communist China would be little different from communist Russia or communist Vietnam in their dealings with Southeast Asia. That break would remove the crucial ethnic element bedevilling China's political relations with ASEAN states that had substantial Chinese populations, and open the way to a resolution of the Cambodia issue on its merits by stopping it from being held hostage to ASEAN nations' view of China as an ethnic player. Although Vietnam's occupation of Cambodia was reversed in 1991 only in the context of a larger turn of events — the disarray and then the disintegration of the Soviet Union whose support Vietnam had enjoyed — it is correct to say that Singapore's relentless efforts to keep the Cambodian issue high on the international agenda reflected a determination to ensure that the security of small states like itself should not collapse by default because of a failure of international will to uphold their sovereignty, because of the fact that a superpower was behind the aggressor, and because of the confounding effects of ethnicity on the international relations of Southeast Asia. The international balance of power must not be allowed to go against Singapore.

India's Response

If China's approach to the Indochina conflict and Southeast Asian security revolved on its interpretation of the intention and capabilities of Vietnam, the pivot of India's response to the conflict was its deep suspicion of the role of China, which had been revitalized by the Sino-U.S. *rapprochement*. This was where Vietnam and Indonesia proved vital to Indian interests.

According to Indian analyst K. Subrahmanyam, India had a large stake in ensuring that Chinese pressure on the Indochinese states was contained. "That has been our basic policy from the fifties. The only country that can do this is Vietnam, the most capable nation of the region. That is where the strategic interest[s] of India and Vietnam coincide."[57] Also, in Indira Gandhi's *realpolitik*-driven vision of Southeast Asia, a strong and anti-Chinese Indochina would "guard the flank of the Indian sphere of influence in South Asia. There was thus a convergence of Vietnamese and Indian views. Both were concerned with checking the southern advance of Chinese power".[58]

The other country of interest to India was Indonesia. Indigenous Indonesians' view of the affluent ethnic Chinese minority in their country as being exploitative; the Indonesian elite's strong aversion to the communist character of the Chinese regime; China's attempt to intervene in Indonesian affairs in the 1950s by using the issue of the status of overseas Chinese; and Beijing's perceived role as the mentor of the Communist Party of Indonesia were factors that alienated Jakarta from Beijing, notwithstanding the "aberration" of Sukarno's last years, when Indonesia teamed up with China to confront what the Indonesian leader perceived as Anglo-American designs in Southeast Asia injurious to Indonesian interests.[59] If there was an Indian "grand design" regarding Southeast Asia, Indonesia and Vietnam formed its two main pillars.[60]

As for the Soviet presence in Southeast Asia, it made strategic sense for Moscow to reinforce its military capability in the South China Sea by using Cam Ranh Bay in Vietnam if Moscow feared China's entry into the Indian Ocean or an increase in the American naval presence there.[61] In any case, the Soviet presence in Southeast Asia was not considered detrimental to regional security; instead, it was the American presence that attracted vocal criticism in Indian policy and scholarly circles. Referring, no doubt, to the circumstances in which the United States had to withdraw from Vietnam, Subrahmanyam hoped that the Americans "have learnt the lesson that their presence in mainland Southeast Asia is not only unwelcome but is militarily unsustainable".[62] And if, as Vietnam's critics pointed out, its invasion of Cambodia occurred in the context of Hanoi's links with Moscow, it was no less true, another Indian commentator exclaimed, that China had invaded Vietnam with the "tacit approval of a super power" — the United States. "An aspiring super power invaded India in 1962... The invasion was apparently undertaken to 'teach India a lesson'. For the same reason, Vietnam was invaded in 1979..."[63] The Soviet Union also was preferable to the United States because, unlike the latter, it rarely had permitted its strategic interests in South Asia to overshadow India's vital interests, and it had accepted India's pre-eminence and managerial role in South Asia.[64]

If the United States was excoriated for giving succour to Beijing and if the Soviet Union was seen as but responding to Sino-U.S. moves to contain it, Singapore's vociferous opposition to the Vietnamese invasion was seen in two-fold terms. First, Washington had a "very reliable ally" in Singapore because the city-state saw the American presence as a protection in case it came under pressure from Malaysia and Indonesia.[65] The second point, Indian policy-makers decided, was that Singapore's anti-Soviet and hence anti-Vietnamese stance was not based on the merits of the case but on a strategy of enhancing American interest in the city-state's economic fortunes by playing its anti-Soviet card and by convincing Washington of the close link between Singapore's prosperity and its strategic value.[66] Such sentiments left no one in doubt about how Indians viewed the source of the problem in Indochina. While it was the Vietnamese invasion of Cambodia that was making diplomatic waves, the real problem lay with China's desire to dominate Indochina in particular and Southeast Asia in general, as Indians saw it.

The Indian Government's stance initially was measured, however. It was even-handed under the Janata Party government of Morarji Desai, which did not recognize either the Democratic Kampuchea Government of the Khmer Rouge ousted by Hanoi or the People's Republic of Kampuchea regime installed by the Vietnamese. Even when China's attack on Vietnam in 1979 began to tilt New Delhi towards Hanoi on the Cambodian issue, India tried to be even-handed.

Thus, when the contentious issue of Cambodian representation was raised at the Sixth Non-Aligned Summit held in Havana in September 1979, India's position was that the seat should be left vacant. It was Indira Gandhi's return to power in January 1980 that drove Indian policy markedly in a pro-Hanoi direction, and New Delhi recognized Heng Samrin's regime in July 1980. (India recognized the Soviet-supported Babrak Karmal government in Afghanistan as well.) The decision, which came in the wake of a Vietnamese attack on Thai territory, caused the Indian-ASEAN Foreign Ministers' dialogue to be aborted. New Delhi stood its ground. However, by the mid-1980s, it began to realize that its endorsement of Vietnam's position on Cambodia — a position opposite to that of an ASEAN which wanted to see the Vietnamese military presence there come to an end — was becoming counterproductive. Vietnam's inflexible position was hurting Indian interests by highlighting the coincidence between ASEAN's formal approach and China's; and by underscoring the convergence of Chinese and American interests in Southeast Asia because of their common refusal to accept the military presence of Soviet-supported Vietnam in Cambodia.[67] Indian policymakers therefore went about trying to narrow differences between Vietnam and ASEAN.[68]

As for Singapore, the Indian recognition of the Vietnamese-installed government placed the city-state and New Delhi "on opposite sides of an issue crucial to peace and stability in Southeast Asia". At the Commonwealth Heads of Government Regional Meeting in the Indian capital in 1980, Lee Kuan Yew disputed Indira Gandhi's dismissal of the value of condemning armed intervention across frontiers, with the Singapore leader arguing that the Vietnamese and

Soviet occupations of Cambodia and Afghanistan were establishing "a new doctrine of justifiable intervention outside the framework of the UN Charter, setting precedents for open and armed intervention". The two countries argued again over Cambodia at the Commonwealth Heads of Government Meeting in New Delhi in November 1983.[69]

Kripa Sridharan makes the important point that Indian policy on Indochina confirmed "the operative condition in a derived relationship", which is that "crucial foreign policy interests determine choices towards a secondary area of concern".[70] India's overriding interests were to prevent China from exploiting the Vietnamese invasion of Cambodia to create a coalition of Southeast Asian countries willing to accept Beijing's regional assertiveness in exchange for reversing Hanoi's unacceptable gains in the area; and to balance against this goal India's stake in upholding the interests of Vietnam, its closest partner in Southeast Asia apart from Indonesia. For India, the key lay in enabling Hanoi to withdraw from Cambodia without suffering serious reverses to its security in the form of a regionally strengthened China. As noted earlier, the Cambodian conflict ultimately was resolved as a part of the dramatically unexpected implosion of the Soviet Union. However, what the conflict did was to reveal the extent of the divergence between ASEAN's and India's approaches to Southeast Asian security, notwithstanding concerns over China's role that New Delhi shared with Jakarta. Between India and Singapore lay a gulf of difference in the terminal phase of the Cold War.

The Indochina conflict and its diplomatic aftermath reversed Singapore's close relations with India and its suspicions about China in 1965. It is true to say of the

1980s that Singapore never had been closer to China and never had been farther from India. But the end of the Cold War changed that situation. As the international system created by the old bipolarity came crashing down, the disappearance of the certainties that it had sustained forced countries to abjure habits of thought and reflexes of action inherited from decades of bipolar animosity. So it was for China, India and Singapore. What occurred globally was not only the bloodless defeat of one superpower by another but the collapse of an historical challenge to the primacy of the capitalist order espoused by an America-led West. Save for two peripheral enclaves of defiance — Cuba and North Korea — countries now had a menu of only one world system to choose from. China effectively had joined that system in 1978 with its reforms; in 1991, India no longer excluded the West from a defining role in its destiny. However, a geopolitical fact that would have a bearing on Singapore's relations with Beijing was that, though Moscow's disappearance as a major global and Asian player benefited Beijing, as it did Washington, the Chinese relationship with the US lost "the degree of shared interest and strategic convergence that were present when confronting the Soviet Union and its regional allies during the second phase of the Cold War".[71] Instead, China's economic rise and the consequential growth of its political and military influence became the source of the greatest potential challenge to American global supremacy. Relations between Washington and Beijing became a key fact of the times, especially in Southeast Asia, which lay on China's periphery. India was yet to feature that prominently on the American radar. These were among the defining circumstances in which Singapore moved on to cement its ties with the two Asian protagonists.

NOTES

1 For an overview of early Singapore-China relations, see Lee Lai-to, *China's Changing Attitude Towards Singapore, 1965–1975* (Singapore: University of Singapore, Department of Political Science, November 1975). This work examines in detail the Singapore Government's prosecution of the Bank of China in Singapore in the late 1960s because of its inability to observe banking relations, and the fall-out from that affair, pp. 21–25. See also his "The Lion and the Dragon: A View on Singapore-China Relations", *Journal of Contemporary China* 10, no. 28 (August 2001): 415–25.

2 Michael Leifer, *Singapore's Foreign Policy: Coping with Vulnerability* (London: Routledge, 2000), pp. 111–12. Trade between Singapore and China, hugely in China's favour, went up from S$197.5 million in 1964 to almost S$770 million in 1974. See, Lee Lai-to, *China's Changing Attitude Towards Singapore*, p. 47.

3 Lee Kuan Yew, *From Third World to First: The Singapore Story, 1965–2000* (Singapore: Singapore Press Holdings and Times Editions, 2000), pp. 636–37.

4 Lee Lai-to, *China's Changing Attitude Towards Singapore*, p. 29.

5 Leifer, op. cit., p. 110.

6 Lee Kuan Yew, op. cit., pp. 638–39.

7 For more on this point, see Lee Lai-to, *China's Changing Attitude Towards Singapore*, pp. 27–28.

8 This paragraph draws on Lee, op. cit., pp. 640–49.

9 Chin Kin Wah, "A New Phase in Singapore's Relations with China", in Joyce K. Kallgren et al., eds., *ASEAN and China: An Evolving Relationship* (Berkeley: University of California, Institute of East Asian Studies, 1988), p. 277. Deng's role in ending China's support for communist insurgencies in Southeast Asia is covered in Lee Kuan Yew, op. cit., pp. 664–67.

10 Leifer, op. cit., p. 114.

11 Somkiat Onwimon, "India's Relations with the ASEAN Countries, 1966–1975: A Transaction Analysis", a dissertation presented to the Graduate Faculties of the University of Pennsylvania in partial fulfillment of the requirements for the degree of Doctor of Philosophy, 1981, pp. 236–43. Onwimon places these economic indicators of Indo-Singapore relations in the context of the trading volumes of both countries.

12 Lee Kuan Yew, op. cit., pp. 30–31.

13 Onwimon, op. cit., p. 150. He examines in some detail the problem that arose between the two countries over Indian workers on British bases. See pp. 151–54.

14 Kripa Sridharan, "The Evolution and Growth of India-Singapore Relations", in Yong Mun Cheong and V.V. Bhanoji Rao, eds., *Singapore-India Relations: A Primer* (Singapore: Singapore University Press, 1995), p. 23.

15 Ibid.

16 Kripa Sridharan, *The ASEAN Region in India's Foreign Policy* (Aldershot and Brookfield: Dartmouth, 1996), pp. 37–38.

17 Ibid., p. 38.

18 Ibid.

19 Sridharan, "The Evolution and Growth of India-Singapore Relations", p. 24.

20 The course of the crisis is charted in Asad-ul Iqbal Latif, "India and the Emergence of Bangladesh: A Study in Diplomatic History", a thesis submitted to the University of Cambridge for the degree of Master of Philosophy in International Relations, 1988.

21 Richard Sisson and Leo E. Rose, *War and Secession: Pakistan, India, and the Creation of Bangladesh* (Berkeley, Los Angeles and Oxford: University of California Press, 1990), p. 242.

22 Sridharan, "The Evolution and Growth of India-Singapore Relations", p. 25.

23 Thu-huong Nguyen-vo, *Khmer-Viet Relations and the Third Indochina Conflict* (Jefferson, North Carolina, and London: McFarland & Company, 1992), pp. 133–34.

24 Werner Draguhn, "The Indochina Conflict and the Positions of the Countries Involved", *Contemporary Southeast Asia* 5, no. 1 (June 1983): 95.

25 Ibid., p. 96.

26 Thu-huong Nguyen-vo, op. cit., p. 83.

27 Stephen J. Morris, *Why Vietnam Invaded Cambodia: Political Culture and the Causes of War* (Stanford: Stanford University Press, 1999), pp. 230–31.

28 Ibid., pp. 229–30.

29 Nguyen-vo, op. cit., p. 123.

30 For an analysis of this factor, and related factors, see Morris, op. cit., pp. 232–34.

31 *Su That Ve Quan He Viet Nam-Trung Quoc Trong 30 Nam Qua* [The Truth About Relations between Vietnam and China in the Past Thirty Years], translated and cited in Nguyen-vo, op. cit., pp. 85–86.

32 Morris, op. cit., pp. 232–34.

33 Draguhn, op. cit., pp. 106–7.

34 Nguyen-vo, op. cit., pp. 137–38.

35 Bruce Elleman, "Sino-Soviet Relations and the February 1979 Sino-Vietnamese Conflict", <http://www.vietnam.ttu.edu/vietnamcenter/events/1996_Symposium/96papers/elleviet.htm>.

36 Chang Pao-min, *Kampuchea Between China and Vietnam* (Singapore: Singapore University Press, 1985), pp. 88–89.

37 Nguyen-vo, op. cit., pp. 138–39.

38 Lee Kuan Yew, op. cit., pp. 669–70.

39 Elleman, op. cit.

40 *Straits Times*, 6 March 1979, cited in Chang, op. cit., p. 89.

41 *From Phnom Penh to Kabul* (Singapore: Ministry of Foreign Affairs, September 1980), p. 14.

42 Ibid.

43 Ibid., p. 13.

44 Ibid., p. 12; p. 13.

45 Ibid., p. 21.

46 Ibid., p. 35.

47 Ibid., p. 31.

48 For a study of the maximum and minimum objectives, see Peter Schier, "The Indochina Conflict from the Perspective of Singapore", *Contemporary Southeast Asia* 4, no. 2 (September 1982): 226–35.

49 Ibid., p. 226.

50 Ibid.

51 For an overview of Singapore's actions, see Lee Kuan Yew, op. cit., pp. 374–82.

52 Ibid., pp. 661–62.

53 Ibid., pp. 663–64.

54 Ibid., pp. 671–72.

55 Ibid., pp. 673–74.

56 Ibid., p. 674.

57 K. Subrahmanyam, "Indochina — Strategic Perspectives", in T.N. Kaul, ed., *India and Indochina: Perspectives of Cooperation*

82 *Between Rising Powers*

(New Delhi: Patriot Publishers, on behalf of the Indian Centre for Studies on Indochina, 1987), p. 43.
58 John W. Garver, "Chinese-Indian Rivalry in Indochina", *Asian Survey* 27, no. 11 (November 1987), cited in Mohammed Ayoob, *India and Southeast Asia: Indian Perceptions and Policies* (London and New York: Routledge, published under the auspices of the Institute of Southeast Asian Studies, Singapore, 1990), p. 56.
59 Ayoob, op. cit., p. 37.
60 Ibid., p. 38.
61 Subrahmanyam, "Indochina — Strategic Perspectives", p. 42.
62 Ibid., p. 43.
63 R. Rama Rao, "Common Interests", in Kaul, op. cit., p. 44.
64 Ayoob, op. cit., pp. 75–76.
65 Subrahmanyam, "Indochina — Strategic Perspectives", p. 42.
66 Ayoob, op. cit., p. 62.
67 This analysis of India's position is drawn from ibid., pp. 55–58.
68 For a detailed study of the intricacies of India's diplomatic initiatives on Cambodia and their impact on its relations with ASEAN, see Sridharan, *The ASEAN Region in India's Foreign Policy*, Chapter 6, pp. 134–62.
69 Lee Kuan Yew, op. cit., pp. 453–54.
70 Sridharan, op. cit., p. 135.
71 Michael Leifer, "China in Southeast Asia: Interdependence and Accommodation", in David S.G. Goodman and Gerald Segal, eds., *China Rising: Nationalism and Interdependence* (London and New York: Routledge, 1996), p. 157.

CHAPTER IV

ENGAGING CHINA
Interlocution

China's reforms straddled the global transition from the Cold War. China's future had hung in the balance in the late 1970s after the excesses of the Great Leap Forward and the Cultural Revolution. Following the death of Mao Zedong in 1976, Deng Xiaoping rose to power, determined to reform a failing system. Deng was opposed by those who believed that he would place the whole socialist project in jeopardy. The contest between the two sides came to the fore clearly at the Fifth National People's Congress in early 1978, when the Hua Guofeng faction (which would come to be branded as leftist) and Deng's moderates clashed. Within the year, there were signs that Deng had won. At the Third Plenum of the 11th Congress of the Chinese Communist Party in December, the party line calling for protracted class struggle was repudiated in favour of the Four Modernizations of agriculture, industry, research and development, and the military. The Four Modernizations,[1] which reoriented China towards the market, marked four successive phases of reform: agricultural and industrial devolution from 1979 to 1983; the second phase of reform from 1983 to 1987 that abolished communes and saw greater emphasis being placed on the establishment of special economic zones; the third phase from 1987 to 1993, during which the private sector was legalized as a complement to the public sector; and the fourth phase from 1993, when the socialist market economy was codified in the Constitution.[2] It was clear that the Dengists were charting China's future anew.

However, Satya J. Gabriel argues that even when Marxian ideas ceased to determine public policies in post-Mao China, there remained among the Chinese leadership "a latent Marxian ontology of economic life as a continuous series of tensions and struggles…".[3] History had shaped the jagged contours of that ontology. Both the leaders of China and its masses could draw on a common pool of memory of how their country had been forced to open its markets to Western traders in the 19th century through a series of "unequal treaties", notably the Treaty of Nanjing in 1842 that had ceded Hong Kong to Britain. But a suspicion of Western motives did not outweigh the felt need to open up to the world to recover from the Great Leap Forward and the Cultural Revolution. Placing Deng Xiaoping's reforms in the context of their precursors from 9A.D., Chi Wang notes that Deng responded to his opponents, who criticized his ideas as being pro-Western, by characterizing the reforms as socialism with Chinese characteristics.[4] The Dengists insisted that China was not selling its history or even the early achievements of its communist past in re-engaging the world. China was reformulating its strategy of survival and success on the basis that "opening up is just a means to an end, rather than an end in itself".[5]

Formulations containing words such as "socialism" did not go down well abroad, however. Reformist China's entry into global economy in the closing decades of the 20th century was a political event as well. After the disappearance of the Soviet Union and the end of the Cold War in 1991, liberal democracy became the dominant mode of governance, preferred in both the advanced economies and adopted in word, if not practised always in deed, in the states born out of the dissolution of the colonial European and Soviet empires. Among the nations arguing for liberal democracy as the defining principle of the post-Cold War era was the United States, whose victory over the Soviet Union led to exuberant calls to replace the Cold War strategy of containment with a "strategy of enlargement — enlargement of the world's community of market democracies".[6] The economic rejuvenation of a billion Chinese certainly made their country a welcome addition to the community of markets, but the problem was that China, with nuclear weapons and a veto at the United Nations Security Council, was not a democracy and had no desire to become one. Its socialism with Chinese characteristics — or Market-Leninism, the form in which the combination was popularized in the West — was a model where the market generated economic growth without challenging the hegemony of a one-party state structured along Leninist lines of legitimacy and authority. Should such an apparent anachronism be allowed to enter the economic club led by the advanced democracies? Or should praetorian China be expected to follow the Soviet Union into ideological oblivion? Would it thereby keep its *rendezvous* with the end of history, that moment of *dénouement* when the Berlin Wall fell to the latest assault in "humankind's long Darwinian search for an optimally efficient political-economic system"?[7]

The jury was out on this question, for China was both a bustling marketplace for foreigners and an *agora* with its own peculiar sense of the past. American businessmen could eat at the world's biggest McDonald's in Beijing and indulge in the "centuries-old foreign dream of selling one of everything to each Chinese".[8] Market-driven Americans might take heart from the curious historical detail that no two countries with McDonald's had warred with each other since hosting the fast-food restaurant,[9] this conjuncture being an extrapolation from the idea that countries prosperous enough to boast McDonald's had a stake in a peaceful international system where interlocking economic interests softened the warring instincts of states. However, the issue was not prosperity *per se* but a prosperous democracy — and that, China was not. Here, more convincing than a McTheory of international relations was democratic peace theory, which argues that the "distinctive domestic institutions and political values of liberal democracies ensure peace among them, but not between liberal democracies and non-democracies".[10] Thus, the need to see a democratic Beijing was an essential part of the desire to make China a peaceful country whose domestic norms would be consonant with the expectations of an America-led international system.

Yet, that was only one view. Sitting in Beijing, Americans might imagine that their democratic values were being universalized in the world's largest country through icons of popular consumption such as Big Macs and Coca-Cola. But the truth was that Americans in business and public policy often failed to remember that "in the world of political economy, you aren't necessarily what you eat".[11] Or drink. Big Macs and Coca-Cola were not necessarily franchised oases on the road leading out from China's communist past to democracy. China's own Darwinian experience of embattled centres, warring states, fears of disintegration, foreign invasions, rebellions against obstreperous barbarians, and an overall fear of chaos provided much clearer signposts to the future. The Beijing leadership could tap into this ingrained fear of chaos when it argued that the West was engaged in "peaceful evolution", a policy of subversion meant to undermine the party's hegemony in Chinese society without attacking China militarily. Whether that argument was a case of special pleading is not the issue: the point is that Chinese leaders could make the argument because it was true to the historical grain of a nation whose autonomy had been subverted without direct colonization. The force of national memory, utilized by Beijing but emanating authentically nevertheless from the deep consciousness of an intensely historical people, is what many Westerners and some Asians failed to understand or refused to acknowledge. The failure created the real gap between the reality of even modernizing China and the expectations that its democracy-minded global partners had of it. China simply refused to modernize its economy on others' political terms. This was the gap between it and the West.

It was this gap into which Singapore inserted itself. Psychologically speaking, the city-state belonged sufficiently to the West and China to speak credibly of one to the other. Singapore was a colonial creation by a Western adventurer; independent Singapore stayed true to its Western heritage, which included the institution of universal suffrage in Britain, by giving each adult the vote and choosing the rule of law. But that was about the extent of the homage it paid to its colonial past. Independent Singapore's soft-authoritarianism — which curtailed political and social liberties on the argument that democracy should not encourage a populist competition for votes based on divisive issues of ethnicity and class — ensured that governance took precedence over democracy in the "administrative state".[12] True, the political means through which Singapore ensured stability drew the wrath of scribes, but the wrathful do not invest — businessmen do — and scribes do not form the majority of voters. So long as investors were drawn to Singapore by the profits that they could make from its stability, as they were; and so long as the majority of voters did not prefer the freedoms of Western democracy to the economic advances that they were making, which they appeared not to prefer, Singapore's government had little to worry about. In the ruling party's compact with pragmatic Singaporeans, they would, and did, give it votes in return for the jobs, homes, highways and foreign holidays that the government delivered efficiently. This compact formed a basis of the Asian values that Singapore began to propagate in the final decades of the 20th century; we shall address later the role of value systems in Singapore's engagement of China.

The point is that if Singapore, a city-state of a few million people with hardly any natural resources, could thrive in the global market in spite of its authoritarian political system, there was no compelling reason why a billion-strong and resource-rich China could not do so. Singapore, the only Chinese-majority state outside Greater China, was the natural interlocutor between a modernizing China and a West that included those who apparently wished to transform the oldest existing civilizational nation into a Chinese suburb of the Western hemisphere. No such catastrophe need occur: such was the message from Singapore that resonated in Beijing.

It is important to emphasize the importance of Singapore's political foothold in China in assessing its engagement of Beijing and in comparing that access with Singapore's engagement of New Delhi. India's normative inheritance of Westminster-style democracy, the rule of law, an independent judiciary and an apolitical civil service made it unnecessary for any country to act as an interface between New Delhi and the West. The key difference between the take-off in Singapore's relations with China, and its ties with India, was the political one — the overtures to Beijing on which Singapore based its desired role of interlocutor. That role shaped itself around the many public interventions on China's behalf that Singapore's leaders, primarily Lee Kuan Yew, made to international audiences; and around his substantial access to Chinese leaders spearheading economic change. Singapore became a part of China's re-engagement with the world as Deng and his radical economic reformers, facing leftist opposition at home, encountered democrats' opposition to their political conservatism abroad.

Singapore could play this role because foreigners bent on democratizing China were not being helpful to the reformers trying to bring it into the global system. Chi Wang exclaims that, "encouraged by the outcry of a handful of Chinese students and intellectuals, who have little idea of life beyond their Westernized cities, some U.S. policy makers would like to see the 4,000 years of Chinese tradition change overnight".[13] In its opposition to foreign pressure on China, Singapore's message was that the flag does not have to follow trade: the Chinese Communist Party did not have to cede political control along with economic space. While Singapore hardly shared the Marxian ontological premises of Deng's pragmatic conservatives, it understood that their purpose was to revitalize China and preserve its ruling party. Their purpose was not to abolish the party's centrality and their own power in the affairs of the nation that the party had reclaimed from warlords at home and foreign predators three decades earlier. In providing a vote of support for the Four Modernizations from a foreign yet culturally familiar country, Singapore was saying in effect that there was a third way between the material poverty that Mao's autarchic Chineseness had inflicted on China while incontestably giving it autonomy in world affairs, and the danger that a prosperous China would become a global Chinatown with Western characteristics. That third way lay through Singapore's record of modernizing its economy in a non-Westernized polity. Among Asia's Newly-Industrialized Economies whose prowess the Chinese admired, colonial Hong Kong could not play the role of re-introducing China to the world; nor, obviously, could estranged Taiwan. Singapore could. It could show China the path back to a world defined, not by McDonald's Golden Arches under which the global nomads of commerce ate, drank and dreamt of changing China, but by the ancient arches of retreat that the cunning turns of history now had cleared for China's re-entry to the world.

It was a powerful message, combining enough of market possibilities with due regard for the Chinese leadership's Leninist role to go down very well in Beijing. Indeed, when Deng toured southern China in

1992 to accelerate his reforms, he specifically called for "learning from Singapore" to promote what he defined as "rapid economic development with good social order". "The choice of Singapore's economic and social model as the archetype (of) Chinese development was a carefully scripted and rehearsed effort on the part of Deng Xiaoping... His message to the party cadres was to prioritize robust economic achievements over inter- or intra-party politics."[14] Beijing searched for "non-Western experiences" because it deemed the political cost of adopting Western-style democracy to be too high. In later years, Singapore's political system — which a Chinese scholar defined as "electoral authoritarianism" — caught the attention of party school officials, who believed that it was very likely that Beijing would adopt a modified Singaporean style of limited democracy.[15] By 1996, Singapore became the foreign country that Beijing residents favoured the most.[16] Singapore's interlocutory role took off in China.

Interlocution has two sides. To China, Singapore presented itself as a politically safe economic bridge to a Western-led world. To the West, Singapore presented China, not just as a land of economic opportunity but as a player in the larger arena of war and peace. During the Cold War, when speaking at a joint meeting of the United States Congress in Washington, D.C., in 1985, Lee Kuan Yew said: "I want to refocus your attention, distracted by the problems of trade imbalance, job loss, high value of the dollar, and budget deficits, back on the basic issues of war and peace."[17] More than the atom bomb had been responsible for the four decades of relative peace since World War II, he said. Decolonization; the establishment of an open and fair trading system under the General Agreement on Tariffs and Trade; and the creation of a stable currency exchange system under the

original International Monetary Fund Agreement at
Bretton Woods had laid the basis of a world order in
which the explosive growth in trade, banking and finance
had provided nations with a realistic alternative to
seeking power through territorial aggrandizement. Japan
had taken off, followed by South Korea, Taiwan, Hong
Kong and the ASEAN countries.[18]

Placing post-Maoist China's decision to modernize
its economy firmly within the possibilities of this
peaceful economic order, he reminded his audience
that a "poor but ideologically fervent China" had been
a "ceaseless spoiler of other countries' economic plans"
from 1949 to 1976, undermining their stability by
exporting revolution.[19] China had discontinued
support for guerilla insurgencies in Southeast Asia
"for the present",[20] Lee said in a pointed reminder of
what Beijing could relapse into doing should it be
rebuffed by the international system. Hailing the
significance of China's decision to modernize for
peace, stability and growth in Asia, he framed his
remarks against the contest between democracy and
the free market *versus* communism and the controlled
economy, the ideological binaries through which Cold
War Americans viewed and judged the world. He
asked Americans whether they wanted to abandon
the contest for Third World hearts and minds that
they nearly had won. Calling on American legislators
to abjure protectionism, he asked their country to
uphold rules of international conduct that reward
peaceful, cooperative behaviour and that punish
transgressors.[21] "In every age, the leading power has
to carry the burden of encouraging the peaceful
acceptance of the status quo," Lee observed.[22]

That observation did not lose its edge with the end
of the Cold War; if anything, the disappearance of the

Soviet Union renewed the urgency of Washington drawing Beijing into the *status quo* because the United States now was not only the leading global power but the only superpower.

Emerging as ASEAN's most ardent advocate of engagement with China, Singapore leaders touched on the need for engagement in almost every speech they made or interview they gave on East Asian affairs.[23] In 1994, Lee said: "For the world's stability and security, integrating China into an international framework is not a question of choice but of necessity. The world does not need another Cold War."[24] Lee encapsulated Singapore's expectations of China's role in 1996, when the Nixon Center for Peace and Freedom honoured him with the Architect of the New Century Award. Groatian undertones were heavy in Lee's speech on the occasion. "Trade does not prevent wars, but it does require peace," Lee quoted Richard Nixon as writing in his book, *Beyond Peace*.[25] He drew on the former U.S. President's words to argue that China should be engaged. "China has repeatedly stated that it will never become a hegemon. It is in everyone's interest that before that moment of choice arrives, China should be given every incentive to choose international cooperation which will absorb its energies constructively for another 50 to 100 years," Lee declared.[26] His Groatian emphasis on economic cooperation as a source of peace was accompanied by a ready reminder of the other strand of Singapore's approach to global affairs: the city-state's belief in a balance of power among major international players, a balance that should be supple enough to incorporate rising powers that might otherwise threaten the *status quo*, but a balance by whose rules the rising power must play as well. Thus, if China did not have

economic opportunities to grow peacefully, the world
would have to live with a "pushy" Beijing, Lee said.
In that case, however, the United States would not be
the only country to be concerned about what China
would do when it was able to "contest the present
world dispensation".[27] Asian countries shared the
concern: would China seek to re-establish its
traditional pattern of international relations in which
vassal states had a tributary relationship with the
Middle Kingdom? "Any signs of this will alarm all
the countries in the region, and cause most countries
to realign themselves closer to the US and Japan,"
Lee forecast.[28] His warning, that a revisionist China
would cause other Asian countries to balance it by
moving towards the United States and Japan, was
directed, no doubt, at Beijing. That done, his larger
message was meant for the West, including the United
States. "The world will not be better off with a China
that is not bound by its rules," Singapore's elder
statesman declared.[29]

Lee's remarks summed up Singapore's case for
engaging a rising China, a case that was two decades
old when he spoke at the Nixon Center. He placed
these remarks within the context of America's role in
Asia. Lee recalled how East Asian industrialization had
been hastened by America's military interventions in
Japan, Korea and Vietnam; and by its economic
initiatives, from the reconstruction of Japan, to helping
South Korea rebuild, and to buying time in Vietnam to
enable Southeast Asia to get its act together and lay the
foundations of ASEAN's growth. China's entry into
this East Asian industrial system had "sparked off the
most spectacular economic transformations in the
history of man". Indeed, Lee forecast, American policies
had initiated a process that in the next two to three

decades would move the world's economic centre of gravity from the Atlantic to the Pacific. The United States now should use the time available to help China integrate itself into the world community and play a role in shaping the international order. Even as he made these points, Lee characterized Nixon as a "pragmatic strategist" who today would engage and not contain China, but the former American leader also would "quietly set pieces into place for a fallback position should China not play according to the rules as a good global citizen". In that eventuality, which would force countries to choose sides, Nixon would make arrangements to win over to America's side Japan, Korea, ASEAN, India, Australia, New Zealand and the Russian Federation.[30] Lee was aware of how decisively the Asian balance of power could shift should an economically resurgent China assert itself strategically. But such a change would occur only after turns down the road — and turns that were by no means inexorable — in the evolution of the post-Cold War security order. What the emerging contours of that order required was not China's containment but its engagement. This goal called for the managers of the global order to take a clear view of their responsibilities.

China's transformation from a political-ethnic threat to Singapore, to an object of intense engagement appears astonishing, but it is important to keep certain continuities in view. Whether during the Cold War or after it, Singapore's objective was to encourage the United States and the other powers to bring China into the international *status quo*. After the Cold War, Singapore had no desire to see Asia regress to a Sinocentric regional order reminiscent of the pre-European tributary system that had reduced states on China's periphery to satellites revolving around the

Middle Kingdom in hierarchical subordination. An effective return to the past was not a stated Chinese intention, of course, but intentions can change with ability, especially for a nation with stubborn memories of its centrality in Asian affairs before the advent of colonialism ended that role and inaugurated a Chinese century of humiliation at Western hands. It was not Singapore's intention to see China alter the norms and practices of international relations as it rose to prominence. Particularly sensitive to how its relations with China would be viewed by its neighbours and the West, Chinese-majority Singapore made it clear that it was not an interlocutor for an ascendant China wishing to exclude the external powers from Asia in a China-led future. All that Singapore was saying was that the external powers, primarily the United States, should not seek to exclude China from supping at the table of existing powers. In 1998, Singapore Minister George Yeo warned: "Together with the European Union, the US and Japan will have to manage carefully and strategically China's incorporation into the global system. The alternative is global conflict."[31] There was no question of Singapore favouring an Asia with Chinese characteristics but, equally, it did not want China to be treated unfavourably merely because Beijing wished to run its domestic affairs as it pleased. The distinction between Singapore wanting to bring China peacefully into the Asian balance of power — which it did desire — and Singapore wanting Asia to become a regional system in China's orbit — which it did not desire — is an important one.

It is difficult to determine what effect the city-state's interlocutory role had on Western, especially American, policies towards China. On the occasion of the Nixon Center award, Henry Kissinger feted Lee for the "seminal role" that he had played "in educating this provincial country, thrown into sudden contact with cultures that it never had to deal with". Kissinger chided Americans for their tendency to demand that "other nations adopt today what it took 800 years of evolution to produce in the West", echoing Singapore's objection to external pressure being brought on China to democratize.

However, the actual course of the American encounter with China has been more complex, of course. Washington's relations with Beijing have reflected attempts by policymakers to "choose between a range of policy options that they hope or believe will have the effect of integrating China into the world order and/or deter China from actions seriously disruptive of the world order".[32] Within this framework, issues of trade, labour, democracy, human rights, religious freedom, weapons proliferation and environmental responsibility — whether championed by legislators or by non-governmental organizations and political lobbies — have risen or receded on the White House's agenda as part of a tactical embrace of Beijing that has veered from close engagement during the Cold War Nixon years, to ambiguous calls for a strategic partnership during the Clinton era, to what reads like strategic containment in all but name.[33] The latest approach to China is embodied in documents such as the United States *National Security Strategy* released in 2002, when President George W. Bush declared that he sought to create "a balance of power that favors human freedom". In that context, the document welcomes the emergence of a strong, peaceful, and prosperous China but insists that the "democratic development of China is crucial to that future". China's leaders have not made yet "the next series of fundamental choices about the character of their state", it says, warning: "In pursuing advanced military capabilities that can threaten its neighbors in the Asia-Pacific region, China is following an outdated path that, in the end, will hamper its own pursuit of national greatness."[34] A balance of power that favours human freedom does not seem to have a great deal to offer Beijing.

This is another way of saying that Singapore's interlocutory role — which has emphasized the importance for the West of engaging China as a power without demanding the reform of domestic Chinese politics as a condition for engagement — has not had a substantial impact on the direction of the Sino-U.S. relationship. But this does not need to be said at all because Singapore has had no illusions about its ability to influence foreign policy outcomes in Washington — or Tokyo or Brussels. There, chanceries would fashion strategies towards Beijing on the basis of their own power, interests and imperatives — much as China would treat these capitals in terms of its own calculus of strength, interests and exigencies, not in terms of Singapore's arguments on behalf of an apposite international system into which it would like to see China incorporated as a great power. Speaking of the city-state's approach to Beijing, Khong declares that engagement is a process in which "interested members of the international community can participate", there being nothing to suggest that "to qualify as an 'engager,' states like Singapore — or Malaysia or Indonesia — must be able to unilaterally move the 'engagee' toward the goal of using its power responsibly".[35] Rather, the interlocutory aspect of Singapore's engagement of China has reflected its leaders' awareness of the importance of "voice" in shaping the terms of a debate.[36] In arguing that China should be engaged and not isolated or contained, Singapore has tried to ensure that China's voice would not be lost in translation into the political parlance of a West where Kissinger's 800 years of development have produced contending discourses of capitalism, liberalism, democracy and human rights, all seeking to define how nations should behave with their own populations and with one another. The rise of China reinvigorated a global debate in which Singapore weighed in.

Over the years, Singapore's interlocutory role has receded as a factor in its relations with China. This is because reformist Beijing does not need an interlocutor as it did in the early years of its entry to the global system. Its own leaders, particularly young, Western-educated technocrats moving up the political and corporate ladders, are more than capable of arguing China's case to the rest of the world. Singapore's interlocutory role also has confronted key issues in Beijing's relations with the world, including the Tiananmen Square killings and their effect on the return of Hong Kong to the mainland. There have been other issues as well, of a different nature: Singapore's espousal of Asian values in an era of China's rise, Beijing's entry into the ASEAN Regional Forum, the fate of the Suzhou Industrial Park, and Taiwan's role in the world's relations with China. To these issues we now turn.

NOTES

1 Zhou Enlai articulated the Four Modernizations in 1975, but Deng Xiaoping transformed them into public policy.
2 Satya J. Gabriel, "Economic Liberalization in Post-Mao China: Crossing the River by Feeling for Stones", China Essay Series, Essay Number 7, October 1998, Mount Holyoke College, Department of Economics, <http://www.mtholyoke.edu/courses/sgabriel/economics/china-essays/7.html>.
3 Ibid.
4 Chi Wang, "Some Historical Reflections on Chinese Economic

Reforms: From Wang Mang to Deng Xiaoping, 9 A.D. to the Present", in A.M. Canyon, ed., *Assessment of China into the 21st Century* (New York: Nova Science Publishers, Inc., 1997), p. 31.

5 Wang Mengkui, chief editor, *China's Economic Transformation Over 20 Years*, organized and sponsored by the China (Hainan) Institute of Reform and Development (Beijing: Foreign Languages Press, 2000), p. 329.

6 Senior American official American Lake in 1993, cited in Sean M. Lynn-Jones, "Why the United States Should Spread Democracy", International Security Programme, Belfer Centre for Science and International Affairs, John F. Kennedy School of Government, March 1998, <www.ciaonet.org/wps/lys02/>.

7 Daniel Burstein and Arne De Keijzer, *Big Dragon China's Future: What It Means for Business, the Economy, and the Global Order* (New York: Simon & Schuster, 1998), p. 14.

8 Ibid., p. 15.

9 The "Golden Arches Theory of Conflict Prevention" is propounded in Thomas L. Friedman, *The Lexus and the Olive Tree: Understanding Globalization* (New York: Farrar, Straus & Giroux, 1999). The so-called theory is critiqued in Jacob Weisberg, "DOS Capitalism: Thomas Friedman embraces the forces of globalization", 18 April 1999, <www.slate.com/id/25365/>.

10 Avery Goldstein, "Great Expectations: Interpreting China's Arrival", in Michael E. Brown et al., eds., *The Rise of China: An International Security Reader* (Cambridge, Massachusetts, and London, England: MIT Press, 2000), p. 33.

11 Burstein and De Keijzer, op. cit., p. 16.

12 Chan Heng Chee, "Politics in an Administrative State: Where has the Politics Gone?" (Singapore: University of Singapore, Department of Political Science, 1975).

13 Chi Wang, op. cit., p. 31.

14 Zheng Yongnian and Tok Sow Keat, *How China Views Singapore* (Singapore: East Asian Institute, Background Brief No. 184, 19 March 2004), p. 6.

15 Ibid., pp. 11–12.

16 Yongnian Zheng, "Nationalism, Globalism, and China's International Relations", in Weixing Hu et al., *China's International Relations in the 21st Century: Dynamics of Paradigm*

Shifts (Lanham, New York and Oxford: University Press of America, 2000), pp. 97–98.

17 Lee Kuan Yew, "Peace and Progress in East Asia", speech to a Joint Meeting of the United States Congress in Washington, D.C., on 9 October 1985, in *Speeches: A Bimonthly Selection of Ministerial Speeches* 9, no. 5 (September–October '85): 5.

18 Ibid., pp. 6–7.
19 Ibid., pp. 7–8.
20 Ibid., p. 8.
21 Ibid., p. 7; pp. 10–11; p. 14.
22 Ibid., p. 13.
23 Ian Storey, "Singapore and the Rise of China: Perceptions and Policy", in Herbert Yee and Ian Storey, eds., *The China Threat: Perceptions, Myths and Reality* (London and New York: RoutledgeCurzon, 2004), p. 217.
24 Storey, ibid., p. 217.
25 Richard Nixon, *Beyond Peace* (New York: Random House, 1994).
26 <www.nixoncenter.org/publications/YEW96.html>.
27 Ibid.
28 Ibid.
29 Ibid.
30 Ibid.
31 Information Minister George Yeo, cited in Storey, op. cit., p. 217.
32 Robert G. Sutter, "Seeking Integration and Deterrence — The U.S. Role in Shaping China's Future", in *China's Economic Future: Challenges to U.S. Policy*, edited by the Joint Economic Committee, Congress of the United States, Studies on Contemporary China (Armonk, New York, and London, England: M.E. Sharpe, 1997), p. 499.
33 The evolution of relations is analysed in Derwin Pereira, "Congress, the Presidency and US-China policy: A comparison of the Bush and Clinton Presidencies", Research Paper for the Master in Public Administration, Harvard University, 2006; and Derwin Pereira, "China Rising: Conflict or Cooperation with the United States?", Research Paper for the Master in Public Administration, Harvard University, 2006.
34 <http://www.whitehouse.gov/nsc/nssall.html>.
35 Yuen Foong Khong, "Singapore: a time for economic and political engagement", in Johnston and Ross, eds., *Engaging China: The Management of an Emerging Power*, op. cit., p. 112.
36 Ibid., p. 113.

CHAPTER V

FROM TIANANMEN SQUARE TO HONG KONG

Tiananmen Square is named ground. The Square is the figurative centre of China's literal centre; it is what a journalist calls "China's state cathedral".[1] Tiananmen, the Gate of Heavenly Peace — the main gate leading from the centre of power to the rest of China and thence the world — is the symbolic space where the emperor could make spiritual contact with his subjects.[2] The spiritualism emanated by power transcended the rise and fall of not just dynasties but ideologies. Tainanmen, which had been a site of the May Fourth Movement of 1919, was the arena where Mao Zedong proclaimed the birth of a new China in 1949. He had the area outside Tiananmen levelled, rebuilding the square into a grander version of Moscow's Red Square, which he might have had in mind. Tiananmen was where Mao met Red Guards during the Cultural Revolution.[3] But if the Square was where the ruler met the masses, it was also where the masses met their ruler. In the post-Mao China of 1978–79, thousands recorded their protests on a stretch of blank wall called "Democracy Wall" to the west of Tiananmen Square. Deng put a stop to this expression of discontent when people began to attack the Communist Party and system. Wei Jinsheng, a dissident who had demanded democracy as the "fifth modernization" to complete Deng's Four Modernizations, was punished severely. Initially, Deng had appeared to believe that economic reforms could not survive without a free discussion of problems and solutions. This idea, which had blossomed during the Prague Spring of 1968, had been adopted by Chinese Communist Party Chairman Hu Yaobang and had been advanced by Soviet leader Mikhail Gorbachev. However, as inflation, corruption and nepotism accompanied China's reforms, the anger of workers, students and intellectuals was sidelined in Beijing's quest to preserve political stability at all costs. When Chinese television announced Hu's death on 15 April 1989, popular mourning over his demise became a channel for the expression of repressed demands for political change, in a replay of the demonstrations at the funeral of Zhou Enlai in 1976. China was in ferment.

On the international front, although the Berlin Wall had several months left to fall, the winds of *glasnost* (openness) released by Gorbachev in 1985 were travelling well. The explosive situation in Eastern Europe, with the Round Table Talks in Poland and the liberalization of the Hungarian Communist Party, offered political parallels that the intelligentsia found impossible to miss in restive China. The year 1989 was also a year of anniversaries: the 200th anniversary of the French Revolution, the 70th anniversary of the May Fourth Movement, and the 40th anniversary of the founding of the People's Republic itself. In another anniversarial irony, Gorbachev himself visited Beijing in May 1989, the first visit by such a senior Soviet figure in the 30 years since Khruschev had come to parley with Mao in 1959.[4] Gorbachev's car was cheered by students in an unequivocal message to the Chinese authorities.

They were concerned already. Towards the end of April, Deng had referred to the international context in which trouble was brewing among the Beijing students, who increasingly were being seen as conspirators and rebels. Deng is said to have told party members: "These people have come under the influence and encouragement of Yugoslavian, Polish, Hungarian and Russian elements who [agitate for] liberalization, who urge them to rise up and create turmoil. They will cause the country and the Chinese people to have no future. We must take measures and act quickly, without losing any time."[5] Party General-Secretary Zhao Ziyang thought otherwise, but he soon would be sidelined as well. In a passionate attempt to get the students to call off their protests, Zhao appeared in Tiananmen Square on the morning of 19 May, and pleaded with the crowd: "We have come too late... We demonstrated and lay across railroad tracks when we were young, too, and took no thought for the future. But I have to ask you to think carefully about the future."[6] He was too late because the previous night, a Politburo Standing Committee meeting hastily had been called to endorse martial law. Zhao had cast the only dissenting vote before meeting the students in Tiananmen and making his exit to *de facto* house arrest, in which he would spend his remaining years.

Martial law was imposed on Beijing on 20 May. But the students did not retreat from their challenge to central authority, in which workers had joined them; and protests had spread to other cities, including Shanghai, Chengdu, and Guangzhou. A replica of the Statue of Liberty named the Goddess of Democracy heretically appeared in Tiananmen Square, although the youthful rebels also sang the *Internationale* and thought of themselves as patriotic heirs of the May Fourth Movement. The Square had come into its own as the interface between the ruled and the rulers. The protesters refused to retreat; violence escalated near Tiananmen; and a hardline faction, which had emerged victorious from divisions in the Beijing leadership over how to handle the challenge mounting outside, decided to use force to end what it saw as a counter-revolutionary plot against the nation. The world watched how China after Mao would deal with the legacy of both its imperial and communist pasts on the named ground that again had turned into a staging post of China's future.

THE TIANANMEN CRACKDOWN

On 4 June 1989, Tiananmen kept its *rendezvous* with history. Who was responsible, and how far, for ordering the crackdown is a point of contention,[7] and the numbers of those killed and injured vary considerably in different accounts.[8] The scale of casualties was modest by the yardstick of lives that had been snuffed out by the Great Leap Forward or thrown to the winds by the Cultural Revolution. However, judged by the expectations that China's re-engagement with the world had roused, Tiananmen marked no less than the closing of a chapter of history. Condemnation arose from around the world.

On the international Left, Trotskyists declared themselves vindicated by the latest expression of obdurate Stalinist continuities from Berlin in 1953 to Budapest in 1956 to Prague in 1968 to suppressed spring in Beijing now. There were other lines of descent as well, inherited from running street battles of dissent. Tiananmen in 1989 took up from the burning May of 1968, when the spontaneous daring of young societies had rocked the brooding power of old states.[9] On the international Right, those who had averred that economic change could not lead to political liberalization in the land of socialism with Chinese characteristics found themselves vindicated as well. On that basis, conservatives such as Senator Jesse Helms and Max Kampelman, head of Freedom House, called for sanctions.[10] The Chinese state had shown its claws, and had drawn fresh blood. China had re-entered the world all right, *via* Tiananmen, the Gate of Heavenly Peace through which imperial power once gazed at its realm, imperturbable in a timeless Mandate of Heaven. The world had changed, but China had not. So much for the world engaging China, the voices of condemnation argued. Engagement was nothing else but appeasement. And appeasement had a recent history: it had led to a world war. This must not happen again.

Although less condemnatory than popular sentiment, official reactions were telling as well. The United States and the European Union announced an embargo on the sale of weapons to China. Washington froze high-level official exchanges with Beijing, imposed a number of economic sanctions, and suspended several trade and investment programmes. At the Group of Seven summit in Houston in 1990, Western nations called for renewed political and economic reforms in China, particularly in the disputed field of human rights. Tiananmen disrupted the U.S.-China trade relationship, with American investors' interest in China dropping dramatically.[11]

But what suffered most was China's image, which changed from that of a reformist ally of the West to a threat to global peace and American interests. Tiananmen provided grounds for arguments against trade liberalization with China since access to world markets only would serve to empower the Chinese leaders at home and embolden them abroad. Tiananmen, a mere incident in the ancient lexicon of China's rulers, became a massacre in the register of contemporary world affairs. China's new symbol was 19-year-old Wang Weilin confronting a column of tanks, forcing them to swerve, and making them come to a halt.[12] Soon after Tiananmen, recalcitrant regimes fell in Romania, Poland, Czechoslovakia, Hungary, and Bulgaria. So did the Berlin Wall, ending German socialism and reunifying Germany. These transformations of once apparently impregnable systems threw into sharper relief the precarious position of Market-Leninism in the international system. When the transformations climaxed with the dissolution of the Soviet Union in 1991, the political divide in the international system was crystal clear. Equally clear, however, was the fact that the Soviet Union had disappeared into history whereas China remained sovereign and united, if defiant — and also a primary factor in the international system. Of course, that primacy made China the natural potential challenger to the United States in post-Cold War Asia.

Singapore's Response

Singapore steered clear of both Chinese under-statements and the global outpouring of angst over the abiding significance of Tiananmen. On 5 June 1989, Lee issued a statement saying that his Cabinet colleagues and he were "shocked, horrified and saddened by this disastrous turn of events". The firepower and violence caused many deaths and casualties and were "totally disproportionate to the resistance unarmed civilians offered". Although Singapore did not condemn the Chinese leadership, it warned that a China where large sections of the people, including the best-educated, were "at odds with the government means trouble, with people resentful, reforms stalled, and economy stagnant". Given its size, such a China could create problems for itself and its Asian neighbours. "We hope wiser counsels will prevail to pursue conciliation, so that the Chinese people can resume the progress which the open-door policies have brought them."[13]

In the aftermath of Tiananmen, five linked motifs mapped Singapore's attitude to China. The first was a defence, not of the military means adopted to put down the protests, but of Beijing's refusal to allow the protests to topple the political system. Secondly, Lee articulated this position on the basis of a long view of Chinese history in which the state saw its primary role as preserving stability and keeping society safe from the threat of chaos. Thirdly, the state's stabilizing role required a hierarchical respect for authority that the protesters unforgivably had breached by mocking their leaders. Fourthly, underscoring his reading of the Chinese mind even before Tiananmen, Lee played down both the utility and the ability of Western-inspired ideals of democracy and human rights to move China, a far more appropriate political framework being the Chinese ordering of reality in which national history and culture loomed large. Consequently, Singapore viewed Tiananmen, not as a part of the trajectory of democratization that had overthrown communist regimes in Eastern Europe and the Soviet Union, but as an aspect of China's own political and social evolution. Fifthly, Lee reiterated post-Tiananmen China's continuing national interest in staying engaged with the world — this reminder also being a way of saying that the world should not punish Beijing by isolating it. At stake down the road was nothing less than the circumstances in which Hong Kong's return to China, agreed on with the British in 1984, would occur. Tiananmen had tarnished China's reputation, but what mattered was that international manoeuvrings should not exploit the shock felt by Chinese in the British-ruled territory to derail its beneficial re-incorporation into China on schedule by 1997.

In a word, Singapore's response to Tiananmen confirmed and extended its strategy of getting the great powers to integrate Beijing into the global order by requiring it to conduct its international relations by international rules, but not to demand as well that it give up its autonomy to manage its domestic affairs. The culturalist assumptions in Singapore's response drew criticism from those in the West and elsewhere who saw the city-state acting as an apologist for a China that had revealed its true political face within a mere decade of apparently softening economic reforms; the memory of Singapore's response would add grist to the mill of those who would criticize it for its role in enunciating Asian values in the 1990s. However, Singapore well could argue that, in its response to Tiananmen, it was being consistent in extending to Beijing what all nations, including itself, enjoyed by virtue of their sovereignty: their right to manage their domestic affairs so long as the consequences did not threaten other nations. The Tiananmen crackdown did not threaten the international system. Needless to add, this stance endeared Singapore to China — and advanced the city-state's own engagement with it — at a time when Beijing was a target of intense international opprobrium.

Lee presented Singapore's position on Tiananmen in a series of media interviews and on public occasions, the essence of the message appearing in his memoirs as well. He was clear that, in spite of his and Singaporeans' disquiet over the use of tanks against civilians, Deng's refusal to give in to the protesters had saved China. "A veteran of war and revolution, he saw the student demonstrators at Tiananmen as a danger that threatened to throw China back into turmoil and chaos, prostrate for another 100 years... But for him the People's Republic of China would have collapsed as the Soviet Union did."[14] Zhao Ziyang, by contrast, had not shown "that toughness needed in the leader of a China on the verge of *luan* (chaos). Orderly protesters had been allowed to become defiant rebels. If not firmly dealt with, they could have triggered off similar disorder throughout the vast country. Tiananmen is not London's Trafalgar Square".[15] Nor was Chinese history British, American or Indian history. "History and culture decides the evolution of societies... In China there is no such thing as a mass, peaceful resistance or dissident movement as in India. That's a different culture," Lee observed. "(In) China, when a dynasty falls, it is always by revolution. The Chinese word for revolution is 'qi yi', the arising of righteousness. In other words, the ruler is unjust, wicked, cruel, oppressive. Therefore the people arise in righteousness. That will be a disaster for China. It means maybe back to warlordism because it's such a big country," he noted in a possible reference to the Republican Revolution of 1911 that had overthrown the Qing dynasty but had triggered a process marred by the warlordism of the pre-communist era. What the students forgot was that they were in that China. There, Deng had "fought with his life to defeat the warlords".[16]

Recalling the context that had moulded Deng, Lee cited the scale of his encounter with history. Deng took part in the epic Long March, where 90,000 began the journey and fewer than 10,000 arrived in Yenan a year later. Deng's thinking was "framed and frozen" by the millions in China who had died fighting the Japanese. When the Japanese advanced across the Yellow River, the dykes were broken to flood the area and stop the invaders. That led to the Henan famine of 1938 in which six to eight million people died. But the Japanese were stopped. The Deng who had helped to stop them commanded the communist armies that crossed the Yangtze and chased Chiang Kai-shek's armies to Taiwan. "Are 100,000 students going to dispute his right to govern China? You must see it in that historic perspective, and you know nobody but nobody will change him."[17]

Looking further back into history, Lee placed Deng's revolutionary credentials for governing China, earned in the thick of battles that settled the fate of hundreds of millions, firmly within an earlier imperial tradition in which the ruler's personal prestige embodied the inviolability of the system. It was one thing for the students to demand reform to improve the system, in which case one faction or the other of the party could have adopted their demands without destroying the entire political structure. But it was another thing when the historical youngsters attacked Li Peng: then, it was not possible for any faction to defend them because that was not the way in which even an anti-Li faction would go about getting rid of a premier. And when the students ridiculed Deng and compared him unfavourably with Mao, "I felt in my bones that they had tempted providence, and that they were doomed".[18] Lee dwelt on this point on another occasion in which he criticized the students for having attacked Deng personally. "The day they came out with a slogan 'Down with Deng' and they have a ditty, a doggerel in Chinese which I read and I heard on the radio, I said, 'It's finished.' You cannot mock a great leader in an Asian Confucian society. If he allows himself to be mocked, he is finished. There can be only one emperor in China, and Deng understands that."[19] Lee's public interventions embody the strands of Singapore's stance mentioned earlier: its defence of Beijing's refusal to allow the political system to be toppled; its understanding of the Chinese leadership's historical self-perception as society's guardian against chaos; and its disapproval of the students' dreadful misreading of China's social milieu when they exceeded permissible forms of protest by defying cultural norms of authority in their personal attack on leaders.

The emphasis on Chinese exceptionalism also informed Lee's terse disapproval of attempts to link Tiananmen with post-communist Eastern Europe. "To quote Eastern Europe as examples of how Communist regimes have broken down because they were not democratically elected in simplistic," he said. The Europeans had revolted because they were "miserable and impoverished". Communist governments had been imposed by an occupying Red Army in 1945 on those countries, which had a history and tradition of elections and liberal governance. "They reverted to tradition", a case in point being Czechoslovakia, where democrats and patriots had fought the Nazis and had stood up to the communists.[20] Also, Chinese leaders were different from Soviet leaders, who "aspire to be Europeans and are troubled when condemned as failures by European standards. The Chinese do not have such aspirations. They are happy to be Chinese, to be Asians not Europeans".[21] Unlike Gorbachev, who had put *glasnost* before *perestroika*, or economic restructuring, Deng "believed in restructuring before opening up"; *glasnost* could wait. The Chinese leader understood that unless the forces of change were released in a controlled way, the system would collapse. "He saved the country from an implosion like the Soviet Union."[22] On the theoretical point about the economic need for liberal democracy, Lee was adamant. "You can have a successful free market or capitalist economy without a democratically elected government," he said, pointing to South Korea's and Taiwan's record under martial law.[23] "I do not accept the simplistic view that you must have liberal democracy on top of free enterprise in a free-market to succeed."[24] In any case, it was futile of anyone to coerce Beijing into a different form of governance.[25] No country could or would "fight the battles of the Chinese people to establish the kind of government they want. That struggle has to be by Chinese people themselves who will have to pay the price. If it costs lives it will have to be Chinese lives." As for economic sanctions, they would hurt China's government and people, but they would not force the Chinese to give up or share power.[26] Lee appeared to be saying that the political *status quo* in post-Tiananmen China was a *fait accompli*.

However, what he did not say was that this *status quo* was destined to last forever. Mindful of the brake — temporary, as it turned out to be — that the Tiananmen eruption had placed on Deng's economic reforms, Lee had a message for Beijing as well: do not let a political setback derail economic change. "The Chinese people will not revert to contented isolation. TV is a great destroyer of icons." The Chinese knew that "they are not the centre of the world, the Middle Kingdom".[27] Television, foreign businessmen and tourists in China, visitors from Hong Kong, Taiwan and elsewhere, and letters from friends and relatives had shown the Chinese how the rest of the world worked and lived. The Chinese wanted a change in their lives. "If China's policies do not give them the prospect of catching up with Taiwan or Hongkong, then I think something dramatic can happen."[28] Reiterating one of the key tenets of Singapore's own political culture, Lee declared that, in the longer run, "a government's right to govern depends upon being able to give its people a better life".[29] The Long March veterans, in their 70s and 80s, had earned their unchallengeable right to govern China through their role in the anti-Japan war and the civil war. However, when a new generation of leaders took over, their legitimacy would depend on their ability to improve the lives of the people. That would require them to free the economy and plug into the trade and investment flows generated by the free-market economies of Japan and the West. "If they do not, the outcome may be as dramatic as the events in the Soviet Union and Eastern Europe. We shall know the outcome in 5, at the outside, 10 years," Lee said in February 1990.[30] The key point remained: "Tiananmen has not altered China's potential as the biggest economic player in the region, and indeed in the world."

Although Lee's support for China was contingent on it continuing with economic reforms, there was no doubt over where Singapore stood on the question of Tiananmen. What happened on the Square on that fateful day in June did not detract from the wider logic of China's integration into the global order, which would benefit both the country and the world. Singapore's attempt to prevent the Tiananmen killings from diverting international attention away from the larger picture was an intrinsic part of its own engagement of China.

Yet, this danger of diversion was playing out in a territory whose impending return to China was an aspect of China's return to the world. Hong Kong's reunification with China was under pressure.

HONG KONG'S RETURN TO CHINA

The Sino-British Joint Declaration of 1984 provided the framework of Hong Kong's return to China on 1 July 1997. Article 3(5) states: "The current social and economic systems in Hong Kong will remain unchanged, and so will the life-style. Rights and freedoms, including those of the person, of speech, of the press, of assembly, of association, of travel, of movement, of correspondence, of strike, of choice of occupation, of academic research and of religious belief will be ensured by law in the Hong Kong Special Administrative Region. Private property, ownership of enterprises, legitimate right of inheritance and foreign investment will be protected by law." Article 4 adds: "The Government of the United Kingdom and the Government of the People's Republic of China declare that, during the transitional period between the date of the entry into force of this Joint Declaration and 30 June 1997, the Government of the United Kingdom will be responsible for the administration of Hong Kong with the object of maintaining and preserving its economic prosperity and social stability; and that the

Government of the People's Republic of China will give its cooperation in this connection."[31] These and other provisions of the Joint Declaration reflected Beijing's agreement to preserve Hong Kong's capitalist way of life for 50 years and give it a high degree of autonomy under a special one country, two systems formula that acknowledged a thriving Hong Kong's importance to reforming China. "One country, two systems" meant precisely what it said. Hong Kong being different from the mainland, China was different from Hong Kong. There was no suggestion that China would gravitate politically towards Hong Kong. The intentions contained in the Declaration were codified in the Basic Law of 1990, meant to serve as the territory's post-1997 constitution.

In between came Tiananmen. One million Hong Kong residents took to the streets in protest, the stock and property markets collapsed, and a tide of emigration lasting five years revealed the extent of anxiety over the territory's approaching reversion to China. Political leaders in Hong Kong decided to hasten the pace of building democracy, with the executive and legislative councillors agreeing in July 1989 that at least half the legislature should be elected directly by 1995 and the entire body and the chief executive by 2003. Hong Kong Governor David Wilson urged London to restore full British nationality to Hong Kong citizens, including the right to live in Britain, so as to provide an escape route should 1997 and beyond prove calamitous. In early July 1989, a parliamentary foreign affairs report urged full democracy for the territory before 1997 so as to help it preserve a high degree of autonomy later. In early July as well, the Hong Kong government said that it would draft a Bill of Rights, which was done in March 1990 and went into effect a year later.[32]

But in what mattered — the drafting of the Basic Law — London's attempts only moderately were successful with a Beijing extremely wary of what was happening in Hong Kong under transition. "For every safeguard demanded in Hong Kong's name, Beijing inserted a provision to enhance its own interests"[33] although the Hong Kong government remained committed to the principle of convergence, known popularly as the "through train" on which colonial Hong Kong would make its transition to being a Special Administrative Region of China.

But then came the collapse of the Soviet Union in 1991 on the back of the dissolution of communist rule in Eastern Europe, a geopolitical momentum that "evidently emboldened London to strengthen its management of Hong Kong's transition to Chinese rule".[34] Suzanne Pepper believes that Britain might not have embarked on its reform programme without "the massive shift in opinion against China after Tiananmen and, more importantly, in the global balance of power that followed the Soviet Union's demise".[35]

The strengthening of British management took shape with the appointment in 1992 of the Conservative politician Christopher Patten as Hong Kong's last colonial Governor. He went about introducing electoral reforms that essentially were meant to make an enlarged franchise a *fait accompli* before the handover. The changes were resisted by Beijing for being inconsistent with the political shape of Hong Kong envisaged in the Joint Declaration. Patten has justified his reforms on the basis that Hong Kong was a "Chinese city with British characteristics, not like any other Chinese city"; a city whose six-million people produced a gross domestic product that was more than a fifth that of 1.2-billion-strong China; that Hong Kong was "the only example of a free society which was being handed over to a society which had, to put it mildly, a different notion of freedom";[36] and that, in spite of Hong Kong's reputation as an economic city, "you can't make a distinction between economic man or woman and political man or woman". Patten argued: "What I felt very strongly when I read about Asia, when I met Asians, when I governed an Asian city, was that the things that I believed constituted a decent society were pretty much the same in Asia as they would be in Europe or North America. I found the relativist approach to values offensive."[37]

China found not only offensive but decidedly subversive attempts by a departing colonialist, no product of Hong Kong democracy, to bequeath on the colony a political system that the British had not introduced during almost 150 years of undemocratic rule. The eventual abolition of the Legislative Council formed on the basis of Patten's expanded electorate signified Beijing's determination to dismantle what it saw as a political edifice mischievously constructed by a departing colonial power.[38] In any case, Britain was Hong Kong's past and China was its future: that was the view taken in Beijing.

But matters were not as simple as that. Modern-day Hong Kong had been built on the enterprise and initiative of Chinese who had fled communism for the economic freedoms of the British colony. Most Hongkongers did not identify themselves with either Britain or China: they identified themselves with Hong Kong so long as it remained a land of economic opportunity. The majority of them might have no particular fascination for London's belated attempt to introduce democracy — an attempt, in fact, whose popularity was never tested in a referendum — but they had no passion either for living under a system where the tanks of Tiananmen might crush one day the economic freedom to which they were accustomed in the colony. Hong Kong was a fragile social creation sustained by its people's, and foreign investors', confidence in its economic future. If Britain's attempts to politicize the island before abandoning it were a threat to its economic well-being, so would be China's refusal to acknowledge that Hong Kong's value depended on the territory's appeal to its notoriously fleet-footed residents. Hongkongers, by deciding to stay or to quit, could make or unmake the economic destiny of an island whose return to China was important for Beijing because the territory's millions showed what more than one billion Chinese were capable of achieving economically. It was the residents of Hong Kong who mattered. Neither last-minute political improvisations in London nor time-honoured political reflexes in Beijing did. Hong Kong's political future admittedly lay in China, but its economic future primarily lay within itself. In a word, Hong Kong could be broken both by London and by Beijing. Beijing, as the incoming power, owed it to Hong Kong to sustain its success and to itself to preserve the city's value to China's reforms. The key lay in the relationship between the people of Hong Kong and China.

Singapore's Response

This understanding of the Hong Kong Chinese psyche, where a pragmatic political culture and a gypsy-like cult of mobility accompanied the collective worship of Mammon, guided Singapore's response to Hong Kong's insecurities following Tiananmen. "Your right as a Hongkonger is to continue to make a reasonable living as a law-abiding resident of Hongkong. If they don't give you the living that you have been accustomed to, then you have to leave," Lee Kuan Yew declared.[39] Six weeks after Tiananmen, Singapore offered to give 25,000 Hong Kong families Approval In-Principle (AIP) permanent residence, the AIP being valid for five years and extendable for another five. After a year, double the intended number of AIPs was granted. The point about this scheme was that those selected did not need to move to Singapore until they felt the need to do so, thus giving them an exit strategy without drawing them away at a time when Hong Kong was passing through great uncertainty. Thus, although 50,000 AIPs were granted, only 8,500 moved to Singapore by 1997.[40] As for companies shifting some of their operations to Singapore to keep staff threatening to leave, Singapore did not encourage the trend but it did not refuse to accept them because "we think by doing this we are helping the main operation to continue in Hongkong".[41]

While emphasizing Hong Kong residents' right to argue with China over economics, Lee was adamant that they should not argue about politics.[42] Speaking of the leaders in Beijing, he said: "My guess is that when it comes to the crunch, they will not do anything which will threaten or negate Hongkong's usefulness to them economically. Politically, it's different. They are not prepared to have Hongkong become a model of what China ought to be."[43] Beijing was prepared to let Hong Kong continue to make money and benefit China so long as the territory did not constitute a problem for the mainland, "including the problem of how Chinese in China see themselves and their government". If Chinese on the mainland saw Hong Kong's success as resulting from a one-man-one-vote system livened by political debate, they would want the same kind of democratically-elected legislature and government themselves, this being "total anathema" to the communists in Beijing. When the Chinese agreed to a one country, two systems formula, they agreed to a system for Hong Kong that basically was the same as under the British, with a few changes. "They did not envisage a democratically elected government in Hongkong, one totally different from theirs."[44] Indeed, even a fully-democratic legislature in the territory standing up to Beijing would not ensure that the formula for returning to China would work because post-1997 Hong Kong would be subordinate to Chinese sovereignty. "Your separate way of life and different way of doing things will only continue if you don't challenge their way of doing things in China."[45] Patten's proposals "slip into the blank spaces of the Basic Law and the Joint Declaration",[46] but what was far more important than the fate of his reforms was the fate of Hong Kong. It was a mistake to believe that "the economy would look after itself" merely if the territory's residents protected democracy and human rights in an "irreversibly democracy-minded" Hong Kong being handed over to China.[47] Politically, British-emboldened Hong Kong was no match for China, and those who thought otherwise were deluding themselves. But once this reality was understood in the territory, it was possible for its residents to talk economics with China — which, in fact, was what they had done with the British. Singapore's approach to Hong Kong was based on the unsentimental *realpolitik* of business.

In his memoirs, published after the territory had reverted to Chinese rule without the collapse that some had feared, Lee sums up his views on Hong Kong's future. It cannot be just another Chinese city, because then it will be of no value to the mainland. What make the city useful are its institutions, management expertise, sophisticated financial markets, rule of law, a cosmopolitan lifestyle and its use of English as the language of business. Admittedly, Hongkongers need to work with Chinese officials produced by a different social, economic and political system, but the city must retain the characteristics that "made it an indispensable intermediary between China and the world, as during British rule". Calling Hong Kong people a "special sub-group of the Chinese nation", Lee hopes for convergence with the mainland over the remaining years to 2047, when "they meet in one country, one system". That would take two more generations. "If the changes that have taken place in the one generation since Chairman Mao died continue at the same pace, the convergence should not be too uncomfortable."[48]

That this attitude — evident in Singapore's reaction to the unfolding crisis in Hong Kong and encapsulated by Lee later — upheld China's sovereign right to maintain Hong Kong's political contours in terms of the Joint Declaration and the Basic Law is obvious; Singapore's position was of a piece with its objection to the Tiananmen protests causing political instability that would ruin China's economic reforms. However, what the city-state's response to Hong Kong underscored was a nuanced appraisal of the colonial city's role in China. Even as Singapore acknowledged Beijing's upper hand in Hong's Kong's political affairs, a hand that it would be futile for the departing British and their local supporters to resist, Singapore suggested that it would be unwise for Beijing to think that because it had the stronger hand it politics it could play this hand as it chose in the economic realm. If the legal and social institutions that made Hong Kong thrive under the British were destroyed, the city would cease to have value to the mainland, causing its return to China to be little more than an historical transition resonating with nationalist pride but a pyrrhic economic victory. Hence, even as Lee advised Hong Kong residents to put their economic interests ahead of political demands that would subvert their relations with Beijing, his message to Beijing was to treat Hong Kong as the economic prize that it was. Indeed, it might be said that there were intimations of the Singapore system in his subtle message that authoritarian was legitimate, but only if it produced the economic goods that citizens wanted. Beijing's handling of Hong Kong therefore would be judged, not by itself, but by whether it succeeded in preserving the economic confidence and enterprising zeal that had made Hong Kong one of the Asian Tigers.

Lee could afford to make this distinction and still be received warmly in Beijing because, unlike Western leaders arguing to keep Hong Kong vibrant economically, soft-authoritarian Singapore's political motives were not suspect in China. But the premium that Singapore put on Beijing's need to handle sensitively Hong Kong's talented and instinctively mobile professional class was unambiguous. In engaging China, Singapore was careful to make a distinction between market economics and Leninist politics, giving each its due. Over Hong Kong, when Singapore argued that the territory's residents should keep economics separate from politics, its simultaneous message to Beijing was that it, too, should keep its political right to guide Hong Kong's destiny separate from the economic space that the city needed in order to thrive.

NOTES

1 Orville Schell, *Mandate of Heaven: A New Generation of Entrepreneurs, Dissidents, Bohemians, and Technocrats Lays Claim to China's Future* (New York: Simon & Schuster, 1994), pp. 15, 17 and 18.

2 Yuan-Li Wu, *Tiananmen to Tiananmen: China Under Communism 1947–1996*, Occasional Papers/Reprint Series in Contemporary Asian Studies, Number 1 — 1997 (138) (Baltimore: University of Maryland, School of Law), p. 2.

3 Ibid., pp. 2–3.

4 For a discussion of these developments, see Anna M. Cienciala, *The Rise and Fall of Communist Nations 1917–1994* (Lawrence, Kansas: University of Kansas, 1996), Chapter 10, <http://raven.cc.ku.edu/~eceurope/communistnationssince1917/ch10.html>.

5 Han Minzhu, ed., *Cries for Democracy: Writings and Speeches from the 1989 Chinese Democracy Movement* (New Jersey: Princeton University Press, 1990), p. 67, cited in Cienciala, ibid.

6 Andrew J. Nathan and Perry Link, eds., *The Tiananmen Papers*, compiled by Zhang Liang (New York: Public Affairs, 2001), p. 217.

7 Nathan and Link, eds., *The Tiananmen Papers*, provides an account from leaked sources of what happened inside the highest echelons of the party as the students mounted their challenge to the government.

8 See Gregory Clark, "The Tiananmen Square massacre myth", *Japan Times*, 15 September 2004, and <www.sinomania.com/CHINANEWS/tiananmen_perspective.htm> for "Tiananmen Square Uprising: A Perspective". "Tiananmen Square, 1989: The Declassified History" contains a selection of documents relating to the crackdown, in <www.gwu.edu/~nsarchiv/NSAEBB/NSAEBB16/documents/>.

9 For a critique from the Left of the crackdown, see Charlie Hore, *The Road to Tiananmen Square* (London, Chicago and Melbourne: Bookmarks, 1991).

10 See David Skidmore and William Gates, "After Tiananmen: The Struggle Over U.S. Policy Toward China in the Bush Administration", <www.drake.edu/artsci/PolSci/personal webpage/tiananmen.html>.

11 "Background Note: China", U.S. Department of State, Bureau of East Asian and Pacific Affairs, March 2005, <www.state.gov/r/pa/ei/bgn/18902.htm>.
12 Hore, op. cit., p. 134.
13 *Lee Kuan Yew on China and Hongkong after Tiananmen*, edited by Lianhe Zaobao (Singapore: Shing Lee Publishers, 1990), p. 1.
14 Lee Kuan Yew, *From Third World to First: The Singapore Story, 1965–2000*, op. cit., p. 695.
15 Ibid., p. 698.
16 *Lee Kuan Yew on China and Hongkong after Tiananmen*, pp. 110–11.
17 Ibid., pp. 116–17; p. 142.
18 Ibid., p. 32.
19 Ibid., p. 136.
20 Ibid., p. 53.
21 Ibid., p. 4.
22 See <www.pbs.org/wgbh/commandingheights/shared/minitextlo/tr_show02.html> for the transcript containing Lee's remarks on the PBS programme, Commanding Heights.
23 *Lee Kuan Yew on China and Hongkong after Tiananmen*, p. 52.
24 Ibid., p. 51.
25 Ibid., p. 8.
26 Ibid., p. 62.
27 Ibid., p. 85.
28 Ibid., p. 41.
29 Ibid., p. 63.
30 Ibid., p. 86.
31 Hungdah Chiu, *Hong Kong's Transition to 1997: Background, Problems and Prospects (With Documents)*, Occasional Papers/Reprint Series in Contemporary Asian Studies, Number 5 — 1993 (118), (Baltimore: University of Maryland, School of Law), p. 26; p. 27.
32 Suzanne Pepper, "Hong Kong on the Eve of Reunification with China", in William A. Joseph, ed., *China Briefing: The Contradictions of Change* (Armonk, New York, and London, England: M.E. Sharpe, published in cooperation with the Asia Society, 1997), pp. 158–59.
33 Ibid., p. 159.
34 Ibid., pp. 157–58.
35 Ibid., p. 161.
36 Interview with Harry Kreisler, Conversations with History,

Institute of International Studies, University of California at Berkeley, 8 April 1999, <http://globetrotter.berkeley.edu/conversations/Patten/patten99-con3.html>.

37 Ibid., <http://globetrotter.berkeley.edu/conversations/Patten/patten99-con4.html>.

38 For a close analysis of Patten's reforms, China's response and the effects of both on Hong Kong's politics till just before the handover, see Pepper, op. cit., pp. 161–94.

39 *Lee Kuan Yew on China and Hongkong after Tiananmen*, op. cit., p. 96.

40 Lee Kuan Yew, *From Third World to First: The Singapore Story, 1965–2000*, op. cit., pp. 608–9.

41 *Lee Kuan Yew on China and Hongkong after Tiananmen*, op. cit., pp. 126–27.

42 Ibid., p. 119.

43 Ibid., p. 131.

44 Ibid., pp. 49–50.

45 Ibid., p. 76.

46 Lee Kuan Yew, *From Third World to First: The Singapore Story, 1965–2000*, op. cit., p. 610.

47 Ibid., p. 618.

48 Ibid., pp. 618–19.

CHAPTER VI

ASIAN VALUES

Singapore's intensely political engagement of China, apparent in the previous chapters, went into higher gear during the Asian values debate of the late 1980s and the 1990s. Singapore's international advocacy of Asian cultural exceptionalism, reflecting a conservative approach to democracy and human rights deemed to be beneficial to economic growth, paralleled its defence of Chinese political exceptionalism. Combined with an emphasis that emerged earlier on Confucian values, transmitted through Mandarin, as constituting a cultural ballast for Singapore's Chinese majority, the Asian values initiative provided an expansive ideological framework for Singapore's evolving relations with China. There, Confucianism had emerged as one of the strands of the new nationalism, which itself had arisen as a response to the Chinese Communist Party's experience of crises of faith in Marxism and Maoism since the 1980s; the need to protect China from disintegration brought on by economic decentralization;

the need to reverse the worship of Western culture; and a sense of pride in a great tradition that had allowed the country to reform itself without breaking up, unlike the Soviet Union.[1] At the national level, Confucianism could be a panacea for the familiar anomie of individuals in the industrialized West that now was seeping into post-communist China. At the international level, a pragmatic or mainstream Confucian-nationalism, contrasted with the conservative and irrational strains of Confucian fundamentalism[2] that once had made the Chinese backward-looking, would help China to find its place in the world. The non-antagonistic premises of Confucianism were preferable to the social Darwinism on which Western civilization rested;[3] moreover, the fact that Confucianism did not possess a strong sense of salvation gave the civilization an advantage in a world where "relations between different religions are competitive because there is only one God".[4]

It is possible to detect in the Confucian revival in China a change in philosophical direction among members of the intelligentsia even as the state sought a new source of legitimacy in the rediscovery of a national past relevant to a post-communist future driven by the market. It would be questionable to claim that Singapore espoused Confucian or Asian values to advance its relations with rising China. However, the debate over values, in which Singapore participated eagerly, reflected the geopolitical contours of an era in which Asia's economic growth and expectations, fueled in no small measure by China, made it possible for many Asian governments to advance their version of the possible. They did so against models that claimed to be universal but were rooted in the West's historical experience and were transmitted globally through its dominance of the economic and ideological landscape.

That Western dominance was being attacked by events and trends, from the breakdown of the Bretton Woods system and the oil price hikes of the 1970s to America's retreat from Vietnam and the American overstretch required to maintain U.S. preponderance in the post-Cold War world. Paul Kennedy's scholarly work on the rise and fall of the great powers became a popular bestseller in the 1980s by resonating with the anxious mood of the times in America.[5] What caught the reading public's attention was his assessment of the interaction between economics and strategy, of how the steady alteration of a great power's position in peacetime is as important as how it fights in wartime.

Grappling with the insecurities of decline, Americans and others in the West looked for the lessons that Kennedy had gleaned from half a millennium of history. Reassurance arrived when Francis Fukuyama argued that liberal democracy — victorious over the successively rival ideologies of hereditary monarchy, fascism and communism — might embody the end of human ideological evolution and constitute the final form of human government, heralding thereby the "end of history".[6] However, Fukuyama's triumphalism was dealt a sobering blow by Samuel Huntington's thesis that the West, far from enjoying victory at the end of history, faced a challenge to its very identity from a clash of civilizations.[7] Huntington's formulation encouraged interpretations of global trends focusing on cultural distinctiveness, particularly the distinctiveness associated with geographical regions. Asia, being transformed by the rising power of China, became a candidate in the civilizational struggle. East Asia had been transformed dramatically since Gunnar

Myrdal's apocalyptic view of Asia in 1968 as a continent of teeming masses and low technology.[8] What fomented change was the appearance of Asian "alliance capitalism". "Until the mid 1990s Asian alliance capitalism generated the highest sustained economic growth rate for any region in world history."[9] East Asia changed into a "flying-geese" formation of countries to which development spread from the dynamism of the Japanese economy. The strong state in Asia, relatively free of domestic pressure groups, intervened in the economy to act as patron and pick industrial winners, providing them capital through state-managed banks. The strong state produced not only growth but equity, comparable to levels in the OECD countries even without the presence of Western welfare systems. Asia was home to the idea that "developing countries require government to take on a more central and powerful role than many Western countries imagine... Rather than distrusting and limiting it as the United States and liberal theorists do, the strong state is largely trusted in Asia".[10]

The strong state also tended to emphasize development over political freedom; indeed, it made a *causal* connection between the two options. Unlike claims to tradition that enjoyed little international credibility — such as those made by sub-Saharan African dictators in the 1970s to rationalize their rule — Asian rulers "won the attention of Western elites primarily because they were making cultural claims for authoritarianism that were matched by impressive economic results".[11] In an extensive essay studying the debate as an experiment in soft power, Alan Chong writes: "Singapore's discourse on Asian Values is a form of discursive power premised upon the ability of an SMD (Singapore Model of Development), culturally-derived and uniquely synthesized, to deliver material and spiritual goods from an exceptionalist standpoint which is labelled non-Western in origin and 'shocking' in its selective non-conformity towards the presumptively liberal norms of post-Cold War international order."[12] The debate was precipitated by a set of factors, including the advent of the William Clinton presidency in 1993 in which the primacy of democratization and human rights "proselytizing" became a centerpiece of a New World Order, with European states not lagging far behind. The searchlight fell on issues such as Tiananmen, Hong Kong, East Timor, North Korea, the Middle East and Cuba. Singapore was concerned deeply over the possible repercussions for China's stability of democratic enlargement targeting the country's economic transition.[13] Responding to perceived Western "sermonizing", Singapore sought "normatively to assert Asian countries' political equality with the West after the divisions of the Cold War".[14] "A soft threat was to be met by soft power."[15]

The Asian values debate that occurred in the closing years of the 20th century was, therefore, as much about the relativities of power as it was about the normative force of arguments. The endeavour to promote instrumentalist values conducive to economic success, in which Malaysia's Mahathir Mohamad played a vital role along with Singapore's Lee Kuan Yew, lost its momentum following the economic crisis that hit the region in 1997 and destroyed culturally particularistic explanations of Asia's economic success. Also, the argument for Asian values itself was not accepted by everyone in Singapore. Chua Beng-Huat, for example, criticized the fact that "cultural elements are constantly invoked as the so-called Asian values that are needed to combat the penetration of " 'undesirable' Western values that may come as the ideological baggage of the borrowed technologies and administrative strategies".[16] But while it lasted, Singapore's public diplomacy on behalf of Asian values reflected a period of regional ascendancy contoured by the rise of China. It represented also the culmination of the Republic's ideological engagement of Beijing.

CONFUCIUS AT HOME

Singapore's espousal of Asian values was the external manifestation of a domestic political culture in which the PAP promoted Confucianism as part of its policies of social engineering. The PAP's controversial turn to cultural tradition, after its initial disparagement of Confucianism as an impediment to China's progress for 2,000 years, has been read variously. Some scholars have seen in the rise of politically-conservative Confucianism an attempt by the party to prevent the growth of opposition politics that drew sustenance from Western frameworks of democracy.[17] That apart, the Confucian thesis provides a restrospective mode of justification for a paternalistic and interventionist state. "The language of Confucian philosophy becomes a conceptual foil to reinterpret the now established practices of the state. What was simply practical and good government becomes retrospectively Confucianist in character."[18] Others contend, less persuasively, that the adoption of cultural tradition as state policy was an effort to establish a new, ambiguous basis of political legitimacy following the government's declining ability to provide social welfare.[19] Yet others argue that Singapore's dominant ideology essentially is not Confucianism but Western conservatism, with aspects of Confucianism being used "*only* when they serve the dominant ideology. Life in Singapore is being shaped by the demands of international capitalism, not by Asian traditions".[20] Others contend, however, that from "the perspectives of classical Chinese political philosophy, Singapore is more Legalist than Confucian". Confucianism emphasizes moderation and self-restraint on the part of rulers, who would set good examples for subjects who would be ruled with the "minimal application of legal sanctions"; Legalism emphasizes the use of generous rewards and severe penalties to make people obey the law.[21] The government, on its part, justified the new programme as a means of protecting Singapore's cultural authenticity, which touched on its economic vitality as well. The argument privileging Confucianist values as the source of growth sought to reverse Weber's castigation of Oriental culture as an impediment to growth along Western capitalist lines, but in doing so, the Asian argument drew attention to the Weberian othering of the Orient.

All in all, however, the "Asianising of Singapore" was a significant project.[22] A key element of the promotion of Confucianism was the Speak Mandarin Campaign, which Lee launched in 1979 to unify Chinese dialect-groups through a common language. The creation of a Mandarin-speaking environment was seen as being conducive to the implementation of the bilingual education programme in which English as the medium of instruction was combined with the study of the mother-tongue, Mandarin, for Chinese Singaporeans. From 1979 to 1981, the campaign's target audience was Chinese Singaporeans in general. Beginning in 1982, it targeted specific groups, for example, hawkers, public transport workers, white-collar workers and senior executives. The primary message to Chinese Singaporeans was an invitation to speak Mandarin in place of dialects so that they would better understand and appreciate their culture and heritage. But when research showed that Mandarin was losing ground among English-educated Chinese Singaporeans, the campaign began targeting this group from 1991. In 1994, it focused on English-educated business professionals and working adults.[23] Behind the campaign's riverine turns lay a desire to reverse the Westernization of consciousness in the city-state, a felt need that would characterize its defence of Asian values as well. Mandarin, which was believed to be the most effective way of transmitting Confucian values, became a marker of Chineseness, which itself was portrayed as a traditional culture in which were embedded discipline, respect for authority and a sense of commitment to the community.[24]

The publication of two government reports around the time that the Speak Mandarin Campaign was launched provided further impetus to the use of education to promote beneficial values. The first, the Report of the Education Study Team led by Goh Keng Swee (the Goh Report) dealt with bilingualism and multiculturalism in schools; and the second, the Report on Moral Education (the Ong Teng Cheong Report) delved into the need for moral education. Bilingualism was seen as a way of inoculating the young against the decadent influences of Westernization, and this goal of inoculation "provided the starting point for the policy of bilingualism and the later search for Asian values; thereafter the process developed into a search for an ideology to legitimize social discipline and an exploration of substitutes for the Protestant work ethic".[25] In 1980, the government initiated the elite Special Assistance Plan (SAP) schools project as part of an "overall objective to Asianise Singapore and restore the Chineseness of the Chinese".[26] In spite of the fact that these schools would prepare students to be equally proficient in English and Mandarin, their linguistic and cultural ambience was essentially Chinese.[27] Thus, their products, among those youth groomed for national leadership, could be expected to help set the tone for Singapore's cultural identity. Then, in 1983, the government sponsored the foundation of the Institute of East Asian Philosophies (IEAP), whose initial purpose was to help reinterpret and adapt Confucian philosophy to answer contemporary concerns.[28] About the same time, Singapore introduced a course on religious knowledge and Confucian ethics as part of the secondary school curriculum, the texts for the course being commissioned especially by the Ministry of Education.[29] The IEAP ultimately was unsuccessful in promoting any genuine Confucianization of Singapore, and it no longer exists in its original form; the Confucian ethics course in schools also was abandoned[30] (as was the religious knowledge programme itself). Nevertheless, the use of Confucianism "was carried out quite explicitly against the West in general, and Western notions of democratic politics in particular".[31]

It needs to be emphasized that the PAP took pains to reiterate that Singapore was a multiracial and multicultural country that owed its success to the value systems of its different communities, a message conveyed by the White Paper on Shared Values issued in 1991.[32] Within this shared-values-driven framework for a national ideology, however, Confucianism retained a special place in nation-building and was so justified in the pronouncements of Singapore leaders long after the initiation of the Speak Mandarin Campaign. "The English-educated Chinese community is the dominant community in Singapore. Unless they are taught and instilled with core Chinese values, cultural individualism will force out Confucian dynamism as Singapore's value system," Prime Minister Goh Chok Tong, who took over from Lee Kuan Yew in 1990, declared in 1991. "I want to do what I can to promote the use of Mandarin, to preserve Chinese customs and traditions, to uphold those Confucian values which contribute to Singapore's progress," he said. He had an economic rationale in mind. "My view is that if Chinese Singaporeans lose their core values, it will be a disaster for Singapore. Cultural values of a country do affect its economic performance, and for Singapore more than any other country, if our economy is shaky, Singapore cannot survive."[33]

In 1992, then Minister for Information and the Arts George Yong-Boon Yeo linked cultural developments in Singapore to the possibilities of an emerging Pacific Century: "What we are witnessing is an economic and cultural renaissance of a scale never before experienced in human history. Like the renaissance in Europe a few centuries ago, this East Asian renaissance will change the way man looks at himself..."[34] The implications of the Pacific Century resonated in another speech that he made that year. The cultural influence of an economically ascendant East Asia would reach Australia and New Zealand, and the west coast of Canada and the United States, and Chinese culture would play a major role in the East Asian renaissance, he declared. The Chinese language would grow in importance because the stronger an economy is, the more influential its language grows. "During the Roman Empire, Latin was used throughout Europe. When the Arab empire was at its peak, the Arabic language was used all the way from Spain to Central and Southeast Asia. In the last 200 years, English has become an international language because of the power of the British Empire and the strength of the American economy. Changes in the structure of economic power must lead to changes in the pattern of language use." Singapore had to be a part of this upswing in regional fortunes. "Singapore is geographically, economically and culturally part of East Asia. There is no reason why we should not be part of the East Asian renaissance. However, nothing is inevitable in human history. If we want to be part of the East Asian renaissance we must work towards it." Hence, a conscious effort was necessary to promote Singapore's Asian cultures. The right linguistic choices were critical. It would be "a great tragedy" if the Chinese language were to be neglected. Every effort should be made to keep Chinese language and culture alive and well in Singapore. "We will succeed if we make the effort because the external factors are conducive."[35] Singapore's cultural and linguistic policies were necessary, therefore.

CONFUCIUS ABROAD

The reference to external factors indicates a nexus between the domestic promotion of Confucianism through the use of Mandarin and Singapore's advocacy of Asian values in the context of China's entry into the contemporary world system. Confucianism had been important to the domestic policies of Singapore's leaders, but China's entry transformed the international possibilities for Singapore and other Asian nations that sought to give Asia a stronger voice on the international stage. At stake in the nexus were two controversial variables: the avowed effects of culture on economic performance; and the place of human rights in international relations in the aftermath of the Cold War.

As for the first variable, its importance in the thinking of Singapore's leaders was dramatized in a widely-quoted interview that Lee Kuan Yew gave to Fareed Zakaria in 1994. "The dominant theme throughout our conversation was culture. Lee returned again and again to his views on the importance of culture and the differences between Confucianism and Western values," Zakaria wrote.[36] Zakaria asked Lee for his views on a recent World Bank report on East Asia,[37] which had feted the region's governments for creating the conditions for national success by getting right fundamentals such as promoting savings and investment, keeping inflation low and providing quality education. These factors served to explain those countries' extraordinary economic growth more than industrial policies and so on, Zakaria suggested. Lee thought differently, noting of the report that "there are cultural factors which have been lightly touched over, which deserved more weightage. This would have made it a more complex study and of less universal application, but it would have been more accurate, explaining the differences, for example, between the Philippines and Taiwan". The report "makes the hopeful assumption that all men are equal, that people all over the world are the same. They are not", Lee declared. Instead, the truth was that groups of people "develop different characteristics when they have evolved for thousands of years separately. Genetics and history interact", he remarked, citing differences in neurological development and cultural values between Native Americans and East Asian Mongoloids, although both are of the same genetic stock. Culture made the difference; in the words of the article's headline, culture was destiny. But what were the Asian cultural values necessary for economic growth? A checklist of the values that Singapore considered Asian was provided by one of its leading diplomats, Tommy Koh. He enunciated the following East Asian values: (i) the absence of the "extreme form of individualism practiced in the West"; and striking a balance between individual and social interests; (ii) belief in strong families; (iii) reverence for education; (iv) belief in saving and frugality, in contrast to the "Western addiction to consumption"; (v) belief in hard work; (vi) cooperative, not adversarial, relations among social groups; partnership among the government, business and employees; and an ability to forge a national consensus; (vii) an "Asian version of a social contract" between citizens and the state in which the government maintains law and order and provides citizens with basic needs, and citizens reciprocally are expected to be "law-abiding, respect those in authority, work hard, save, and motivate their children to learn and be self-reliant"; also, the state avoids "the Western disease of welfarism"; (viii) an attempt to build communitarian societies by making citizens stakeholders in the country; (ix) the presence of a morally wholesome environment; and (x) a free press that is desired but is not considered an absolute right, with the press acting responsibly.[38] Koh argued that, taken together, these ten values provided an enabling framework for economic prosperity, progress, harmonious relations between citizens, and law and order in East Asia.

The argument for such values came not only from Asian elites: several Western scholars, too, sought to give them intellectual legitimacy. Michael Hill cites three influential books appearing in 1979 that transformed Western discussions of Asian values:

Herman Kahn's and Thomas Pepper's *The Japanese Challenge: The Success and Failure of Economic Success;*[39] Herman Kahn's *World Economic Development: 1979 and Beyond,*[40] produced under the auspices of the Hudson Institute; and Ezra F. Vogel's *Japan As Number One: Lessons for America.*[41] Kahn argued that "the modern Confucian ethic is superbly designed to create and foster loyalty, dedication, responsibility, and commitment and to intensify identification with the organization and one's role in the organization. All this makes the economy and society operate much more smoothly than one whose principles of identification and association tend to lead to egalitarianism, to disunity, to confrontation, and to excessive compensation or repression".[42]

The formulations of scholars such as Vogel appealed to Singaporean leaders who were concerned with upholding social values that gave Singapore and other Asian societies their competitive edge on the global marketplace. The appeal was magnified by the times. The downfall of the Soviet bloc had destroyed one contender for global supremacy. In its ideological wake remained two major contenders within the global capitalist system: a West which was viewed as being under siege within from individualism, consumerism, libertinism, welfarism and other economically sapping ailments; and an Asian, or at any rate East Asian, model that was invigorated by the values of communitarianism, hard work and delayed gratification, moral probity, and reliance on oneself and the family and not the state. Asian values, which had helped Japan modernize after World War II, had been deployed by the Newly-Industrializing Economies, and were spreading to post-communist China. That all these countries and territories — Japan, Hong Kong, Taiwan, South Korea,

Singapore and China — lay within the Confucian sphere was not a coincidence: It was the values inherent in those societies that made it possible to read them as constituting together a model whose dynamism and success made Asia a convincing claimant for ideological supremacy in the post-Cold War world of the 1990s. This was how the region looked to those who believed in the distinctive economic properties of Asian values.

That said, there lay a crucial obstacle to realizing the economic potential of an Asia driven by congenial values. This was the question of human rights, the second variable that was at stake as the liberal-democratic West sought to reorder global affairs following the removal of the Soviet threat to its physical, economic and ideological supremacy.

As human rights were elevated to an aspect of Western state policy in dealings with Asia, many Asian governments saw rights as an underhand weapon used by a region on the wane against one on the rise. Singapore and Malaysia led the Asian counter-charge, with China joining in eagerly. What has come to be known as the Singapore School made several forays into the conceptual debate on the value of values. In an influential essay published in 1993, senior Singapore diplomat Bilahari Kausikan averred that the "economic success of East and Southeast Asia is the central strategic fact of the 1990s".[43] He recalled the Western promotion of human rights during the Cold War, when the West had deployed it as an ideological instrument in the East-West struggle.[44] Following the end of that war, the West might use human rights as an instrument of economic competition. "As American and European apprehensions about their competitiveness rise, the West is emphasizing values like openness and equal opportunity and relating them to broader issues of freedom and democracy."[45] Taking a stand against such attempts, he suggested that Asia did not have to fall in with Western demands. East and Southeast Asian countries tended to find the key to their economic success in "their own distinctive traditions and institutions".[46] Thus, Asian countries were dismayed by the propensity of Westerners to place more emphasis on civil and political rights than on economic, social and cultural rights. The Asian experience upheld the need to view order and stability as "preconditions for economic growth, and growth as the necessary foundation of any political order that claims to advance human dignity".[47] Kausikan did not frame his comments on the basis of Asian exceptionalism to which human rights were inimical, but he implied the converse: that the Western sponsorship of human rights as universal reflected exceptionalism of its own kind, in that these rights had grown out of Western history and culture. Taking his stand between West and Asia, he argued for the need to find an agnostic position between "a pretentious and unrealistic universalism and a paralyzing cultural relativism".[48] The balance represented by that position would not be achieved if the Western, especially American, media, non-governmental organizations (NGOs) and rights activists pressed the human rights dialogue "beyond the legitimate insistence on humane standards of behavior by calling for the summary implementation of abstract concepts without regard for a country's unique cultural, social, economic and political circumstances".[49] Kausikan's defence of the Singapore position avoided the Manichean absurdities that found their way into diatribes over values, such as the astonishing Philippic heard in one Asian country that Western-style democracy caused homosexuality, single motherhood

and economic slowdown.[50] However, his conclusion —
that the needs of economic advance should take
precedence over civil and political rights — upheld the
essence of the view advanced by several Asian
governments.

That was the message of another influential essay
as well, written by senior Singapore diplomat Kishore
Mahbubani in 1992. Warning against ahistorical
attempts to put democratic carts before economic
horses, he noted that most Western societies had
benefited from economic development that had created
working and middle classes whose vested interest in
stability had insulated them from the centrifugal
appeals of "demagogic democratic politicians" making
capital out of ethnic and other sectional differences.[51]
That path had been taken also by East Asian countries
that had made a successful transition to democracy.
But, today, the West was promoting democracy before
economic development.[52] Mahbubani did not argue
that democracy had to impede development; indeed,
he acknowledged that authoritarianism could block
progress, as it had done in the Philippines. However, it
was equally true that some authoritarian governments
had been good for development, South Korea and
Taiwan in the early years being cases in point.[53] "In the
long run, it may be wiser for the West to encourage a
more viable process of transition in developing societies,
one that puts the horse before the cart — promoting
economic development through good government
before promoting democracy."[54] Here, again, was an
affirmation of the need to place Asia's circumstantial
evidence for economic advance over claims for civil
and political rights, signifying a rejection of Western
ideological premises wherein lay the sources of a
seemingly absolutist commitment to individual liberties

that culminated in a demand for democracy with Western characteristics. The Singapore elite defined the region's agenda very differently from the agenda created by the Western focus on civil and political liberties.

In China's case, its stance was defined by a historical materialist understanding that saw the rise of human rights in the West two centuries earlier as the work of enlightened bourgeois thinkers challenging the authority and privileges of aristocrats and the clergy. An official treatise written during the early years of the transition from communism summarized the Chinese case on human rights. The struggle against feudal autocracy had been a progressive one. However, that conflict itself had masked the bourgeoisie's desire to supplant feudal lords and establish its own power through ownership of private property. The right to pursue happiness had become the right to exploit labour, whose rights, as Marx and Engels noted, were considered a privilege.[55] But rights "develop as history develops, and so do human rights". Hence, economic and social changes, the emergence of new political forces, and development of international struggles had turned the concept of human rights into "something bigger, richer and broader than what was defined by the Western bourgeoisie in the 17th and 18th centuries".[56] Human rights were not "an abstract slogan or an isolated question but are closely related to international politics", which is why imperialists and the Western bourgeoisie used rights to "attack and slander" China and try to "infiltrate China ideologically".[57] The international practice of human rights should safeguard the right of Third World countries to develop; using "the slogan of human rights to interfere in other countries' essentially internal affairs is intolerable" and China would brook no such encroachment on its sovereignty.[58] Anybody free of prejudice could see that rights stipulated in the Chinese Constitution were superior to the Western bourgeoisie's concept of "individual human rights", although implementing the constitutional rights fully would take time in a developing socialist country because "the rights enjoyed by the citizens of a state are first subject to its social system and then to its economic, cultural and other objective conditions".[59]

Essentials of that argument cohered as Beijing joined the international economic order. The premises of the Singapore and Chinese positions were different, not least on the question of whether there could be a degree of convergence between Western and Asian practices of human rights. The Singapore school of thought appeared to leave that possibility open, not quite arguing that there was something inherently destabilizing in civil and political rights of the Western-sponsored variety that made them a threat to economic growth and harmony at any time. No such ambiguities troubled the Chinese thesis, which seemed to rule out convergence since the socialist rights offered in China already were superior to bourgeois human rights — in which case Beijing and Western capitals were journeying on two irreconcilable historical trajectories. Differences between the Singapore and Chinese doctrines notwithstanding, however, there was an interesting degree of overlap between them on the issue of weighing individual rights in the entire basket of rights and in opposing Western attempts to privilege political liberties over economic imperatives.

The focus of the human rights debate, on the consequences of rights for prosperity and order, obscured contradictions in the Western position.

Western arguments celebrating universal values, many born of the European Enlightenment, glossed over some of its less advertised features: colonialism, racism and environmental imperialism. The European discovery of the New World had entailed the genocide of a native population that had never declared war on Europe. Nor had Africans, kidnapped for slavery, declared war on America. Nor had Indians, Africans and Australian aborigines declared war on anyone. Yet they became unwilling beneficiaries of universal progress unfolding through expanding worlds of conquest and pacification, objects of a *mission civilisatrice* undertaken by colonial traders, proconsuls and priests, visionary exemplars of their times. In time arrived two world wars, tied umbilically to Western antagonisms. Fascism and communism made their debut in the West. The Cold War carved out the rest of the world into proxy spheres dying to uphold the contending ambitions of Washington and Moscow.

In an article on the frightening spread of illiberal democracy around the world, Fareed Zakaria notes an ideological benchmark of sorts, that in the 1970s, "Western nations codified standards of behavior for regimes across the globe" based on the Magna Carta, the Fundamental Orders of Connecticut, the American Constitution and the Helsinki Final Act.[60] However, Arundhati Roy reveals discordant truths that lay behind the celebration of universal standards. Drawing attention to the nature of the "peace" achieved after World War II, she notes that, since 1945, the US warred with Korea, Guatemala, Cuba, Laos, Vietnam, Cambodia, Grenada, Libya, El Salvador, Nicaragua, Panama, Iraq, Somalia, Sudan, Yugoslavia and Afghanistan. This list should include Washington's "covert operations in Africa, Asia, and Latin America, the coups it has engineered, and the dictators it has armed and supported".[61] As the West broke bread with despots in Central American satellites and oil-royals in Middle Eastern rentier states, a Salvador Allende fell here and a Shah rose there. Ronald Reagan's "democracy enhancement" programmes in Central America reinvigorated an already formidable tradition. Noam Chomsky notes, for example, how Reagan's covert war against Nicaragua's Sandinista government using a mercenary army left the country the second poorest in the hemisphere. "About 60 per cent of Nicaraguan children under age two are afflicted with anaemia from severe malnutrition — only one grim indication of what is hailed as a victory for democracy."[62] Asians were more familiar with Indochina. "Indochina provided the lush, tropical backdrop against which the United States played out its fantasies of violence, tested its latest technology, furthered its ideology, examined its conscience, agonized over its moral dilemmas, and dealt with its guilt (or pretended to)."[63]

When many Asians (and sympathetic Westerners, Latin Americans and Africans) thought of universal values and human rights spreading across Asia, they thought of the road to My Lai or the road from Trang Bang, where a superpower convinced a little Vietnamese girl that it was more powerful than she. They thought of the direct hit of napalm that Kim Phuc had taken. They thought of the carpet-bombing of neutral Cambodia. They thought a lot. Of course, war is violent, and Asian history — the terrain of Asian values — could lay claim to acts of violence that spectacularly rivalled the West's. Ashoka's Kalinga War of 266B.C. or the Mongol Sack of Baghdad in 1258 numbed the senses to numbers. However, Asia did not become the centre of the world system and go on to prescribe the reordering of international affairs. Had it done so, it might have argued for universal values emanating from an Asian Enlightenment rooted in Ashoka's anguished renunciation of violence after Kalinga, or Akbar's ecumenical quest for a faith of all faiths in Mughal India. Such universal values would then have been tainted, like their counterparts emerging in the West, by the viciousness of Asian history. In the event, the history of genocide, slavery, colonialism and war accompanying the rise of the West subverted the Western discourse of human rights infused by the universality of values.

If several strands of the championing of Asian values insinuated bad faith on the part of the West, critics of such positions mocked what they saw as special pleading at best and a cover-up at worst. Asia was too diverse culturally and politically to be able to produce a single set of Asian values; and if by Asian values was meant the values of East Asia, even there, Confucianism shared cultural space with Islam, Buddhism and Hinduism as sources of belief and action.[64] Indeed, Confucianism was not the only intellectual tradition in China itself; and, indeed, Confucius himself had not been hostile to liberal values, for the great humanist had noted the importance of social justice and political dissent even in the ordering of a disciplined, obedient and hierarchic society. It was Imperial Confucianism that had suppressed radical strands of justice and dissent in order to extol conveniently those words of the Master that prescribed submission to the established authorities.[65] The re-invention of Confucianism in subsequent Chinese society created a confessional politics that all but elevated states to religions in which penitent citizens gathered faithfully. In a more fundamental critique that moves beyond China and the region, Michael Hill shows that Asian values, delineated in contradistinction to the West, had ironical origins. He argues that they lay actually in a "largely Western social scientific artefact which was later adopted by Asian leaders as an ideological component of their nation-building projects", leading him to say that Singapore exemplifies the case for viewing Asian values as a Western project best labelled reverse Orientalism.[66] "This process entailed the attribution of a set of cultural values to East and Southeast Asian societies by Western social scientists in order to contrast the recent dynamic progress of Asian development with the stagnation and social disorganization of contemporary Western economies and societies… While originating in the conceptual constructions of Western social scientists, these 'Asian values' were widely assumed to embody a concrete distinction in the cultures of East and West," Hill writes.[67]

Inoue Tatsuo notes another irony: the concept of socioeconomic rights that Asia was emphasizing had been developed by Western countries themselves since the late 19th century as part of their attempt to cope with the class struggle. After World War II, these rights had been upheld by a consensus cutting across political parties in the Western welfare states until the onset of the Reagan-Thatcher revolution, and even then, the fundamental social security net had not been dismantled completely. Certainly, there might be some cultural resources in Asia for developing those rights, such as the Confucian idea of public ownership of the public realm, but these resources demonstrated merely that socioeconomic rights were not alien to Asian traditions, not that they were peculiar to Asian traditions. "The peculiarity lies in how the Asian values discourse exploits this concept, by resorting to socioeconomic rights as an excuse to restrain political liberties," Inoue comments. "In the social democratic tradition, these rights support arguments for regulation of the market, not arguments against political participation."[68] Amartya Sen provides further grounds for rescuing rights from the East-West dichotomy in which they found themselves. He points out the fallacious tendency, present in the West, to extrapolate backwards from the present in making its case for values. "Values that (the) European Enlightenment and other relatively recent developments have made common and widespread cannot really be seen as part of the long-run Western heritage — experienced in the West over millennia," Sen argues. "What we do find in the writings by particular Western classical authors (for example, Aristotle) is support for selected *components* of the comprehensive notion that makes up the contemporary idea of political liberty." But support for such components can be found in Asian traditions as well, for example in Buddhism and in Ashoka's championing of egalitarian and universal tolerance. Asian thinking and statecraft did value freedom, Sen remarks in a rejoinder both to those who saw the West as the historical bastion of rights and to those who would make Asian history an argument against rights.[69]

Moving beyond conceptual arguments, Errol P. Mendes looks at the *realpolitik* dimension of the rights issue.[70] He points out that during the Cold War, many Asian governments took advantage of the geopolitical struggle to win Western support for their authoritarian systems by participating in the struggle against communism. That option disappeared with the Soviet Union's demise and China's entry into the market system. Many Western countries and international human rights NGOs began to focus more critically now on authoritarian Asian states, Mendes says. What was clear was that much of the vaunted growth of these countries came from a low-cost, export-driven strategy of industrialization that thrived in a political environment that discouraged independent trade unionism and pluralism. Seeking to cover up the real nature of their political economy, Mendes implies, authoritarian governments deflected attention towards a contrived pan-Asian culture and value system that they set about defending from the West's putative use of human rights to battle Asia's booming economies. The quixotic battle over values was in reality a war between capitalism anchored in civil and political rights and authoritarian capitalism. These values belonged to the phenomenology of global affairs. Asians, like everyone else, instead led anthropological lives as members of villages, towns, nations and states where the sun rose in daily defiance of any finalities, Asian or otherwise.

The case for human rights — supported not only by Western organizations and segments of the public but, in differing degrees, by opposition parties, dissidents, civil society groups and members of the intelligentsia in Asia as well — was quintessentially that human rights were universal and were threatened by the divisive demand for culturally-specific rights. To the more pugnacious advocates of human rights, it was not only permissible but necessary for Western governments to use their power, including economic sanction, to rectify the behaviour of errant Asian states. These states prospered because their peoples were unfree; they owed their economic successs in no small measure to their access to Western markets; and their competitiveness, bought by withholding from their workers rights and protective regulations familiar in the West, created an uneven playing field on which Western workers suffered because unfree Asian labour produced goods at low costs that free labour could not match. Western governments owed it to their workers to protect them from the politically-skewed economies of the East; and these governments had an international obligation as well to Asian citizens and workers to rein in the authoritarian systems that flourished at the expense of Asians' own economic and political rights.

BANGKOK AND VIENNA

China, driven by its own compulsions, became an important player in the discursive battle over rights. Responding to international criticism of the Tiananmen killings, Beijing had published a White Paper on human rights in 1991. Its fundamental approach was to place the greatest priority on "the right to subsistence and economic development as a precondition to the full enjoyment of all other human rights".[71] The White Paper emphasized the stability that made subsistence and development possible. Beijing won an important opportunity to go international with its case — also achieving thereby "a major coup" for Asian values — when, in December 1991, it secured the organizing of regional preparatory conferences ahead of the 1993 Vienna Conference on Human Rights.[72] Opposition by the West to the regional conferences, which it saw as unnecessary because human rights were universal, failed, and an "alliance forged by China" managed to articulate Asian values at the March 1993 Asian regional meeting in Thailand.[73] Singapore participated in the meeting, along with more than 30 Asian states. The Bangkok Declaration, which expressed the "aspirations and commitments of the Asian region", recognized that human rights were universal in nature, but it qualified that observation by adding that "they must be considered in the context of a dynamic and evolving process of international norm-setting, bearing in mind the significance of national and regional particularities and various historical, cultural and religious backgrounds".

Asian exceptionalism was writ large in that crucial proviso. In the same spirit, the Declaration reaffirmed "the interdependence and indivisibility of economic, social, cultural, civil and political rights, and the need to give equal emphasis to all categories of human rights", and reiterated that "all countries, large and small, have the right to determine their political systems, control and freely utilize their resources, and freely pursue their economic, social and cultural development". The right to development articulated in that call amplified the Asian insistence that civil and political rights should not overshadow economic rights. So as not to leave any doubt about the significance of this point, the Declaration, which upheld state sovereignty in the realm of human rights, made clear Asian opposition to the use of rights as an instrument of political pressure or as conditionality for extending development assistance.[74]

The Bangkok Declaration — which reflected China's human rights doctrine and the "good governance" argument[75] propounded by the Singapore School — marked a diplomatic victory for participating Asian governments by codifying into an international document what had been till then a verbal debate on values carried out at fluctuating levels of sophistication and credibility. It cemented what Denny Roy, speaking broadly of the soft-authoritarian challenge from Singapore and China, terms the "rhetorical alliance" between the two countries emerging from "Singapore's bold philosophical break from the West", its defence of China against Western criticism, and "Asia's interest in soft authoritarianism".[76] NGOs from Asia and the Pacific, which had gathered in Bangkok before the conference to coordinate their position, opposed attempts by China, Indonesia, Singapore and Malaysia to promote an Asian concept of human rights. Articulating a vision of rights that differed radically from those of Asian governments, the NGOs "helped redefine priorities for the human rights movement in a way that rendered obsolete the old division of labor among human rights, development, women's rights and environmental organizations".[77]

The result was the Bangkok NGO Declaration on Human Rights, which insisted that because human rights were universal, the advocacy of human rights could not be considered to be an encroachment on national sovereignty. While noting the importance of cultural pluralism in the region, the NGOs declared: "Those cultural practices which derogate from universally accepted human rights, including women's rights, must not be tolerated."[78] In reaffirming the indivisibility of political and economic rights, they stated: "Violations of civil, political and economic rights frequently result from the emphasis on economic development at the expense of human rights."[79]

Notwithstanding the intervention by the NGOs at Bangkok, the case for Asian values found its way into discussions at the world human rights conference that brought together delegates from more than 180 countries in Vienna in the summer of 1993. The path lay through claims of cultural and historical relativism and the crucial need for development advanced powerfully by Chinese Deputy Foreign Minister Liu

Huaqiu. He said: "The concept of human rights is a product of historical development. It is closely associated with specific social, political and economic conditions and the specific history, culture, and values of a particular country. Different historical development stages have different human rights requirements." He declared: "Thus, one should not and cannot think of the human rights standard and model of certain countries as the only proper ones and demand all other countries to comply with them. For the vast number of developing countries, to respect and protect human rights is first and foremost to ensure the full realisation of the rights to subsistence and development...".[80]

The Chinese statement came in response to remarks by U.S. Secretary of State Warren Christopher, that "we cannot let cultural relativism become the last refuge of repression" and that the universality of human rights set a single standard of acceptable behaviour across the world.[81] "We reject any attempt by any state to relegate its citizens to a lesser standard of human dignity. There is no contradiction between the universal principles of the UN Declaration and the cultures that enrich our international community. The real chasm lies between the cynical excuses of oppressive regimes and the sincere aspirations of their people," Christopher declared. With an eye on the Asian clamour for economic rights, he said that democracy was good for the economy because "nations that are committed to democratic values create conditions in which the private sector is free to thrive and to provide work for their people". Indeed, the promotion of democracy was the front line of global security because a "world of democracies would be a safer world". In a nutshell, "democracy is the moral and strategic imperative for the 1990s. Democracy will build safeguards for human rights in every nation. Democracy is the best way to advance lasting peace and prosperity in the world".[82]

The American challenge to the Asian position was obvious. On the contentious question of linking economic aid to human rights, Indonesian Foreign Minister Ali Alatas asked the industrialized nations to show greater "flexibility" in their approach to the implementation of rights elsewhere, but his appeal was rejected by the Japanese representative, who said that Tokyo regarded developmental aid as being instrumental to the promotion of human rights.[83]

The two themes — relativism and development — in the Chinese statement resonated in the speech made by Singapore Foreign Affairs Minister Wong Kan Seng. He ruled out repugnant extremes such as murder or torture being rationalized under the rubric of cultural diversity, but he insisted that "the very idea of human rights is historically specific" and that differences in the history, culture and background of different societies could not be ignored.[84] He remarked that the United States, Britain and France had taken 200 years or more to evolve into full democracies. "Can we therefore expect the citizens of the many newly independent countries of this century to acquire the same rights as those enjoyed by the developed nations when they lack the economic, educational and social pre-conditions to exercise such rights fully?"[85] He agreed that the non-derogable rights in the International Covenant on Civil and Political Rights were among core rights that were truly universal, but he reiterated his belief that development, too, was an inalienable right. "Our experience is that economic growth is the necessary foundation of any system that claims to advance human dignity, and that order and stability are essential for development."[86] Human rights would not be accepted if they were seen to impede progress, and there was evidence that "at some stage" excessive emphasis on individual rights became counter-productive. Development and good government required a balance to be struck between individual and community rights, with the precise point of the balance varying for different countries at different points of their history. Early into a country's development, excessive emphasis on individual rights over community rights would retard progress. But as the country developed, new interests had to be accommodated, perhaps leading to a "looser, more complex and more differentiated political system." However, the assumption that this accommodation must lead to "a 'democracy', as some define the term" was not warranted.[87]

Wong's remarks put on record Singapore's rejection of Western premises seen as enshrining an absolutist emphasis on civil and political liberties, and underlined the Republic's disavowal of any corresponding notion of teleological development towards democracy along Western lines. The closeness of that position to China's stand was clear. However, the Singapore position was rather more complex. It adopted a "strategic fuzzy logic" in "drawing up a median position between Asian value exceptionalism and accommodation to the West on the intellectual level of value and systemic differences. Moreover, it then leaned towards a hardline exceptionalism on the level of normative governing differences, and returned to flexibility on specific policy-political consequences". This finessing was an attempt to avoid "total alienation of Western stakes in the Asia-Pacific".[88]

The adoption of the Vienna Declaration "concealed intense differences" between Afro-Asian and Arab countries; and Western countries, Japan and the majority of the Commonwealth of Independent States. Also, about 1,500 NGOs that, at Chinese insistence, had been excluded from the drafting of the final declaration, issued a separate statement criticizing the conference for "failing to commit governments to adopt tougher measures to protect human rights".[89] At both Bangkok and Vienna, countries espousing exceptionalist lines — China, Indonesia, Malaysia, Myanmar, Bangladesh and Pakistan — adopted a hard approach based on cultural exclusivity. Opposition to them and to the Singapore School came from Western countries, the Philippines' pro-Western tilt, and Japan's and Thailand's "ambivalence". The hardline argument based on Asian values was supported by an Arab-Islamic bloc consisting of Iraq, Iran, Libya, Syria, Yemen and the Palestine Liberation Organization, plus Cuba. This "Asian-Islamic opposition coalition" faced a number of ex-Soviet bloc, African and Latin American states that supported universalist and Western positions. In the event, Singapore was not marginalized. "Singapore's strategic fuzzy logic appears to have benefited its diplomatic image and goals at Vienna."[90] Indeed, the Singaporeans were asked to be a mediator behind the scenes in the final drafting sessions at Vienna.[91]

The official declaration affirmed the qualified universality and the indivisibility of human rights — much as the Bangkok Declaration had done — and incorporated several manifestations of cultural relativism, such as the contention that the right to development was "as universal and inalienable a right as other fundamental human rights".[92] In this regard, proponents of Asian values had stood their ground. How well they had done so was clear at the 26th ASEAN

Ministerial Meeting held in Singapore in July 1993. The joint *communiqué* released at the end of the meeting exuded quiet satisfaction over the stand taken by Asian countries at Vienna and reiterated its key tenets. Thus, welcoming the "international consensus" achieved at Vienna, ASEAN Foreign Ministers argued that civil, political, economic, social and cultural rights should be promoted "with due regard for specific cultural, social, economic and political circumstances". They emphasized that the promotion and protection of human rights should not be politicized; insisted that development is an inalienable right; opposed the use of human rights as a conditionality for economic cooperation and development assistance; and emphasized that the international protection and promotion of rights should respect national sovereignty, territorial integrity and non-interference in the internal affairs of states. The ministers "reviewed with satisfaction the considerable and continuing progress of ASEAN in freeing its peoples from fear and want, enabling them to live in dignity", and they agreed that the grouping should consider the establishment of an appropriate regional mechanism on human rights.[93] The ASEAN meeting upheld the main Asian lines of reasoning at Vienna.

THE ASIAN CRISIS

However, change was round the corner. Observers like Mendes had reasoned that, even if Asian economies could deliver increasing incomes to all their people over time, a questionable assertion, "the promise of higher incomes may already be declining in relative utility as compared to rights and participation".[94] Authoritarian regimes therefore would have to reform their institutions, including delegating power, to retain their legitimacy.

In the event, however, reforms were necessitated, not by middle-class demands for political space generated by economic growth, but by the economic violence that hit the region in 1997. Indonesia's authoritarian government fell and a deadly leadership struggle in Malaysia led to the sacking of the deputy premier as capital flight battered currencies and stock markets across the region, cutting a swathe of dislocation, shock and pain from Bangkok to Seoul. An estimated 50 million people out of more than 300 million in Indonesia, South Korea and Thailand fell back below the nationally-defined poverty line in the year from mid-1997. The middle-class confidence of many more millions was shattered, the cutting of public expenditure created social deficits that matched economic and financial retrenchments, and nature was pillaged as the calamity drove people to forests, land and sea in desperation.[95]

While some Asian elites blamed international currency speculators for their undeserved misfortune, sarcastic Western observers revelling in *Schadenfreude* drew attention to corruption, cronyism and a lack of transparency in Asia, traits that they all but labelled silent Asian vices that had accompanied the trumpeted march of Asian values. "Why do you need to be authoritarian to deliver a sensible macroeconomic policy? Which economic-modellers can demonstrate some sort of connection between political repression and GDP growth?" Christopher Patten asked. "Economic growth is surely the result more of business-friendly policies than of people-*un*friendly ones, to do more with sensible dependence on markets than with brutal dependence on phone-tappers and armed policemen."[96]

In a more convincing critique, Robert Wade situates the crisis, not in cultural venality but in the conjunction of material factors that implicated both Asian and Western greed: domestic financial fragility that pre-dated the crash; the growth of excess liquidity in the major industrial nations during the decade that found its way into the hands of money managers seeking high short-term returns; the opening of the capital account by Asian governments in the first half of the decade; and a surge of "momentum-driven private-to-private capital inflows into Asia that were largely unregulated by governments".[97] Villains in analyses such as Wade's include avaricious Wall Street investment banks; the "Washington Consensus" on market liberalization as an almost religious verity that made it possible to elevate Asia into a miraculous continent; conniving Asian policy elites; and the cruelty of the rescue operations mounted by the International Monetary Fund.

Interestingly, the Asian crisis did not hurt China heavily, not least because the non-convertibility of the renminbi insulated the economy. The vigilance of Singapore's financial regulatory institutions was among the factors that enabled the Republic, too, to escape the worst effects of the crisis. However, the regional mood of confidence that had propelled its push for Asian values came to an abrupt end. In a far cry from articulations of Asian cultural recipes for economic success, proponents of Asian values were "reduced to pleading that they were not to *blame* for the recent economic downturn".[98]

Thus ended an era — modest in historical terms, for it had lasted no longer than two decades, but significant in the discursive power that it had exercised over many Asian minds even as it had incensed cultural universalists around the world — in which Asian values had provided an expansive ideological framework for Singapore's engagement of China. Singapore had sought Beijing's incorporation into the global economy without the destruction of the domestic Chinese order. That goal had been achieved in spite of the Tiananmen crackdown and the difficulties that it had created for Hong Kong's return to China. But a bolder attempt to influence the course of Asia's destiny by articulating a set of culturally-specific values that were friendly to growth floundered on the unsuspected shoals of a crisis in which both Asia and the West were implicated. An entire, geopolitical dimension of Sino-Singapore relations vanished from view almost overnight. The Asian retreat began, charted by magisterial Western prescriptions of the need for "the rule of law, freedom of information, and skepticism towards authority in modern economies".[99] When Asian countries returned to growth, they did so without citing values. Asian values descended from the discursive peaks of global affairs and disappeared into silence.

NOTES

1   Yongnian Zheng, *Discovering Chinese Nationalism in China: Modernization, Identity, and International Relations* (Cambridge: Cambridge University Press, 1999), p. 19; p. 39; p. 77.
2   Ibid., p. 72.
3   Ibid., p. 78.
4   Ibid., p. 81.
5   Paul Kennedy, *The Rise and Fall of the Great Powers: Economic Change and Military Conflict from 1500 to 2000* (New York: Random House, 1987).
6   Francis Fukuyama, "The End of History", *The National Interest* 16 (Summer 1989): 3–18, expanded into *The End of History and the Last Man* (New York: The Free Press, 1992).
7   Samuel Huntington, "The Clash of Civilizations?", *Foreign*

Affairs 72, no. 3 (1993): 22–47, expanded into *The Clash of Civilizations and the Remaking of World Order* (New York: Simon and Schuster, 1996).

8 Gunnar Myrdal, *The Asian Drama: An Inquiry into the Poverty of Nations* (New York: Twentieth Century Fund, 1968).

9 Robert Wade, *Governing the Market: A Decade Later*, LSE Development Studies Institute, Working Paper Series, No. 00-03 (March 2000), p. 5.

10 Simon S.C. Tay, "Human Rights, Culture, and the Singapore Example", *McGill Law Journal* 41 (1996): 755–56.

11 Mark R. Thompson, " 'Asian Values' as 'Zivilisationskritik'?", <www.essex.ac.uk/ecpr/events/jointsessions/paperarchive/mannheim/w4/thompson.pdf>.

12 Alan Chong, "Singaporean Foreign Policy and the Asian Values Debate, 1992–2000: Reflections on an Experiment in Soft Power", *Pacific Review* 17, no. 1 (March 2004): 103.

13 Ibid., p. 102.

14 Ibid., p. 104.

15 Ibid., p. 105.

16 Beng-Huat Chua, *Communitarian Ideology and Democracy in Singapore* (London and New York: Routledge, 1995), p. 65.

17 Stephanie Lawson, "Confucius in Singapore: Culture, Politics, and the PAP State", in Peter Dauvergne, ed., *Weak and Strong States in Asia-Pacific Societies* (St Leonards and Canberra ACT: Allen & Unwin in association with the Department of International Relations, Research School of Pacific and Asian Studies, Australian National University, 1998), p. 128.

18 Beng-Huat Chua, op. cit., p. 161.

19 Amod Lele, "State Hindutva and Singapore Confucianism as Responses to the Decline of the Welfare State", *Asian Studies Review* 28 (September 2004): 268; 267.

20 Joseph B. Tamney, *The Struggle Over Singapore's Soul: Western Modernization and Asian Culture* (Berlin and New York: Walter de Gruyter, 1996), p. 183. Author's emphasis.

21 Chung Kwong Yuen, "Leninism, Asian Culture and Singapore", *Asian Profile* 27, no. 3 (June 1999): 232.

22 This term is taken from Raj Vasil, *Asianising Singapore: The PAP's Management of Ethnicity* (Singapore: Heinemann Asia, 1995).

23 <www.mandarin.org.sg/smc/history.html?pg=8&mlid=8>.

24 Lawson, op. cit., p. 126.
25 Michael Hill, *'Asian Values' as Reverse Orientalism: The case of Singapore*, Working Paper, No. 150, (Singapore: National University of Singapore, Department of Sociology, 2000), pp. 16–17.
26 Vasil, op. cit., p. 75.
27 Ibid.
28 Lawson, op. cit., p. 127.
29 Ibid.
30 Ibid., p. 128.
31 Ibid., p. 129.
32 Vasil, op. cit., p. 81.
33 "Cultural Values and Economic Performance", *Speeches '91: A Bimonthly Selection of Ministerial Speeches*, Ministry of Information and the Arts, Singapore, p. 6; 8; 10.
34 "An East Asian Renaissance", *Speeches* 16, no. 6, 1992, pp. 131–32.
35 "Promoting Chinese Culture in a Multi-racial Singapore", *Speeches* 16 no. 3, 1992, pp. 39–40.
36 Fareed Zakaria, "Culture is Destiny; A Conversation with Lee Kuan Yew", *Foreign Affairs* (March/April 1994), <www.fareedzakaria.com/articles/other/culture.html#top>.
37 World Bank, *The East Asian Miracle: Economic Growth and Public Policy* (Oxford: Oxford University Press, 1993).
38 Tommy Koh, "The 10 Values That Undergrid East Asian Strength and Success", *International Herald Tribune*, 11 December 1993.
39 (New York: Thomas Y. Crowell, 1979).
40 (Boulder, Colorado: Westview, 1979).
41 (Cambridge, Massachusetts: Harvard University Press, 1979).
42 Cited in Hill, op. cit., p. 9.
43 Bilahari Kausikan, "Asia's Different Standard", *Foreign Policy* 92 (Fall 1993): 28.
44 Ibid., p. 26.
45 Ibid., p. 28.
46 Ibid., p. 34.
47 Ibid., p. 35. For a rejoinder to Kausikan, see Aryeh Neier, "Asia's Unacceptable Standard" in the same issue of *Foreign Policy*, pp. 42–51. For another critique of Asian values, see Amartya Sen,"Culture and Human Rights", in *Development as*

Freedom (New York: Anchor Books, 2000), pp. 227–48; and "Democracy as a Universal Value", *Journal of Democracy* 10.3 (1999): 3–17, where Sen speaks of Singapore, South Korea and post-reform China as "disciplinarian states": p. 6.

48 Kausikan, ibid., p. 32.
49 Ibid., p. 33.
50 Chris Patten, *East and West* (London and Basingstoke: Macmillan, 1998), p. 150.
51 Kishore Mahbubani, "The West and the Rest", *The National Interest* 28 (Summer 1992), reprinted in Kishore Mahbubani, *Can Asians Think?* (Singapore and Kuala Lumpur: Times Books International, 1998), p. 47.
52 Ibid.
53 Ibid., p. 48.
54 Ibid., p. 52.
55 Shen Baoxiang, Wang Chengquan and Li Zerui, "Human Rights in the World Arena", *Hongqi* 8 (1982) republished in Zhou Guo, ed., *China & the World* (3) (Beijing: *Beijing Review*, Foreign Affairs Series, 1983), pp. 49–51.
56 Ibid., p. 52.
57 Ibid., p. 58; p. 59.
58 Ibid., p. 60; p. 61.
59 Ibid., p. 63.
60 Fareed Zakaria, "The Rise of Illiberal Democracy", *Foreign Affairs* (November 1997), <www.fareedzakaria.com/ARTICLES/other/democracy.html>.
61 Arundhati Roy, "The Loneliness of Noam Chomsky", *The Hindu*, 24 August 2003, <www.hinduonnet.com/thehindu/thscrip/print.pl?file=2003082400020100.htm&date=2003/08/24/&prd=mag&>.
62 Noam Chomsky, "From Central America to Iraq", *Khaleej Times*, 6 August 2004.
63 Roy, op. cit.
64 Patten, op. cit., pp. 155–58; Sen, op. cit., p. 232.
65 Simon Leys, Foreword to the translation of *The Analects of Confucius* (New York: W.W. Norton, 1997), cited in Patten, op. cit., p. 162.
66 Hill, op. cit., p. 1.
67 Ibid., p. 6.
68 Inoue Tatsuo, "Liberal Democracy and Asian Orientalism", in

Joanne R. Bauer and Daniel A. Bell, eds., *The East Asian Challenge for Human Rights* (Cambridge: Cambridge University Press, 1999), pp. 34–35.

69 Sen, op. cit., pp. 233–36. Author's emphasis.
70 Errol P. Mendes, *Asian Values and Human Rights: Letting the Tigers Free*, Human Rights Research and Education Centre, University of Ottawa, 1996, <www.cdp-hrc.uottawa.ca/publicat/asian_values.html>.
71 Ibid.
72 Ibid.
73 Ibid.
74 For the text of the Bangkok Declaration, see <www.unhchr.ch/html/menu5/wcbangk.htm#III>.
75 Inoue, op. cit., p. 34.
76 Denny Roy, "Singapore, China, and the 'Soft Authoritarian' Challenge", *Asian Survey* 34, no. 3 (March 1994), p. 238.
77 Human Rights Watch, <www.hrw.org/reports/1994/WR94/Asia.htm>.
78 Cited in ibid.
79 Cited in ibid.
80 Cited in Alice Erh-Soon Tay, " 'Asian Values' and the Rule of Law", Jura Gentium, Centre for Philosophy of International Law and Global Politics, <www.tsd.unifi.it/jg/en/index.htm?surveys/rol/tay.htm>.
81 *Keesing's Contemporary Archives* (June 1993): 39537.
82 "Democracy and Human Rights: Where America Stands", remarks delivered by US Secretary of State Warren Christopher, World Conference on Human Rights, 14 June 1993, Vienna, Austria, Office of the Spokesman, US Department of State, <dosfan.lib.uic.edu/ERC/briefing/dossec/1993/9306/930614dossec.html>.
83 *Keesing's Contemporary Archives*, op. cit.: 39537.
84 Wong Kan Seng, "The Real World of Human Rights", Singapore Government Press Release, 09-1/93/06/16, p. 4. For the text of the Vienna Declaration and the official report on the conference, see <www.unhchr.ch/huridocda/huridoca.nsf/(Symbol)/A.CONF.157.24+(PART+I).En?Open Document>.
85 Wong, op. cit., p. 5.
86 Ibid., pp. 6–7.

87 Ibid., p. 8.
88 Chong, op. cit., pp. 106–7.
89 *Keesing's Contemporary Archives*, op. cit.: 39537.
90 Chong, op. cit., p. 107.
91 Ibid., p. 108.
92 Mendes, op. cit.
93 <www.aseansec.org/2548.htm>.
94 Mendes, op. cit.
95 Wade, op. cit., p. 2.
96 Patten, op. cit., pp. 152–53. Author's emphasis.
97 Wade, op. cit., p. 8.
98 Mark R. Thompson, "Pacific Asia after 'Asian values': authoritarianism, democracy, and 'good governance' ", *Third World Quarterly* 25, no. 6 (2004): 1079. Author's emphasis. He cites Koh, but Koh was not alone.
99 Matt Steinglass, "Whose Asian Values?", *The Boston Globe*, 20 November 2005.

CHAPTER VII

SUZHOU
INDUSTRIAL PARK

The Asian values debate, cut off abruptly by the Asian
crisis, revealed the international limits of the discursive
framework for the evolution of Sino-Singapore ties,
but it did not have a bearing on those relations
themselves. By contrast, the hobbled fortunes of the
Suzhou International Park (SIP), an ambitious attempt
to build a Chinese township with Singapore
characteristics,[1] tested the limits of Singapore's
engagement of China. The SIP, which began as a 65–35
joint venture between Singapore and China,
encountered problems that ceased only when the two
stakes were reversed. The Asian crisis played a role in
the park's problems by exacerbating its competition
for investment with a neighbouring industrial park,
but the causes of the conflict in Suzhou went deeper: to
a seemingly intrinsic incompatibility between the
Singapore and Chinese ways of doing business in spite

of ethnic affinity and empathy with each other's political systems.

The SIP's origins were economic. They lay in an attempt to supplement Singapore's economy with earnings made abroad. Singapore's regionalization strategy, which was formulated in the mid-1980s, encouraged overseas investment by Singapore companies and joint ventures to "combine the competitive strengths of Singapore and its partners to attract international investors".[2] The strategy led to official initiatives to establish growth triangles and overseas industrial parks. Thus, the SIJORI growth triangle became a partnership between Singapore, Johore in Malaysia, and Riau in Indonesia that "links the infrastructure, capital, and expertise of Singapore with the natural and labour resources of Johore and Riau".[3] Industrial parks in India and Vietnam, too, became a part of Singapore's efforts to develop an external wing for its economy to overcome the scarcity of its land and human resources, tiny domestic market, and its loss in comparative advantage as a result of rising costs. "Neighboring emerging economies serve as extensions or frontiers toward which Singapore transfers management know-how and administrative skills such as clean and efficient government (software)."[4] Replicating its successful development experience served Singapore's aspirations to be a gateway for multinational corporations wishing to invest in the region.[5]

Suzhou embodied the possibilities of engagement with China. Approached in 1992 by Suzhou Mayor Zhang Xinsheng to invest some of Singapore's reserves in turning that grand but dilapidated city into a "miniature Singapore",[6] Lee Kuan Yew, who was Senior Minister then, was sceptical at first. But an intervention by Deng Pufang, Deng Xiaoping's son, through his father's office gave the project all-important political credibility. In May 1993, when Lee met Vice-Premier Zhu Rongji in Shanghai, the Singapore leader explained his proposal, which was for "a government-to-government technical assistance agreement to transfer our knowledge and experience (what we called "software") in attracting investments and building industrial estates, complete with housing and commercial centres, to an unbuilt site of about 100 square kilometres in Suzhou".[7] Backed by a consortium of Singapore and foreign companies in a joint venture with the Suzhou authorities, the project was seen as taking more than two decades to complete. "I explained that my proposal was in response to many delegations that had come from China to study us in a piecemeal manner but would never understand how our system worked."[8]

In that sense, SIP's genesis was Deng's 1978 visit to Singapore, where he had admired the city-state's ability to combine growth and order. That admiration was made explicit during his tour of southern China in 1992, when he exhorted Chinese to learn from Singapore as a model of development. Soon after his endorsement, more than 400 Chinese officials visited the Republic. "We chose Suzhou because the Central Government in Beijing had planned to develop Shanghai as China's main international centre and drive development up the Yangtze river valley. Also Suzhou had well-educated high quality workers who would be fast learners."[9] In February 1994, Lee signed the Suzhou Agreement with Vice-Premier Li Lanqing in Beijing, witnessed by Singapore Prime Minister Goh Chok Tong and Chinese Premier Li Peng.[10]

In keeping with the general direction of Singapore's regionalization strategy, the move into Suzhou had ethnic overtones. Singapore encouraged enterprises formed by ethnic Malays to look for investment opportunities in Malaysia and Indonesia, while Indian Singaporean companies were asked to look towards India.[11] It would be going too far to claim that the emphasis on ethnicity was emblematic of the link that the propagation of Asian values sought to make between cultural values and economic success. After all, Western markets were the locus of substantial Singaporean interests as the source of investments and the destination of exports. However, ethnicity did play a role in Singapore's regionalization as Asia boomed. There was nothing surprising, therefore, when the Singapore authorities cited culture as one reason for identifying China as a target of their regionalization strategy.[12]

The Chinese reciprocated the cultural argument, drawing on their experience of attracting foreign investment during the 1980s, when foreign partners from Hong Kong, Taiwan and Macau accounted for more than 70 per cent of all joint ventures registered on the mainland. The "overseas Chinese" utilized ancestral, kinship and hometown ties to establish *guanxi* networks typically closed to investors from America, Europe and Japan.[13] "What ethnic Chinese from Hong Kong, Macau and Taiwan did was to demonstrate to a sceptical world that 'guanxi' through the same language and culture can make up for a lack in the rule of law, and transparency in rules and regulations," Lee declared at a world Chinese entrepreneurs' conference in Hong Kong in 1993. "This 'guanxi' capability will be of value for the next 20 years at least, until China develops a system based on the rule of law, with sufficient transparency and certainty to satisfy foreign investors."[14] Lee concluded that it would be a mistake for Singapore entrepreneurs not to participate in "one of the greatest transformations of our age, the industrialization and modernization of the countries of East Asia, and not least of China. And we would be foolish not to use the ethnic Chinese network to increase our reach and our grasp of these opportunities".[15] Although Singapore was situated outside Greater China, it was accorded an honorary role in the extended Chinese family where business ties expressed the bonds of cultural affinity. The SIP was built not only on economic foundations but on this sense of cultural affinity.[16]

While the Suzhou park affirmed cultural affinity — which Beijing shared with Sinic territories on its periphery — it went beyond culture and boasted a feature that those territories' interactions with China did not possess. The SIP was a joint venture between two sovereign governments, not merely between companies bonding through *guanxi*. An act of political collaboration as much as an economic and cultural initiative, the park was visualized as the prototype for a capitalist-authoritarian China. What Singapore brought to the table was a system, described aptly as an administrative state by Chan Heng Chee, in which politicians, bureaucrats, technocrats and businessmen worked together to achieve national ends defined by the executive. In this system, the presence of government-linked companies gave the state itself a powerful role and stake in economic outcomes. Singapore, which Raffles had visualized as the Manchester of the East, was a "miracle of post-colonial discipline and development",[17] organized, methodical and seamlessly predictable from top to bottom. The science-fiction writer William Gibson is unnerved by his experience of confronting Singapore. "If IBM had ever bothered to actually possess a physical country, that country might have had a lot in common with Singapore," he exclaims. However, he acknowledges the value of the premium the state placed on infrastructure, both physical and social. "Ordinarily, confronted with a strange city, I'm inclined to look for the parts that have broken down and fallen apart, revealing the underlying social mechanisms; how the place is really wired beneath the lay of the land as presented by the Chamber of Commerce," he writes. "This won't do in Singapore, because nothing is falling apart. Everything that's fallen apart has already been replaced with something new."[18] The software to be transferred to China was embedded in this almost total organization of society. Transferring that system was quite another thing.

A PARTIAL SUCCESS

The SIP, which was given the same status as China's Special Economic Zones and the Shanghai Pudong development zone, was one of the most successful zones for attracting foreign investment between 1994 and early 1997. However, from the last quarter of 1997 until mid-1999, the zone became uncompetitive and lost money.[19] The Asian economic crisis hit the park by affecting existing tenants, including multinational corporations, which were not expanding operations; and by reducing the number of potential new tenants.[20] However, the primary problem was the "aggressive marketing strategy" adopted by a rival industrial zone, the Suzhou New District (SND),[21] which had begun three years before the SIP. The Suzhou Municipal Authority had offered the SND to Singapore as a site for the inter-governmental project with China, but the Republic had turned down the offer because the SND did not provide sufficient space and because it wanted the SIP to be independent of ties with local governing bodies.[22] The SND avenged itself by copying the SIP's practices while undercutting it in land and infrastructure costs. The SND "simply looked over the fence, understood what made the Suzhou Industrial Park successful and replicated it".[23] "Things came to a head in mid-1997 when the vice-mayor of Suzhou, who ran SND, told a meeting of German investors in Hamburg that President Jiang did not support SIP, that they were welcome to SND and did not need Singapore," Lee writes. He raised the problem with Jiang in December 1997. The Chinese leader assured him that the SIP remained his top priority and that problems at the local level would be resolved.[24]

There were hopes that things would change in 1998. The new mayor of Suzhou declared that the SIP was "the priority of all priorities", Premier Zhu Rongji gave the park his personal backing, a Jiangsu party secretary apologized publicly for the park's fortunes, and it was exempted from a new national tax on foreign investments in January 1999.[25] But these gestures did not change fundamentals on the ground, where Suzhou did not stop promoting the SND in competition with the SIP. The park was in dire straits by the end of 1998.[26] Then Deputy Prime Minister Lee Hsien Loong told Parliament in 1999 that statutory boards and government-linked companies had invested US$147 million in the SIP project till then.[27] In June 1999, it was announced that Singapore would cut its stake in the project to 35 per cent and hand over the park's management on 1 January 2001. This took place, and after seven years of financial operational losses, the SIP, now under the stewardship of the Chinese partner, announced a profit of US$7.6 million earned in 2001.[28] At its 10th anniversary celebrations, Lee declared that Singapore "is honoured to have played a small role in China's growth and transformation",[29] but his memoirs, published earlier, reveal his disappointment over what turned out to be "a chastening experience", "a partial success" although not "a total failure".[30] He put the Suzhou episode in grand historical context. "After two centuries of decline that began with the Qing dynasty, China's leaders face the formidable task of installing modern management systems and changing the mindsets and habits of officials steeped in the traditions of the imperial mandarinate."[31]

The high expectations aroused by the confluence of economics, culture and politics gave a spectacular dimension to Singapore's decision to cede control of the project. What had gone wrong? It is undeniable that the Suzhou municipal authorities had played a crucial role. They were angered when Singapore declined their offer of the SND early on, and they were rankled by the fact that Singapore marketed the SIP as being not a typical Chinese estate, thus implicating the SND.[32] They viewed as arrogance the fact that the Republic insisted on dealing directly with Beijing. Since tax revenues collected from foreign businesses in the SIP were remitted directly to Beijing, by-passing the Suzhou Municipal Authority, it had no financial incentive in wanting to see the park succeed. While the SIP did contribute to Suzhou's economy, it did not benefit the Authority directly. Instead, it was a competitor to the SND, which was the Authority's own responsibility.[33] Thus, Suzhou officials moved away from the "core objective", recognized in Beijing, of effecting the transfer from Singapore of software on how to create a total pro-business environment capable of attracting high-quality foreign investment; the officials had a parochial interest in the hardware of roads and infrastructure, which "brought direct and immediate benefits to Suzhou and credit to its officials".[34] Moreover, there was an important difference between Singaporeans, who "take for granted the sanctity of contracts", and the Suzhou authorities, to whom a signed agreement could be "altered or reinterpreted with changing circumstances".[35] The challenge from the municipal officials would have been expected, but what explained Beijing's refusal or inability to bring its authority to bear on them? One argument that has been advanced is that the Chinese, being minority shareholders, felt little sense of ownership. In any case, it was a "win-win situation" for Beijing: its primary objective of getting Singapore's software transferred to Suzhou was successful and, as for foreign direct investment, it really did not matter much to Beijing if investment went to the SND instead of the SIP.[36] A more charitable view is that Beijing did not exercise total control over provinces and cities, especially in an open season of competition among regions for foreign investment. Each territorial entity did what it deemed necessary to thrive in an era of economic decentralization ushered in by reforms.

The tricky reality of decentralization in post-communist China touches on causes of the Suzhou problem that lay partially in Singapore. Accustomed to a centralized polity, officials of the city-state perhaps did not realize sufficiently the proverbial lay of a land where "the mountain is high and the emperor is far away".[37] Captivated by its own model of "state-driven capitalism", Singapore did what few businessmen would have done: take the "audacious gamble" of replicating itself in "mercantilist" China. Singapore's bureaucrats, "invincible at home, believed they could replicate one overseas". Competent technocrats though they were in Singapore, they could not be expected to operate as successful entrepreneurs abroad without a political climate at home that rewarded free enterprise.[38] While such arguments have a point, they tend to be made only when Singapore bureaucrats fail abroad, not when they succeed. Moreover, failure in China was not limited to risk-averse technocrats from safe and boring state-capitalist Singapore: Business warriors from liberal democracies, too, had fallen off the cunning ramparts of the Great Wall of business. That said, what really was at stake in Suzhou was the viability of grafting Singapore's software, embedded in its political history, onto a China with high mountains and an emperor far away. This was not possible. Although in the decade from its start in 1994, the SIP sent 88 batches of personnel, totalling about 1,360 people, to Singapore for training in urban planning and management, economic development and management, and public management, Suzhou illustrated the limits of cultural affinity in international relations.

NOTES

1 Dana M. Liu, *The China-Singapore Suzhou Industrial Park: Singapore's Role in China's Development* (Baltimore: The Johns Hopkins University, The Paul H. Nitze School of Advanced International Studies, no date), p. 2.

2 Chia Siow Yue, "Singapore: Advanced Production Base and Smart Hub of the Electronics Industry", in W. Dobson and Chia Siow Yue, eds., *Multinationals and East Asian Integration* (Ottawa and Singapore: International Development Research

Centre and the Institute of Southeast Asian Studies, 1997), <www.idrc.org.sg/en/ev-68138-201-1-DO_TOPIC.html>.

3 Ibid.

4 Liu, op. cit., p. 5.

5 Ibid.

6 Lee Kuan Yew, *From Third World to First: The Singapore Story, 1965–2000*, p. 719.

7 Ibid., p. 720.

8 Ibid.

9 Lee Kuan Yew, speech at the ceremony to mark the achievements of the Suzhou Industrial Park's 10th anniversary, Suzhou, 10 June 2004, <stars.nhb.gov.sg/data/pdfdoc/2004061102.htm>.

10 Lee Kuan Yew, *From Third World to First*, p. 721.

11 Alexius A. Pereira, *State Collaboration and Development Strategies in China: The case of the China-Singapore Suzhou Industrial Park (1992–2002)* (London and New York: RoutledgeCurzon, 2003), p. 40.

12 Ibid.

13 Ibid., pp. 18–19.

14 Lee Kuan Yew, "Developing a global guanxi", *Speeches* 17, no. 6, 1993, pp. 36–37.

15 Ibid., p. 42.

16 Pereira, op. cit., p. 19.

17 Christopher Lydon, "My Singapore Sling", *The Transom Review* 2, issue 5 (June 2002): p. 3, <www.transom.org/guests/review/200206.review.lydon.html>.

18 William Gibson, "Disneyland with the Death Penalty, *Wired*, issue 1.04 (Sep/Oct 1993), <www.wired.com/wired/archive/1.04/gibson_pr.html>.

19 Pereira, op. cit., p. 115.

20 Ibid., p. 117.

21 Ibid., p. 120.

22 "To what extent does the Suzhou Industrial Park project reflect both the potential and pitfalls of the Singapore-China connection?", <www.comp.nus.edu.sg/~malliped/SIP.pdf>.

23 Pereira, op. cit., p. 123.

24 Lee Kuan Yew, *From Third World to First*, p. 722.

25 Pereira, op. cit., pp. 130–32.

26 Ibid., p. 141.

27 Agence France-Presse report, 3 August 1999.
28 Pereira, op. cit., p. 156.
29 Lee Kuan Yew, speech at the ceremony to mark the achievements of the Suzhou Industrial Park's 10th anniversary, op. cit.
30 Lee Kuan Yew, *From Third World to First*, pp. 723–24.
31 Ibid., p. 724.
32 General manager cited in Pereira, op. cit., p. 134.
33 Ibid., pp. 137–38.
34 Lee Kuan Yew, *From Third World to First*, pp. 721–22.
35 Ibid., p. 723.
36 "To what extent does the Suzhou Industrial Park project reflect both the potential and pitfalls of the Singapore-China connection?", op. cit.
37 Proverb cited in Foo Choy Peng and Barry Porter, "Suzhou: Sino-Singapore bid fails test", *South China Morning Post*, 30 June 1999.
38 Salil Tripathi, "Innocents Abroad", *Asiaweek*, 19 January 2001.

CHAPTER VIII

TAIWAN

Ironically for the two sides of the Taiwan Strait that have one of the most hostile relations in the world, Singapore's ties with China were foreshadowed by its relations with Taiwan soon after the city-state became independent. Three sets of factors underscored the similarity: economics, politics and culture. Taiwan and Singapore were two Newly-Industrializing Economies that had taken off as part of the Japan-led Flying Geese formation. Politically, Taiwan and Singapore were authoritarian, although the Republic of China began life as a military dictatorship imposed on the island by a party that, having lost the civil war, was determined to recapture the mainland; and Singapore was an authoritarian democracy led by civilians determined not to return humbled to a Malaysia from which the island had been ejected. Taiwan and Singapore were united in their hostility towards communism.

"Apart from my good personal chemistry with (Generalissimo Chiang Kai-shek's son and Taiwanese leader) Chiang Ching-kuo, the foundation of our relationship was that we were both against communism. The Chinese Communist Party was his mortal enemy and the Malayan Communist Party, which was linked to the Chinese Communist Party, was mine. We had a common cause," Lee Kuan Yew writes in his memoirs.[1] Culturally, Taiwan and Singapore (like Hong Kong) were inhabited by maritime Chinese communities. Referring to Taiwan and Hong Kong, Lee writes: "The rapid progress of these two maritime Chinese communities gave me great encouragement. I picked up useful pointers. If they could make it, so could Singapore."[2] These aspects of Singapore's relations with Taiwan presaged its engagement of China as Beijing moved away from communism in its economic planning, settled for hard authoritarian politics, and unearthed a Chinese cultural self that had been subsumed by the demands of proletarian internationalism. Singapore's relations with Taiwan bore an uncanny resemblance to its relations with post-communist China.

This is true but for a crucial proviso: Singapore's ties with Taiwan are strategic, and its ties with China are not. Just two years into independence, land-scarce Singapore began discussions with Taipei on building up its military forces. The Israelis could not offer the facilities that the Taiwanese could to train pilots and naval officers.[3] Since then, Singapore's military forces, including artillery, armour and infantry troops, have trained in Taiwan and, in recent years, Singapore has extended the training to include air force and naval drills, with ground force exercises focusing on heavy artillery practice.[4] Concerned, China offered Singapore military training bases in Hainan province — its first such gesture to a foreign country — to woo it away from Taiwan.[5]

Singapore's relations with Taiwan represent a delicate balancing act with its engagement of China. The balance was achieved by sticking to two complementary fundamentals. The first fundamental, made clear early on, was that Taiwan could not expect diplomatic recognition in return for the provision of military training facilities.[6] Singapore's policy was that "there was 'one China', and "the reunification of the PRC and Taiwan was an internal matter to be resolved between the two".[7] When the UN resolution for the admission of the People's Republic came up, Singapore "voted for the resolution to admit China but abstained on the resolution to expel Taiwan".[8] The second fundamental was that Singapore's diplomatic recognition of China could not come at the cost of its training programmes in Taiwan.[9]

Within these twin realities — its security links with Taipei and its diplomatic relations with Beijing — Singapore received President Lee Teng-hui in 1989, the first visit by a Taiwanese President to Southeast Asia. In a semantic indication of the niceties that the balancing act required, Singapore referred to the visiting dignitary in its public statements as President Lee "from Taiwan", not "of Taiwan". However, the visit had the effect of raising his political profile in the region.[10] Significantly, instead of the visit proving injurious to relations with Beijing, these ties were formalized when Singapore extended diplomatic recognition to China the following year. Indeed, so comfortable were both Beijing and Taipei with Lee Kuan Yew's role as a "channel for messages" between them that they chose Singapore as the venue of their

first-ever talks, in April 1993. The Wang-Koo talks —
named after Wang Daohan, chairman of China's
Association for Relations Across the Taiwan Strait,
and Koo Chen-fu, chairman of Taiwan's Straits
Exchange Foundation — did not improve bilateral
relations because the two sides had different agendas.
Taipei was interested in technical matters, not trade
liberalization, let alone reunification, while China
had hoped that the technical preliminaries would
lead to "substantive discussions on reunification".[11]
Nevertheless, the talks widely were seen as being
historic, and Singapore's role as their venue signified
the trust that Lee Kuan Yew enjoyed at the highest
levels of decision-making in Beijing and Taipei.

That role soon would come to be tested, as Lee
Kuan Yew's memoirs show. Lee Teng-hui had inherited
the historical mantle of the Kuomintang (KMT), a party
that, notwithstanding its visceral rivalry with the
Chinese Communist Party, was pledged to China's
reunification and so shared with the CCP the premise
of One China. But in moving Taiwan towards
democracy, Lee Teng-hui placed more native-born
Taiwanese in key posts, sidelining the mainland-born
KMT Old Guard that was dedicated to reunification. In
1994, the Japanese-educated president gave an
interview to a Japanese journalist in which he described
the KMT as a party of outsiders who had occupied
Taiwan and had caused great suffering to the Taiwanese
people. Setting wrongs right, he conferred on himself
the role of Moses leading his people to the Promised
Land.[12] The urgency of dealing with the sudden
appearance of a Taiwanese Moses did not fail to register
itself on the atheists in Beijing. When Lee Teng-hui
visited the United States in 1995 and spoke of the
Republic of China on Taiwan, the stage was set for "the

most serious confrontation between the two sides since the 1958 crisis in Quemoy". In March 1996, Beijing deployed troops and carried out military exercises in Fujian province opposite Taiwan, and fired missiles that landed in waters off the island's west coast. Seeking to moderate the situation, Lee Kuan Yew made a plea. "China's leaders have referred to me as an old friend. I am an older friend of Taiwan. If either one is damaged, Singapore will suffer a loss. If both are damaged, Singapore's loss will be doubled. Singapore benefits when both prosper, when both cooperate and help each other prosper." Beijing rebuffed him gently, saying that it was an internal matter.[13]

The crisis, which also has been read as an attempt by China to intimidate Taiwanese voters from supporting pro-independence forces in definitive forthcoming elections — Taiwan's first direct and popular polls for the presidency — had a dramatic *denouement*. Washington responded by deploying two aircraft carrier battle groups in the waters near Taiwan, the largest concentration of American naval power in East Asia since the Vietnam War. The elections, seen as an index of Taiwan's political development, went forward and Lee Teng-hui won a second term decisively. In this, the first Sino-U.S. military confrontation since the late 1960s, China was confronted by superior U.S. forces, backed down, and an international crisis was averted.[14] However, Lee Kuan Yew notes some of the longer-terms implications of Lee Teng-hui's position. "Lee's policies could only prevail with the support of the United States. By acting as though such support would be forthcoming for all time, he led the people of Taiwan to believe that they did not need to negotiate seriously on Taiwan's future with China's leaders. His contribution to Taiwan's future has been to turn the reunification issue into the most important item on Beijing's national agenda."[15] Indeed, after the 1999 release of Lee Teng-hui's "two states theory" — according to which Taiwan is a separate entity and negotiations with Beijing should occur under the rubric of "special state-to-state" relations — and with the March 2000 elections looming, Beijing published a State Council White Paper warning of the use of force if Taiwan refused to discuss reunification indefinitely. This escalation in the Chinese position was directed at Chen Shui-bian of the independence-minded Democratic Progressive Party. Although he won with a narrow margin of votes, he set relations with China on a dangerous new course.

China's 2004 *White Paper on National Defense* warned: "The separatist activities of the 'Taiwan independence' forces have increasingly become the biggest immediate threat to China's sovereignty and territorial integrity as well as peace and stability on both sides of the Taiwan Straits and the Asia-Pacific region as a whole. The United States has on many occasions reaffirmed adherence to the one China policy, observance of the three joint communiqués and opposition to 'Taiwan independence.' However, it continues to increase, quantitatively and qualitatively, its arms sales to Taiwan, sending a wrong signal to the Taiwan authorities. The US action does not serve a stable situation across the Taiwan Straits."[16] Relations took a dramatic turn when two opposition leaders — Lien Chan of the KMT and James Soong of the People First Party — visited China in 2005 in the first trip by such senior Taiwanese politicians to the mainland since the end of the Civil War. However, relations remain hobbled by the threat to China of Taiwan declaring independence and the threat to Taiwan of a precipitate military response from the mainland.

The other important player in the issue was Japan, an American treaty ally that China saw as a complicating factor in its relations with Taiwan. Although the U.S.-Japan treaty revision guidelines initially were conceived in the early 1990s with different goals in mind, after the 1996 crisis, "there is little doubt that China is one of the foci of the revisions".[17] Indeed, the Japan-U.S. Joint Declaration on Security, which set forth the case for revising the original defence cooperation guidelines of 1978, appeared in April 1996, a month after the Taiwan Strait missile crisis.[18] The revised Guidelines for Japan-U.S. Defence Cooperation were agreed upon in 1997.

The most significant revision to the 1978 guidelines was the provision — legislated with partial amendments in 1999 — for "cooperation in situations in areas surrounding Japan that will have an important influence on Japan's peace and security". The "geographically undefined" reference to "areas surrounding Japan" drew Chinese objections because it might include Taiwan; even though it was vague, the mere possibility of Japanese military intervention encouraged Taiwanese separatism, in Chinese eyes.[19] Tensions across the East China Sea rose when Japan's chief cabinet secretary said publicly that the guidelines were relevant to the Taiwan Strait area. That view had formed in 1997, with a former Japanese foreign ministry official declaring that no one had denied that the Taiwan Strait was included. Tokyo later tried to escape from the controversy by stating that the term was "not geographic but situational", but China did not accept the semantic creativity.[20] Taiwan did not recede from the U.S.-Japan security agenda. In February 2005, defence officials from the two countries issued the "two-plus-two" declaration noting explicitly that peace in the Taiwan Strait was a "common strategic objective" of the United States and Japan. The declaration reminded former Japanese diplomat Hisahiko Okazaki of the 1969 Sato-Nixon *Communiqué* — signed between Japanese Prime Minister Eisaku Sato and U.S. President Richard Nixon — that mentioned Taiwan as an important element of Japan's security. "The Taiwan question is a very delicate issue. People were afraid of mentioning the importance of Taiwan for a long time," Okazaki told a Taiwanese newspaper later. "Nowadays, we say we're interested in the [security] of the Taiwan Strait, but actually in the *communique,* it didn't even say 'Taiwan Strait.' It said 'Taiwan itself.' " Okazaki placed recent developments in the context of a possible surprise Chinese attack on Taiwan, which had become more likely with the passage of the Anti-Secession Law by Beijing in March 2005.[21] Former Singapore diplomat Kishore Mahbubani pointed out that, given "Japan's colonial role in separating Taiwan from China in 1895 and Japan's subsequent invasion of China, Tokyo had long been careful to avoid taking any public positions about Taiwan that could offend China". "When Japan then declared having a strategic interest in Taiwan, the Chinese leadership felt that a red flag was being waved… By concurring in the two-plus-two statement, Washington complicated the matter, leading many Chinese to wonder whether it was trying to moderate or aggravate Sino-Japanese relations."[22]

Key to outcomes in the Strait is the role that the United States would — or would not — play with its policy of strategic ambiguity. This policy of studied ambiguity leaves unclear to both sides the conditions under which Washington would intervene on Taiwan's behalf in a cross-Strait confrontation. The roots of the policy lie in Washington's establishment of diplomatic relations with China in 1979; the abrogation of official ties with Taiwan; and the termination in 1980 of the quarter-century old mutual defence treaty with the island. Congress passed the Taiwan Relations Act, which provided continued security guarantees. As Scott L. Kastner shows, America's initial dilemma was to maintain enough of a commitment to Taiwan's defence to deter a mainland attack on the island, while preserving a constructive relationship with Beijing. This was not an impossible goal. Since the Taipei government in the early 1980s subscribed to the idea of One China and viewed itself as the legitimate government of all of China, the U.S. defence commitment to Taiwan "at worst, from Beijing's perspective" maintained the *status quo*. American aid to Taipei might have delayed the reunification of China on Beijing's terms, "but it did not threaten the fundamental premise of a single China". It was with the appearance of democratizing reforms in Taiwan in the late 1980s and the loss of political control by mainland-born Taiwanese that the stakes changed.[23] Taiwan's democratization, welcomed by a Washington supportive of the global spread of democracy, made it unlikely for the United States to disassociate itself from its commitment to the island's defence against Beijing. However, the American stance complicated relations with China which, during the 1990s, grew more impatient with Taiwan, partly because of the democratization process, and which increasingly saw America's continued support for Taiwan as a sticking point in its relations with Washington.[24]

Critics of strategic ambiguity argue that it could contribute to war in the Strait by fostering miscalculations of American intentions on either side, but defenders of the policy argue that it remains the best way to deter a Chinese attack and restrain Taiwanese moves towards independence.[25] Should the Taiwanese press on and proclaim independence, the policy provides Washington with an honourable exit strategy from its commitment to a democratic, but not an independent, Taiwan. However, it also is argued that, the United States having invested so much strategically in the island, its credibility in East Asia would suffer should it be seen to be abandoning Taiwan in a crisis because of an unwillingness to confront China militarily. This would amount to "a reordering of great-power influence in East Asia" by demonstrating to Japan, South Korea and Australia that Washington is an unreliable ally and to Southeast Asians that it is an "unreliable protector-stabilizer in the western Pacific".[26]

Beyond the current debate over strategic ambiguity, structured on the existing power differential between Beijing and Washington, lies the question of the consequences of China's growing strength. "The United States may be able to stop China from using force for another 20 to 30 years," Lee Kuan Yew writes. "Within that time, China is likely to develop the military capability to control the straits. It may be wiser, before the military balance shifts to the mainland, to negotiate the terms for an eventual, not an immediate, reunification."[27] Singapore's preference clearly is for peace in the Strait, given the alternative: a war that would devastate the economics and stability of East Asia no matter which side, China or Taiwan/the United States, won.

That outlook was reiterated by the visit to Taiwan in 2004 of Lee Hsien Loong shortly before he became Prime Minister. The trip, which the city-state justified as a sovereign prerogative in the teeth of Chinese opposition, reconfirmed Singapore's fundamental opposition to Taiwan declaring independence. At a press conference, Lee Hsien Loong said: "I did notice the stronger Taiwanese identity among the population. I also learnt that most Taiwanese believe that China will not attack them. It seems that most also believe that the US will come to Taiwan's rescue if China does attack. I was troubled by this."

He also said: "None of the friends I met gave me the impression that the Taiwanese leaders were eager for a confrontation across the straits. Several told me that the leaders will not push for independence. They also recognized that what matters is not what the leaders say, but what they do." Singapore's bottom line: "We are long-time friends of both the mainland and Taiwan, and conduct our relations with both in a way that is consistent with our 'One China' policy. We have not allowed and will not allow ourselves to be used to further the cause of Taiwanese independence."[28] His assessment after visiting Taiwan was that there was "a real risk of miscalculation and mishap". Given that peoples on both sides of the strait were Singapore's good friends, it would be faced with a difficult choice if war broke out. "This is something we do not wish to see happen. But if the conflict is provoked by Taiwan, Singapore will not support Taiwan."[29] The message was clear: not even Singapore's strategic links with Taipei would justify its support for an independent Taiwan.

NOTES

1 Lee Kuan Yew, *From Third World to First: The Singapore Story, 1965–2000*, p. 621.
2 Ibid., p. 623.
3 Ibid., p. 620.
4 Dana Dillon and John J. Tkacik, Jr., "China's Quest for Asia", *Policy Review*, No. 134 (December 2005 and January 2006) (Stanford: Hoover Institution), <www.policyreview.org/134/dillon.html>.

5 Agence France-Presse report, 12 February 2001.
6 Lee Kuan Yew, *From Third World to First*, op. cit., p. 620.
7 Ibid.
8 Ibid.
9 Dillon and Tkacik, Jr., op cit.
10 Lee Kuan Yew, op. cit., pp. 628–29.
11 Ibid., p. 629.
12 Ibid., pp. 626–27.
13 Ibid., pp. 630–31.
14 Parris H. Chang, "Lessons From the 1996 Taiwan Strait Crisis for the U.S., Japan and Taiwan", Harvard Studies on Taiwan: Papers of the Taiwan Studies Workshop 3 (2000)," <www.fas.harvard.edu/~fairbank/tsw/chang.html>.
15 Lee Kuan Yew, op. cit., pp. 631–32.
16 <www.fas.org/nuke/guide/china/doctrine/natdef 2004.html#2>.
17 Alastair Iain Johnston, "Is China a Status Quo Power?", *International Security* 27, no. 4 (Spring 2003): 53.
18 Chris Rahman, "Defending Taiwan, and why it matters", *Naval War College Review* LIV, no. 4 (Autumn 2001): 80–81.
19 Ibid., pp. 79–80.
20 Ibid., p. 80.
21 Chang Yun-ping, "Upgrade defence abilities: Japanese expert", *Taipei Times*, 6 November 2005.
22 Kishore Mahbubani, "Understanding China", *Foreign Affairs* 84, no. 5 (September/October 2005): 57.
23 Scott L. Kastner, "Ambiguity, economic interdependence, and the U.S. strategic dilemma in the Taiwan Strait", <www.bsos.umd.edu/gvpt/kastner/Kastnerambiguity.pdf>, pp. 4–5.
24 Ibid., pp. 6–7.
25 This is view of Kastner: ibid., pp. 10–21.
26 Rahman, op. cit., pp. 71–72.
27 Lee Kuan Yew, *From Third World to First*, p. 633.
28 Ministry of Foreign Affairs, Singapore, "Questions and Answers with DPM Lee Hsien Loong on his visit to Taiwan", 19 July 2004, <app.mfa.gov.sg/internet/press/view_press.asp?post_id=1098>.
29 Lee Hsien Loong, English Text of National Day Rally 2004 Speech in Chinese, 22 August 2004, <app.sprinter.gov.sg/data/pr/2004082202.htm>.

CHAPTER IX

ASEAN

Singapore's relations with China reflect its acute awareness of sensitivities in ASEAN over its being the only Chinese-majority state outside China; and its need to strengthen its hand in its dealings with Beijing by placing its China initiatives within a larger regional framework. ASEAN is, therefore, an integral part of Singapore's policy towards China. Singapore drew on ASEAN's ability to provide its members with a multiplier effect in their international relations although it was (and is) not a supranational organization along the lines of the European Union. But in drawing on ASEAN as a diplomatic resource, Singapore keenly was aware that there was more than one view of China among regional states. The crisis over the Vietnamese invasion of Cambodia had revealed fault lines in the ASEAN view, from one extreme in which Indonesia's closeness to Vietnam attested to its suspicion of China, and the other extreme, in which Thailand and Singapore believed that Beijing was the lesser threat to Southeast

Asia. The disappearance of the Cold War and the end of the Vietnamese invasion of Cambodia transformed such perceptions and approaches, but there were residual differences over China in an expanded ASEAN that included, not least, its former nemesis, Vietnam. In emerging as ASEAN's most articulate exponent of the need to engage China, Singapore gave apprehensions of China due weight. However, its response, which emanated from its general policy of engagement, was that a peacefully rising Beijing must be given a stake in the Southeast Asian *status quo* by having its legitimate interests accommodated — even as regional states sought to ensure that America remained the balancer power in East Asia as a whole.

It is outside the scope of this work to describe the evolution of China's relations with the individual states of ASEAN,[1] or to show how the interplay of intentions, interests and behaviour among the external powers — America, China, Japan, Russia and, increasingly, India — influenced the direction of regional affairs. What is important is to recognize that Southeast Asia was not just another region coming to terms with China's rise. How Beijing dealt with its periphery would be a barometer of the rising power's expected behaviour in the world at large.

THE SOUTH CHINA SEA

For the region, the most serious security issue *vis-à-vis* China in the post-Cold War period has been the South China Sea dispute. It centres on the contested ownership of more than 200 small islands and reefs known as the Spratly Islands, claimed in whole or in part by China, Taiwan, Vietnam, the Philippines, Malaysia and Brunei. The Spratlys include valuable fishing grounds and are believed to contain oil and gas deposits; they also occupy a crucial strategic position straddling vital sea lanes of communication that link the Indian and Pacific Oceans through which much of global trade is conducted.[2] China's assertiveness has been evident since the Sino-Vietnamese clash over some Spratlys reefs in the late 1980s. In 1992, Beijing passed the Territorial Law of the Sea, claiming sovereignty over almost all of the South China Sea; it awarded an American company a contract to search for oil in waters off Vietnam; and its forces occupied the Hanoi-claimed Da Lac Reef. Chinese-built structures, found on the Manila-claimed Mischief Reef in 1995, were upgraded into a permanent military installation in 1998. Meanwhile, in 1996, China extended its baseline claims to the Paracel Islands.[3]

Although the issue did not involve all ASEAN members, the region's common stake in resolving it peacefully was underscored by several developments, including Indonesia's decision to play a role by sponsoring informal workshops on managing potential conflicts in the South China Sea.[4] At the official level, ASEAN foreign ministers signed the ASEAN Declaration on the South China Sea in Manila in July 1992. The grouping's first common position on the dispute, the declaration did not deal with the issue of sovereignty but advanced an informal code of conduct consisting of self-restraint, the avoidance of the use of force and the peaceful resolution of disputes. Intimations of the principles of the ASEAN Treaty of Amity and Cooperation of 1976 were clear in the declaration. In spite of the fact that overlapping claims involved some ASEAN states themselves, all the states "shared an interest in promoting Southeast Asian stability and avoiding any conflict with China".[5]

Singapore has no territorial claims in the Spratlys, but its interest as a trading state in the freedom of navigation gives it a stake in a peaceful resolution of the dispute. It saw China's behaviour as arousing mistrust in Southeast Asia over the degree of Beijing's willingness to abide by international law and regional norms in resolving the issue, which might become an index of its possible behaviour towards smaller regional countries.[6] Prime Minister Goh Chok Tong raised the issue of Mischief Reef with his Chinese counterpart Li Peng at a bilateral meeting in Beijing in May 1995. The intervention, by a country that had no territorial claims in the South China Sea, "sent a clear signal to the Chinese leadership that Singapore was at one with its ASEAN partners over the issue and that its relations with the Association took precedence over its ties with China".[7] Singapore also expressed its concern when Beijing announced that it was drawing its baseline claims from the Paracels, an act that widely was interpreted as contravening the 1982 United Nations Convention on the Law of the Sea. Foreign Minister S. Jayakumar asked countries in the region to abide scrupulously by UNCLOS in resolving their territorial disputes, and Defence Minister Tony Tan said that freedom of navigation would be endangered if China extended the principle to the Spratly Islands.[8] Around the turn of the century, Singapore's perspective included a reiteration of the importance of improved relations among all countries bordering the South China Sea region; the need for commitment to regional frameworks; the importance of continued negotiations with China; consideration of the costs of military conflict; and the institutionalization of the regional balance of power, with the United States playing a role as a balancer and deterrent to conflict.[9]

The dispute lost some of its edge when China and ASEAN signed a Declaration on the Conduct of Parties in the South China Sea at the ASEAN Summit in Phnom Penh in 2002. The two sides declared their determination to seek a peaceful settlement and undertook to exercise self-restraint so as not to complicate or escalate the dispute.[10] In March 2005, China, the Philippines and Vietnam moved to implement the declaration by reaching a tripartite agreement on joint maritime seismic studies in the South China Sea. However, the code of conduct is non-binding; in signing the declaration, Beijing did not withdraw its territorial claims in principle to the whole of the South China Sea; and other disputed islands such as the Paracels were not included in the declaration.[11] Since 2002, relations complicated by the dispute appear to have been moving in the right direction, but there is a risk that claimants will become "complacent about the territorial and jurisdictional disputes" until another crisis or major incident occurs, resulting perhaps in an escalation of the conflict. "The construction of a true and lasting peace between China and ASEAN must proceed by building on what little progress we have already made, moving with patience but with persistence to achieve 'peace by pieces' as it were."[12]

MULTILATERALISM

Notwithstanding the resilience of the dispute, the 2002 declaration marked ASEAN's success in getting China to deal with it multilaterally, a departure from the bilateral approach that had given Beijing far greater leverage in its dealings with ASEAN countries, each of them much weaker than it. Indeed, the accord exemplified the spread of multilateralism as a motif in the grouping's relations with China. The trend goes back to 1989, when Chinese Premier Li Peng proposed four principles for relations during a visit to Bangkok: peaceful coexistence in spite of differences in social and political systems; anti-hegemony; expansion of economic relations; and continuing support for regional cooperation and initiatives by ASEAN. Appreciative of ASEAN's refusal to isolate it over Tiananmen, Beijing grew responsive to overtures from the grouping that sought to bring it into networks of trust and cooperation. In 1991, ASEAN invited it to become a consultative partner. In 1994, China became a member of the ASEAN Regional Forum (ARF), an unprecedented dialogue mechanism involving the major powers in Southeast Asian security. In 1995, China and ASEAN set up a forum to discuss political and security issues affecting the region. In 1996, the People's Republic became a full dialogue partner of ASEAN, joining key global players such as the US, Japan and Europe.

The year 1997 accelerated the pace of ties that was gaining momentum. The Asian economic crisis that year witnessed what was seen as Asia's abandonment by the United States. The Clinton Administration did not bail out Thailand when the baht began to collapse; and later, when Washington went to the rescue of Seoul and Jakarta, the International Monetary Fund's bitter medicine was seen as a prescription written out in the United States. "By contrast China did not take a wrong step during this crisis," Chan Heng Chee, Singapore's Ambassador to Washington, notes. "It provided a good aid package to Thailand, Indonesia and even South Korea and refrained from devaluing its currency. This episode did much to draw attention to China as a

" 'responsible' power in the region, with the interests of the region at heart."[13]

It is true that Beijing feared that the contagion would spread and destabilize its vulnerable banking system, but that perhaps was not the primary reason for its moves to restore confidence in Southeast Asia. China had currency controls in place, a currency that was not convertible on the capital account, and large foreign exchange reserves that helped to insulate it from the crisis. In spite of these protections, Beijing did not devalue its currency and instead offered aid packages and low-interest loans to many Southeast Asian states. Its actions, which contrasted starkly with the "dictatorial posture" adopted by the IMF and international creditors, "punctured the prevailing image of China in the region as either aloof or hegemonic and began to replace it with an image of China as a responsible power".[14]

Buoyed by regional perceptions of China as an actor in its own right, Beijing modified its assessment of regional organizations, particularly those related to security issues, and moved from suspicion to uncertainty to supportiveness. After sending observers to meetings of the ARF, the Council on Security Cooperation in the Asia-Pacific (CSCAP) and Track Two meetings, Beijing became "more agnostic" when its analysts discovered that Washington, far from controlling the organizations, tended to dismiss or to ignore them.[15] Chinese delegates realized that the approach to comprehensive security advanced by the organizers was compatible with Beijing's New Security Concept, which reiterated the Five Principles of Peaceful Coexistence enunciated at Bandung in 1955, adding the need for dialogue, consultation and negotiation.[16] In 1997, a group of Chinese diplomatic and military officers touring Asia called for the abrogation of all international alliances, these being Cold War legacies that had outlived their usefulness. They realized that they had gone too far when a number of Asian governments told them that they did not intend to sever their alliances with the United States, and Beijing did not press the issue.[17] However, that setback did not stop it from going on a multilateral diplomatic offensive in Asia. In 2003, China became the first country outside ASEAN to accede to its Treaty of Amity and Cooperation. The same year, ASEAN and China proclaimed a strategic partnership and agreed to work together on non-traditional security and transnational issues such as drug trafficking and infectious diseases. These agreements embodied concrete advances in political relations following the economic framework agreement signed in 2002 to provide for a China-ASEAN free trade area.

China's integration with the Greater Mekong Sub-region (GMS) is an important aspect of its engagement with Southeast Asia. The GMS, which was formed in 1992 with assistance from the Asian Development Bank, consists of Myanmar, Laos, Thailand, Cambodia and Vietnam. It is a distinct organization from the Mekong River Commission (MRC), formed in 1995 with the participation of Cambodia, Laos, Thailand and Vietnam. Although China's decision not to join the MRC might arise from its reluctance to give downstream nations a voice in its decisions to dam the upper Mekong, and although environmental concerns stemming from the river's damming and channelling may become a source of tension, the GMS nevertheless has the potential of bringing southern China and Southeast Asia closer through economic development.[18] Governments of the sub-region signed a memorandum of understanding on cross-border transport and agreed on a plan to establish a regional power grid that would coordinate hydroelectric projects in the river system at the November 2002 summit in Phnom Penh. Transport links are an important part of the expansion of ties, as seen in Chinese-built roads south from Yunnan's capital, Kunming, to link up with three routes from Laos and Myanmar, and the establishment of air routes, such as between Chiang Mai and Jinghong. Taken together, the complex of roads and air routes is intended to create a north-south economic corridor from south central China into Southeast Asia, an economic re-mapping of the region that could improve the standard of living of millions and lead to China's enhanced regional influence.[19]

Yunnan's role in the GMS bears on the effectiveness of the larger China-ASEAN Free Trade Area. This area has two components in terms of economic geography. "One is the maritime track, that is, cooperation between maritime ASEAN countries and China's costal area. The other is the land track, that is, between continental ASEAN countries and China's southwest." Yunnan, an ancient gateway from China to Southeast Asia called the Southern Silk Road, is a base on the land track.[20] The GMS faces challenges, from a lack of capital to invest in sustainable development and inadequate human resources to consumption power and regime types,[21] but if its potential is realized, China's participation in the affairs of the sub-region could contribute to the creation of a "strategic setting for regional economic and political interests".[22]

The suggestion of strategic influence is not far-fetched. Unlike China's expectations of maritime Southeast Asia, which are focused on minimalist conditions such as countries committing themselves to non-alignment, the absence of foreign bases and a nuclear weapons free zone,[23] "Chinese leaders prefer continental Southeast Asian countries not to assume a strategic centrality within this sub-region that would not only impair China's security interests but also question China's regional status".[24] The GMS helps to consolidate China's influence on the sub-region.

THE ASEAN REGIONAL FORUM

China's investment in multilateralism, at which it had baulked (except at the broad level of the United Nations) for constraining its balance-of-power approach to international politics, is a key indicator of contemporary regional relations. In June 2005, Singapore Prime Minister Goh Chok Tong noted that in the past decade, Beijing had launched 27 separate ASEAN-China mechanisms at different levels, while twenty-eight years after the U.S.-ASEAN dialogue was formalized in 1977, there were only seven U.S.-ASEAN bodies and they met only infrequently.[25] China's emphasis is not only on the breadth but on the depth of engagement.

The ASEAN Regional Forum (ARF), within which China has discussed the Spratlys dispute, for example, is a good example. Like ASEAN — whose origins lie in an attempt to turn post-Sukarno Indonesia into a *status quo* player in Southeast Asia by recognizing its weight and the contribution that it could make to the management of regional order — post-Cold War Southeast Asian countries saw the ARF as a means of integrating and entrenching the United States, China, and Japan as the region's security managers as the centrality and certainties of the Cold War disappeared. Expectations were modest at the start given the divergent interests of the main protagonists. Comparisons of the forum with European security institutions such as the Conference on Security and Cooperation in Europe, and its successor, the Organization for Security and Cooperation in Europe, obscure the fact that, unlike them, the ARF is an "enterprise in cooperative security, as opposed to either collective defence or collective security".[26] Its objective is to improve the climate in which regional countries manage their bilateral and multilateral problems. Nevertheless, China responded to the idea of the ARF with suspicion, believing it to be a vehicle for the advancement of American interests in the region following the Cold War. (Ironically, Washington, too, initially was lukewarm to the idea because, like Beijing, it was accustomed to a culture of bilateralism. However, Japan's proposals for a multilateral security dialogue coincided with ASEAN proposals for a similar dialogue, and led to the ARF's formation.[27] Singapore, on its part, played an active role in the original concept paper that established the ARF.) Beijing did not want to be locked into "an institutionalized expression of interdependence". However, it could hardly avoid participating in it because of the ARF's Asia-Pacific-wide remit, and judged pragmatically that the forum would be "better influenced from the inside than from an isolated outside".[28]

Having joined the ARF, it soon began to see it as a platform for the congruence of its security interests with ASEAN's. Three years into the ARF, China co-chaired with the Philippines an intersessional support group meeting on Confidence Building Measures (CBMs) in Beijing in March 1997. Chinese Foreign Minister Qian Qichen noted that this would be the first time that Beijing would be hosting an official

multilateral confidence on security issues.[29] The
"dominant ARF culture" of emphasizing consensus and
incrementalism,[30] and a tentative yet genuine desire to
treat the People's Republic as a *status quo* power (and
so expect it to behave like one), encouraged it to make
"fundamental compromises" in "limiting its own
sovereign interests for the sake of engagement in
multilateral frameworks and pursuit of greater regional
interdependence".[31] In 2003, China circulated a policy
paper that indicated its willingness to address issues
that it had not been prepared to do earlier: from military
doctrines and strategies, and the revolution in military
affairs, to the role of militaries in non-traditional security
matters, and civil-military relations. Importantly, the
paper proposed an ARF Security Policy Conference
involving defence and security officials at the level of
vice-ministers. The first meeting of the new conference
was held in Beijing in 2004 and the second in Vientiane
in 2005. Chinese security specialists have floated as
well the idea of forming an East Asian security
community built upon the ARF.[32] Building on the
momentum generated by the ASEAN+3 process and
the framework for the China-ASEAN Free Trade Area,
the security policy conference "seems to be part of
a broader Chinese strategy to establish political
preeminence in the region".[33]

David Shambaugh notes that although
multilateralism in Asia had a later start than Europe's
and lags behind it considerably in terms of institutional
integration, there is a growing acceptance of common
norms in the region. "Such ideational agreement must
precede the formation of institutional architectures; but
once norms are institutionalized, they can become
binding on members states." Asia's diversity in cultural,
economic and political systems notwithstanding, "there

are increasing signs of normative convergence around the region".[34] In a critique of Shambaugh's thesis, Nicholas Khoo and Michael L.R. Smith contend that while ASEAN states see the ARF and ASEAN+3 meetings as an opportunity to socialize China's into the grouping's norms, it equally could be argued that "China sees its meetings with ASEAN as a way to socialize its members to China's norms and that Beijing has succeeded in doing this" — evident in a decline in ASEAN's support for Taiwan.[35] In response, Shambaugh insists on the beneficial consequences of the increasingly "deep, strong and binding" normative convergence that is taking place between China and ASEAN.[36] In his original article, he concludes that integrating China into the regional order, a long-standing goal of ASEAN, Japan and the United States, is occurring. The United States and China's neighbours should welcome "China's place at the regional table and the constructive role that Beijing is increasingly playing multilaterally in addressing regional challenges".[37]

Indeed, the question now is whether, as Chinese evangelism grows in the multilateral forum, it will continue to be accompanied by what some detect as signs of American agnosticism. In an insightful article, Evelyn Goh cites several reasons for the indeterminacy that Washington brings to the ARF. She recalls the context in which it was drawn to the forum. The demise of the Cold War obliged America to adopt a more regional focus for its East Asia strategy. Notably, the United States had to restrain potential Japanese militarism while promoting a more active role for Tokyo in the region, even as it had to deal with China's growing power while attempting to draw down its commitments to the region.[38] However, this early purpose came to be overlaid with Washington's changing interests in East Asia. Analysing the evolution of the U.S. approach to the forum through the George H. Bush, William Clinton and first two years of the George W. Bush Administrations, she observes that Washington has tended to treat the ARF as a "supporting forum for declaratory statements and (the) garnering (of) support for the perpetration of international norms deemed important by the US, rather than as a potential regional norms generator". This tendency has been manifest in the emphasis that it has placed on human rights and anti-terrorism on the ARF platform.[39] Also, without agreeing completely with the view, she cites observations of a split in the forum between ASEAN and China, which prefer to "concentrate on general dialogue to avoid disagreements", and the United States, Australia, Canada and Japan, which seek practical CBMs and wish to push the forum towards preventive diplomacy and conflict resolution — with Washington suggesting the need for greater institutionalization as well.[40] She concedes that, overall, Washington's "relative reticence" regarding the ARF may be explained by cost-benefit calculations — the costs of joining it have been low, but so have the benefits, since key security issues cannot be dealt with at the forum — and notes that the United States is concerned over possible constraints on its naval deployments and supremacy posed by CBMs. ARF-style multilateralism involves ceding the primacy, in manner if not in substance, of the American identity born of the sense of being the strategic hub from which the spokes of regional bilateral alliances emanate.[41] Another problem is America's preference for bilateral diplomacy with China, which, although not acknowledged as a peer, is still a great power "several levels" above the rest of the regional states. Washington is not keen on having issues mediated through the interests of these states, nor does it want its bargaining power to be diluted by dialogue partners in a multilateral setting.[42]

These elements in the U.S. approach, as Goh suggests, obscure the ARF's possible value to it, which is that the forum is "a site of international society at the regional level"; "reinforces the identity of the Asia-Pacific as a region"; helps affirm America's identity as "an integral regional player with legitimate interests in East Asia"; and offers Washington the possibility of support for "its mixed strategy of engagement with and containment of China".[43]

These are substantial opportunities, and if Washington is too distracted by other concerns and priorities to utilize them, then the ARF could be expected to become a vehicle of Beijing's desire to socialize its periphery through its norms instead of that periphery's ability to socialize China into abiding by the values of the larger world order. The inaugural East Asian Summit in 2005, announcing the regional desire to create an East Asian Community that excludes the United States, suggests one direction in which integration could move. This is not necessarily a decision to bandwagon with China, unless the absence of America's countervailing will and ability makes this necessary for ASEAN countries. The grouping's worst dilemma would be to have to choose sides in a conflict between the two powers.

Meanwhile, "the ARF remains a limited instrument of regional order", but "it also compensates for the risks and uncertainties associated with exclusive reliance on a balance of power approach, anchored on US strategic hegemony and its forward deployed forces".[44] Evelyn Goh reads Southeast Asian strategies differently, believing that they involve integrating

China into the existing international order "without having to make too many significant adjustments to prevailing norms", including America's dominant position. "Southeast Asian states share the American aim of preventing a power transition in the region, but their emphasis is not on containment but on assimilating China as a new great power, but at a tier below the US."[45]

Singapore's position operates within that framework. The origins of its position lie in the redrawing of the strategic terrain caused by the end of the Cold War. In *The Vulnerability of Small States Revisited: A Study of Singapore's Post-Cold War Foreign Policy*, Bilveer Singh notices "landmark changes", evident in a new policy activism that saw the city-state support ASEAN's expansion to include all ten Southeast Asian nations, the ASEAN Free Trade Area (AFTA), the Asia-Pacific Economic Cooperation (APEC) forum, the ARF and the Asia-Europe Meeting (ASEM) process.[46] (Subsequently, Singapore embarked on a drive for East Asia to engage Latin America through the Forum for East Asia-Latin America Cooperation, or FEALAC; spearheaded an East Asian drive to engage Arab nations through the Asia-Middle East Dialogue process, or AMED; and pursued free trade agreements with a host of countries.) "In a sentence, Singapore's foreign policy since 1991 can be described as one of activism in search of political, economic and strategic space."[47]

Singapore's balance of power horizons originally were restricted essentially to Southeast Asia but "recognizing the increasing power and assertiveness of China and potentially of Japan, its interest expanded during the 1990s to subsume wider East Asia".[48] The "promotion of multilateral institutions has been a key aspect of Singapore's balance of power policy. Its sponsorship of the ARF is a key example".[49] A decade after the ARF's formation, the Republic sees it as having evolved into a useful forum that facilitates the discussion of sensitive regional issues and the sharing of concerns on domestic developments between members. "Over the last few years, the comfort level among ARF participants has risen significantly, and discussions have gradually moved from traditional security issues to non-traditional and other transnational issues."[50] Apart from the South China Sea, the ARF has discussed Myanmar and the Korean peninsula.

But while investing politically in the ARF is an effective way of engaging China, the city-state insists that peace and stability require a continuing U.S. presence. Senior Minister Goh Chok Tong declared unambiguously in 2004 that the "key determinant of Asia's stability is American policy". "As China rises it cannot be expected to acquiesce in the *status quo*. It will want its interests accommodated. As the pre-eminent power, the fundamental US interest is to preserve (the) *status quo*," Goh said candidly. "Some degree of competition between the two is healthy; conflict is not."[51] That Singapore view is a useful starting point for an assessment of the American factor in its engagement of China.

NOTES

1   For a recent survey, see Jurgen Haacke, "The Significance of Beijing's Bilateral Relations: Looking 'Below' the Regional Level in China-ASEAN Ties", in Ho Khai Leong and Samuel C.Y. Ku, eds., *China and Southeast Asia: Global Changes and Regional Challenges*, pp. 111–45.

2   Ian Storey, "Singapore and the Rise of China: Perceptions and Policy", in Herbert Yee and Ian Storey, eds., *The China Threat: Perceptions, Myths and Reality*, p. 213.

3 Ibid., pp. 213–14.
4 For a detailed study of the dispute, see Lee Lai To, *China and the South China Sea Dialogues* (Westport and London: Praeger, 1999).
5 Ralf Emmers, *Maritime Disputes in the South China Sea: Strategic and Diplomatic Status Quo* (Singapore: Institute of Defence and Strategic Studies, Working Paper Series No. 87, September 2005), p. 10.
6 Storey, op. cit., p. 214.
7 Ibid., p. 215.
8 Ibid.
9 "Security Implications of Conflict in the South China Sea: Exploring Potential Triggers of Conflict", a Pacific Forum CSIS Special Report prepared by Ralph A. Cossa (Honolulu, Hawaii, March 1998), p. F-4.
10 For the text of the Declaration, see <aseansec.org/13163.htm>.
11 Evelyn Goh, "Singapore's Reaction to a Rising China: Deep Engagement and Strategic Adjustment", in Ho and Ku, eds., *China and Southeast Asia: Global Changes and Regional Challenges*, op. cit., p. 310.
12 Aileen S.P. Baviera, "The South China Sea Disputes after the 2002 Declaration: Beyond Confidence-Building", in Saw Swee-Hock, Sheng Lijun and Chin Kin Wah, eds., *ASEAN-China Relations: Realities and Prospects* (Singapore, Institute of Southeast Asian Studies, 2005), p. 354.
13 Chan Heng Chee, "China and Asean: A Growing Relationship", speech delivered at the Asia Society Texas Annual Ambassadors' Forum and Corporate Conference, Houston, 3 February 2006, <app.mfa.gov.sg/pr/read_content.asp?View,4416,>.
14 David Shambaugh, "China Engages Asia: Reshaping the Regional Order", *International Security* 29, no. 3 (Winter 2004/05): 68.
15 Ibid., pp. 68–69.
16 Ibid., p. 69.
17 Ibid., p. 70.
18 Bruce Vaughn, *China-Southeast Asia Relations: Trends, Issues, and Implications for the United States* (Washington, D.C.: Congressional Research Service, The Library of Congress, 8 February 2005), p. 23.

19   Ibid., pp. 23–24.
20   He Shengda and Sheng Lijun, "Yunnan's Greater Mekong Sub-Region Strategy", in Saw, Sheng and Chin, eds., op. cit., p. 295.
21   Kao Kim Hourn and Sisowath Doung Chanto, "ASEAN-China Cooperation for Greater Mekong Sub-Region Development", in ibid., p. 321.
22   Ibid., p. 323.
23   Haacke, op. cit., p. 117.
24   Ibid., p. 116.
25   Dana R. Dillon and John J. Tkacik, Jr., "China and ASEAN: Endangered American Primacy in Southeast Asia", *Backgrounder*, No. 1886, 19 October 2005 (Washington, D.C.: The Heritage Foundation).
26   Michael Leifer, "China in Southeast Asia: Interdependence and Accommodation", in David S.G. Goodman and Gerald Segal, eds., *China Rising: Nationalism and Interdependence*, op. cit., pp. 164–65.
27   Zainul Abidin Rasheed, Singapore Minister of State for Foreign Affairs, Speech at the opening of the Second Japan-ASEAN Security Symposium, Shangri-La Hotel, 27 October 2004, <www.mfa.gov.sg/internet>. For an intensive study of the ARF and other institutions in Japan's regional policy, see Sueo Sudo, *The International Relations of Japan and Southeast Asia* (London and New York: Routledge, 2002).
28   Leifer, op. cit., p. 165.
29   Rosemary Foot, "China in the ASEAN Regional Forum: Organizational Processes and Domestic Modes of Thought", *Asian Survey* 38, no. 5 (May 1998): 426.
30   Ibid., p. 439.
31   Shambaugh, op. cit., p. 76.
32   Ibid., pp. 87–88.
33   Dillon and Tkacik, Jr., op. cit., p. 3.
34   Shambaugh, op. cit., pp. 96–97.
35   Nicholas Khoo and Michael L.R. Smith, "China Engages Asia? Caveat Lector", *International Security* 30, no. 1 (Summer 2005): 204.
36   Ibid., p. 208.
37   Shambaugh, "China Engages Asia: Reshaping the Regional Order", op. cit., p. 99.

ASEAN   211

38 Evelyn Goh, "The ASEAN Regional Forum in United States
    East Asian strategy", *Pacific Review* 17, no. 1 (March 2004): 50.
39 Ibid., p. 59.
40 Ibid., pp. 59–60.
41 Ibid., pp. 61–62.
42 Ibid., pp. 62–63.
43 Ibid., p. 63.
44 Amitav Acharya, *Seeking Security In The Dragon's Shadow: China
    and Southeast Asia in the Emerging Asian Order* (Singapore:
    Institute of Defence and Strategic Studies, Working Paper No.
    44, March 2003), p. 22. See also his *Constructing a Security
    Community in Southeast Asia* (Oxford: Routledge, 2001). For a
    sophisticated analysis of the ARF as a "counter-realpolitik
    institution", see Alastair Iain Johnston, "Socialization in
    International Institutions: The ASEAN Way and International
    Relations Theory", in G. John Ikenberry and Michael
    Mastanduno, eds., *International Relations Theory and the Asia-
    Pacific*, op. cit., pp. 107–62.
45 Evelyn Goh, *Great Powers and Southeast Asian Regional Security
    Strategies: Omni-Enmeshment, Balancing and Hierarchical Order*
    (Singapore, Institute of Defence and Strategic Studies, Working
    Paper No. 84, July 2005), <www.ntu.edu.sg/idss/
    publications/WorkingPapers/WP84.pdf>.
46 Bilveer Singh, *The Vulnerability of Small States Revisited: A Study
    of Singapore's Post-Cold War Foreign Policy* (Yogyakarta: Gadjah
    Mada University Press, 1999), p. xvi.
47 Ibid., p. 85.
48 Tim Huxley, "Singapore's strategic outlook and defence
    policy", in Joseph Chinyong Liow and Ralf Emmers, eds.,
    *Order and Security in Southeast Asia: Essays in Memory of Michael
    Leifer* (London and New York: Routledge, 2006), p. 145.
49 Jurgen Haacke, "Michael Leifer, the balance of power and
    international relations theory", in ibid., p. 57.
50 Singapore: Ministry of Foreign Affairs, <www.mfa.gov.sg/
    internet/foreignpolicy/io_asean.htm>.
51 Goh Chok Tong, "Change and Stability in Asia", Speech at the
    US-ASEAN Business Council's Second Annual Leadership
    Dinner, Shangri-La Hotel, Singapore, 1 December 2004,
    <app.mfa.gov.sg/internet/press/view_press.asp?
    post_id=1152>.

CHAPTER X

AMERICA

The Southeast Asian dimension of Singapore's relations with China cannot be detached from the Republic's expectations of the U.S. role in East Asia as a whole. The evolution of the U.S.-Singapore relationship provides a context for the way in which Singapore sees its options in the age of Chinese ascendancy.

The Republic's view of the United States as a benign hegemon made it continue to support, after the American withdrawal from Vietnam, an American presence in the region to counter the potentially malign influence of other powers. But it was the collapse of the Soviet bloc and the dismantling of bipolarity in international affairs that saw one of the clearest reaffirmations of Singapore's balance of power outlook. On 4 August 1989, Brigadier-General George Yeo, Minister of State for Foreign Affairs, told Parliament that Singapore was prepared to allow the United States to use some of its military facilities to make it easier for the Philippines to continue hosting the American bases at Clark airfield and Subic naval bay. Singapore's stance basically was that the Philippines government was coming under increasing domestic pressure on the American bases; and although all non-communist Southeast Asian countries enjoyed the protection of the U.S. cover, Manila was the only capital to have to bear the political burden of hosting them. Although the military facilities that Singapore was offering were negligible in physical terms — all of Singapore could fit into the Subic naval base — the move was a pointed gesture of support for the U.S. presence in Southeast Asia. Such gestures were seen as being necessary because the end of the Cold War was coinciding with a deepening of America's economic problems and a strengthening of U.S. domestic sentiments in favour of military disengagement abroad and the diversion of saved resources to the domestic economy. By making it easier for the United States to remain engaged abroad, beneficiaries of its presence would be furthering their own interests in an era when the domestic mood in the United States was in favour of isolationism. What would come to be called the'"places, not bases" strategy adjusted forward deployment to changing strategic and economic needs. The concept — devised in 1991, when the Pentagon had difficulty in moving large numbers of troops and armament to eject Iraq from Kuwait[1] — gained in appeal in the looming closure of America's Subic Bay base in the Philippines in 1992. Essentially staging points, the "places" were a "logistics rather than a strategic concept", and Singapore was the model.[2]

In the Singapore view in the late 1980s, the consequences of a U.S. withdrawal would be severe. The Soviet Union was effectively out of the race; if the

United States, too, went, there would be a power vacuum that the remaining powers, Japan and China, and the emerging powers, India and Vietnam and perhaps Korea, would seek to fill. The result would spell instability for Southeast Asia.

The power-vacuum theory was not fanciful. At the end of the 1980s, Japan, China and India each had the capacity to project power far in excess of all the ASEAN countries combined. Even with defence taking only one per cent of its gross national product, Japan's defence budget was the third largest in the world. Not only was the one-per-cent ceiling not sacrosanct, neither was the "peace constitution", and if trade disputes with the United States led to the point where they threatened the security relationship, Japan might not be immune to militaristic nationalism, which could lead to an extension of its military reach into Southeast Asia, beginning with naval patrols 1,000 miles to the south. As for China, the needs of economic modernization did act as a constraint on foreign military activities in the short term, but a modernized China would possess the economic infrastructure to underpin a serious quest for global importance, beginning with a Southeast Asia that historically fell within its sphere of influence. Unlike China, whose lack of a blue-water fleet constrained its actions in Southeast Asia, India already had a powerful navy that, supported by a modernizing and externally-oriented economy, could form a realistic basis of aspirations to leadership in the Indian Ocean and beyond. A revitalized Vietnam and a unified Korea could not be quarantined from the struggle for supremacy between the powers, which could result in the formation of adversarial blocs in East Asia. Singapore's point was not that the emergence of these powers should, or could, be prevented, but that a new regional order should emerge without causing instability. The U.S. presence made a major contribution towards that end because it was the only power that was capable of holding the balance of power in the region.

Thailand and the Philippines supported the Singapore offer to the United States, but it was criticized in Malaysia and Indonesia. Malaysian Defence Minister Ahmad Rithaudeen invoked the Zone of Peace, Freedom and Neutrality (ZOPFAN), a proposal that Kuala Lumpur had made in 1971 to neutralize Southeast Asia collectively by means of guarantees from Washington, Moscow and Beijing. He said that ZOPFAN's phasing in should follow the phasing out of foreign military bases, and that the *status quo* should be respected in the interim.[3] Prime Minister Mahathir Mohamad said that he would be opposed to Singapore becoming an American base, but it was a different matter if it were only to provide repair services.[4] In Indonesia, General Sumitro, the former security chief, declared that ASEAN "is on the threshold of disintegration" because of Singapore's move and that "Indonesia should save it",[5] while *Pelita* asked in an editorial: "If Singapore is prepared to accept the presence of US military forces on its soil besides the US presence in the Philippines, will Singapore be discussing the presence of military forces of the People's Republic of China in Southeast Asia after the normalisation of diplomatic relations between Jakarta and Beijing?"[6] Foreign Minister Ali Alatas told Parliament that the government would pay close attention to two key points: that the facilities offered strictly would be for servicing and repairs, and that they would mean only an enhancement of existing facilities not amounting to a base. "Quietly, we told them there is a line. You cross that line and we will speak out."[7] Following a meeting between Lee Kuan Yew and Suharto, however, Indonesian State Secretary Murdiono said that the President was "fully satisfied" with the Prime Minister's explanation that there would be no American base,[8] and soon after, Alatas declared the matter closed.[9]

The issue was revived, however, when, following the signing of a Memorandum of Understanding in November 1990 and a visit by President George H. Bush in January 1992, Singapore agreed in principle to accommodate a U.S. naval logistics element from Subic. (Meanwhile, the Philippines had served notice on the United States that it would have to vacate Clark and Subic by the end of 1992.) Again, there was a flurry of criticism in Kuala Lumpur and Jakarta. Malaysian Deputy Foreign Minister Abdullah Fadzil Che Wan reportedly warned that Singapore could become the headquarters of the U.S. Seventh Fleet,[10] while a commentator writing in the Malaysian *Berita Harian* thought that "the US is not only capable of finding excuses, but creating possibilities to force Singapore to accept more US military personnel and hardware".[11] However, Mahathir Mohamad said that the transfer of the logistics element from Subic "was not tantamount to creating a US base on the island".[12] In Indonesia, Lieutenant-General (Retired) Sayidiman Suryohadiprojo, governor of the National Defence Institute, commented that Singapore was seeking U.S. support "in its efforts to expand its political influence through a more outstanding military posture", a development that Indonesia, though it was not a aggressive nation, would not countenance because "it will not agree to the establishment of a military base and will reject any form of neo-colonialism in Southeast Asia".[13] However, what was remarkable was that, unofficial criticism of Singapore's action notwithstanding, Indonesia made its maritime facilities in Surabaya available to the United States, while Malaysia offered its facilities at Lumut naval base in Perak.[14] Singapore responded with delight.

The outcome of the issue disproved the conspiracy theories being circulated, including the implication that Singapore was carrying out American dictates — an intriguing perspective that diverged from the view of Singapore as angling for American protection. If Singapore's objective had been to become an American base in order to protect itself from its neighbours, it should have been disappointed by the Indonesian and Malaysian decisions because these diluted Singapore's utility to Washington. By contrast, the Republic's reaction suggested that it welcomed the developments since they proved that its own action had been correct. If the move was a U.S. ploy to draw Jakarta and Kuala Lumpur into a closer military relationship by stepping up military ties with Singapore, why would Singapore have acquiesced in the ploy, knowing that, again, the security benefits it derived from augmenting the U.S. presence in East Asia as a whole arguably would be offset somewhat by the losses Singapore would incur in the Southeast Asian balance of power altered by closer U.S. ties with its neighbours? If the United States had pressured Singapore into accepting the facilities, why did Indonesia and Malaysia respond the way they did, since by deepening their ties with the United States in the context of Singapore's move, they obviously were succumbing to indirect pressure themselves? Since they did not subscribe to Singapore's power-vacuum theory, what could have been the reason for their capitulation? And if the point is that they decided to deepen their ties with the United States in their own interests, Singapore's action hardly could have been the catalyst, one way or the other. It would appear, therefore, that Singapore's move was motivated by a consistent balance of power approach to security. The Republic's point was that it was necessary to minimize the dangers of instability caused by precipitate changes in the regional balance of power. Preserving U.S. engagement in Southeast Asia was a crucial part of that effort.

Visible demonstrations of this relationship were evident in a series of arrangements between 1990 and 2000 that permitted the United States access to Singapore's military facilities, rotational deployment of F-16 fighters, and the location of the command and logistics arm of the U.S. Seventh Fleet (COMLOG WESTPAC) in Singapore. As logistics agent for the Seventh Fleet, COMLOG WESTPAC plans the resupply of food, ordnance, fuel and repair parts for ships spread over 52 million square miles of the Pacific and Indian Oceans, stretching from the International Date Line to the east coast of Africa, and from the Kuril Islands in the north to the Antarctic in the south. The region is more than 14 times the size of the entire continental United States. More than half of the world's population lives within the Seventh Fleet's area of responsibility. Indeed, more than 80 per cent of that population lives within 500 miles of the oceans, making it an inherently maritime region.[15] When, in 2001, the aircraft carrier USS *Kitty Hawk* berthed at Singapore's Changi Naval Base, it was the first time that an American carrier had been given pierside access to port facilities in the region since the closure of the Subic base.[16] Built at Singapore's own expense to facilitate the deployment of the Seventh Fleet in Southeast Asian waters, the Changi base was not exclusive to the Americans — large Chinese ships, for example, could call there — but given that few countries possessed aircraft carriers, the base clearly was intended to help the United States project its naval power.[17] Indeed, Changi is the only port in Southeast Asia where aircraft carriers can berth.

Following the 11 September 2001 terrorist attacks in the United States, relations grew even closer, and Singapore became a member of the "coalition of the willing" to help in the reconstruction of Iraq after the U.S. invasion. One essential reason for the closing of ranks was the arrest in Singapore in December 2001 of members of the Al-Qaeda-linked terrorist organization Jemaah Islamiyah, which was plotting to attack American, British, Australian and Israeli interests in the city-state.[18] Although the planned attacks were thwarted, they dramatized Singapore's vulnerability to the plans of a regional network, drawing support from a global one, that was dedicated to the violent establishment of an Islamic state in Southeast Asia covering Indonesia, Singapore, Brunei, Malaysia, and the southern parts of Thailand and the Philippines. America's pre-eminent interest and preponderant role in acting against terror networks created a natural confluence of interests with Singapore. In October 2003, Singapore and the United States announced their intention to expand cooperation in defence and security, and to negotiate a Framework Agreement for a Strategic Cooperation Partnership. Singapore vigorously has supported American counter-terrorist initiatives, becoming the first country in Asia to join the Container Security Initiative, which ensures that all containers that pose a potential risk of terrorism are identified and inspected at foreign ports before they are placed on vessels headed for the United Sates. Singapore was also the first country in the region to join the Megaports Initiative that uses radiation detection capabilities at key ports around the world to screen cargo for nuclear and radioactive materials. Singapore participated actively as well in the global Proliferation Security Initiative aimed at stopping shipments of weapons of mass destruction, their delivery systems, and related material worldwide.[19] Countering the threat of maritime terrorism in the Malacca Straits in particular was another objective that drew Singapore and Washington together. Singapore now has the strongest security relationship with the United States in Southeast Asia even though it is not an ally, as are the Philippines and Thailand.[20] Although not articulated publicly, China's view seems to reflect a certain wariness over Singapore's apparent tilt towards the United States in security matters at a time when Beijing's relations with Washington are being tested by global developments.[21]

Singapore has not assumed an alliance relationship with the United States because it does not wish to upset its immediate neighbours or China, but it identifies much more closely with Washington than with Beijing in security terms.[22] Singapore wants to see China "enmeshed in regional norms, acting responsibly and upholding the regional *status quo*", Evelyn Goh writes. It attaches great importance to China becoming "a second benign great power in the region, balanced tacitly by, and enjoying a *modus vivendi* with, the benign superpower".[23] That *modus vivendi* is not inherently impossible. America's key regional interests lie in promoting stability and the balance of power, with the strategic objective of keeping Southeast Asia free of domination by any hegemon; preventing itself from being excluded from the region by another power or group of powers; ensuring freedom of navigation and the protection of sea lanes; pursuing trade and investment interests; supporting treaty allies and friends; and in promoting democracy, the rule of law, human rights, and religious freedom.[24] China's regional objectives, stemming from its strategic agenda, are to maintain a stable political and security environment, particularly on its periphery, that would facilitate its growth; expand trade routes through Southeast Asia; gain access to regional energy resources and raw materials; develop trade relationships "for economic and political purposes"; isolate Taiwan; and gain influence in the region to "defeat perceived attempts at strategic encirclement or containment".[25] While Washington's objectives diverge from Beijing's over democracy and Taiwan, their interests and stated goals do overlap. The question is whether the overlap is broad enough to underpin a new Asian order.

Yes, perhaps a divided Asian order, Robert S. Ross suggests. In an interesting hypothesis, he sees Pacific Asia as two complementary spheres of influence: a mainland sphere in which China is the incumbent, and a maritime sphere in which America is the incumbent. "Because Chinese and U.S. spheres of influence are geographically distinct and separated by water, intervention by one power in its own sphere will not appear as threatening to the interests of the other power in its sphere. Freed from the worry of great power retaliation, each power has a relatively freer hand to impose order on its allies."[26] East Asian geography allows for maritime balancing. Where China is concerned, apart from having to meet the contending power of Japan, the domination of mainland East Asia cannot give "an aspiring hegemon unimpeded access to the ocean" because the mainland is rimmed with "a continuous chain of island countries" from Japan to Malaysia

boasting strategic location and naval facilities. Access to
these countries permits a maritime power (namely, the
United States) to operate along the perimeter of a
mainland power, dominate regional shipping lines and
project power.[27] Even if China augments naval
capabilities in its coastal waters, American and allied
commercial and military fleets can use secure shipping
lanes that are distant from mainland aircraft and are
dominated by American air and naval forces based in
maritime nations.[28] But just as the United States enjoys
the advantages of being an East Asian maritime power,
so does China enjoy the protection of being an East
Asian continental power. The United States has "no
strategic imperative to compete for influence on the
mainland". This is partly because its experiences in
Vietnam and Korea prove how difficult it is to translate
maritime power into the projection of air and land power
onto East Asian terrain. "The American military
continues to have a 'no more land wars in Asia'
mentality." The difficulty of power projection onto
mainland East Asia thus deters powerfully any U.S.
interest in changing the *status quo*.[29] Should it be possible
to keep the spheres separate, with each power developing
its influence within its zone, the chances of conflict
between the two strategic competitors perhaps could be
reduced. So goes the argument.

Is this separation of spheres a viable arrangement
for an East Asian balance of power? It is difficult to say
so. To begin with, there is no Concert of Powers in
Asia, let alone a Condominium, to allocate spheres of
influence and prevent poaching. Thus, the United States
is expanding its influence in mainland Asia through
the War on Terror, while China is augmenting its
maritime interests. By hosting forces or by providing
overflight permission or by allowing territory to be

used for supply purposes, Central Asian countries such as Kyrgyzstan, Turkmenistan, Kazakhstan and Tajikistan have become partners in the anti-terror war. But the establishment of a permanent U.S. military presence in the region has aroused concern in China, which sees strategic encirclement taking shape on its north-western flank. Meanwhile, China — which sought to entrench its influence in Central Asia through the Shanghai Cooperation Organization, initially formed in 1996 — has embarked on a westward maritime movement through a "string-of-pearls" strategy. This strategy connects the South China Sea to the Persian Gulf through military-related agreements with Thailand, Cambodia, Myanmar, Bangladesh, Sri Lanka, the Maldives and Pakistan, where the Chinese-assisted Gwadar port will overlook energy supplies from the Persian Gulf. Should Gwadar become a Chinese submarine base, pointed both at the Gulf and the western entrance to the Malacca Strait, it would transform China's unfolding Indian Ocean aspirations. A peacefully neat division of Asia into continental and maritime spheres does not appear to be a feasible proposition. China and America inhabit the same strategic space in East Asia.

It is in this regional context that Sino-U.S. competition is unfolding. The larger issue is that what a rising power considers legitimate — the translation of its economic prowess into military power — the incumbent hegemon sees as an intention to enhance the rising power's position at its expense. A Rand report on medium- and longer-term trends relating to economic growth, military spending and military investment in Japan, China, India, South Korea and Indonesia uses the gross domestic products and accumulated stocks of military capital as proxies for the economic and political power of each of the five countries. It draws several inferences from the estimates, including that Japan's relative economic and military power appreciably will diminish in the region over the 2000–2015 period; China's economic and military power will diminish somewhat relative to that of India; but the absolute gap between China's GDP and military capital, and those of the other three countries, will grow substantially.[30] The defence spending and the military modernization of China, although it is rising without the support of an alliance system, are seen as threats to the established world order. The U.S. *Quadrennial Defense Review* of 2001 and the U.S. *National Security Strategy* proposed in 2002 were among early documents signifying a hardening of views on China in the first George W. Bush Administration. The latter document declares: "In pursuing advanced military capabilities that can threaten its neighbors in the Asia-Pacific region, China is following an outdated path that, in the end, will hamper its own pursuit of national greatness."[31]

That cautionary note is palpable as well in the 2005 annual report to Congress on China's military power. "China does not now face a direct threat from another nation. Yet, it continues to invest heavily in its military, particularly in programs designed to improve power projection. The pace and scope of China's military build-up are, already, such as to put regional military balances at risk," the report notes. Given trends in its military modernization, China could have a force capable of "prosecuting a range of military operations in Asia — well beyond Taiwan — potentially posing a credible threat to modern militaries operating in the region". The report acknowledges that Beijing has described "its long-term political goals of developing

comprehensive national power and of ensuring a
favorable strategic configuration of power in peaceful
terms". But it worries that as China's military power
grows, its leaders may be tempted to resort to force or
coercion "more quickly to press diplomatic advantage,
advance security interests, or resolve disputes".[32]
Washington's pessimistic view of the implications of
China's rise is clear.

That pessimism obscures the fact that even as China
outstrips many other Asian nations in computations
of comprehensive national power and strategic
projections, there remains a substantial gap between
American and Chinese capabilities. During the early
part of the post-Cold War era, American defence
spending was larger than the combined defence budgets
of the next six or seven countries. Since then, U.S.
defence spending has grown astonishingly, so that by
2005, its defence budget was nearly the sum of the rest
of the world's defence budgets combined.[33]

The Japanese contribution to American power
makes the differentials clearer. Military cooperation
between Washington and Tokyo is greater now "than
at any time during the Cold War". As early as 1995,
Tokyo agreed to revised guidelines for its alliance with
Washington, "facilitating closer wartime coordination
between the Japanese and US militaries, including use
by the United States of Japanese territory in case of war
with a third country". Since then, Japan has turned
into the "most active" partner of the United States in
developing missile defence technologies. It has agreed
to a five-year plan for the joint production with the
United States of a missile defence system, and it will
contribute US$10 billion by the end of the decade.
"Japanese defense policy now reflects the possibility of
war with China, and the Japanese Defense Agency

now publicly refers to a potential Chinese challenge to Japanese security."[34] Such postures appear alarmist to Beijing, which tries to put its military spending in the context of others' budgets. According to China's 2004 *White Paper on National Defense*, 2003 figures show that its expenditure amounted to only 5.69 per cent of America's, 56.78 per cent of Japan's, 37.07 per cent of Britain's, and 75.94 per cent of France's.[35] Meanwhile, in broader Chinese perceptions of American strengths across the entire spectrum of economic, scientific and technological, military and soft power achievements, the United States is seen as quite possibly remaining the dominant power in the world in the foreseeable future, barring serious mistakes that it might make.[36] Chinese scholars wonder about the urgency, then, of Washington needing to strengthen its military alliance with Tokyo, "bring Taiwan under the protective umbrella of the U.S.-Japan Security Treaty", and take its relations with New Delhi to a higher level — unless it is to set in place a strategy of containing China at reduced cost to the United States.[37]

Are Chinese concerns justified? Or are American concerns justified? The quest to place China's rise in perspective, by comparing its capabilities and intentions with those of the United States, leads to a cottage industry of competing nouns, adjectives, verbs and adverbs inhabiting an entire suburb of the military-industrial complex. Driven by the market in incidents, accidents and events — from Chinese "missile diplomacy" near Taiwan in 1995–96, and NATO's 1999 bombing of the Chinese Embassy in Belgrade, to the EP3 spy plane affair of 2001 — this industry flourishes by recycling Cold War words to meet the passing demands of public consumption. "Encirclement", "containment" and "constrainment"

— all advanced as serious prescriptions for policy — are among the merchandise on sale. Should the demand and supply curves created by the current phase of Sino-U.S. competition be sustained, *"détente"* and *"rapprochement"*, too, no doubt will appear on the shelves of the international strategic economy.

The Chinese reciprocate by drawing on a terminological arsenal minted in their own past, recent or distant. Thus, when not busy selling antidotes to the deadly Western ills of "hegemonism", they merchandise "peaceful rise", rebranded as "peaceful development" to suit the tastes of Asian nations apparently fearful that the Chinese will beat the geopolitical laws of gravity.

In this egregious war labels fly around with the abandon of advertising fliers. Alastair Iain Johnston is among those scholars who sanely argue against labelling Beijing prematurely as a revisionist power. He notes that while its military modernization programme since the mid-1990s aims at deterring or slowing the application of American power in the region, it is "also clear that the immediate and medium-term issue at stake for Chinese leaders is Taiwan, not the U.S. strategic presence in the region per se" nor necessarily a war on the Korean peninsula or power projection far beyond China's periphery.[38] Chinese preparations for dealing with American military power in a Taiwan conflict are not the same as balancing against American power in the region or beyond, and it is unwise to generalize from the Chinese handling of the Taiwan issue to their putative attitudes towards long-term regional distributions of power, to say nothing of global institutions and global rules of the game.[39] (While the Pentagon's 2005 report to Congress worries about China's potential for carrying out military operations beyond Taiwan, it does not suggest any framework of imperatives that might oblige Beijing to do so.)

As for suspicions over external balancing, "China is not trying as hard as it might to construct anti-U.S. alliances or undermine U.S. alliances globally or regionally".[40] Instead, the interdependencies created by China's economic links with the rest of the world are creating constituencies inside China that do not have an interest in hostility towards the United States. All in all, Beijing appears to be unwilling to "bear the economic and social costs of mobilizing the economy and militarizing society to balance seriously against American power and influence in the region, let alone globally".[41]

The logic of that argument is developed in a paper by Paul A. Papayoanou and Scott L. Kastner, who make a strong case for treating internationalist economic constituencies in China as a constraint on national belligerence. They study the behaviour of two non-democratic powers: a largely-responsible Czarist Russia, which became a credible ally for a democratic France with which it had close economic ties; and Wilhelmine Germany, a highly-aggressive power in spite of its economic links with democratic Britain. Drawing analogies with the past and asking which way China might go, they focus on the crucially different roles played by economic and political constituencies in Russia and Germany in determining strategic outcomes. They conclude that a policy of engagement with Beijing is beneficial because it empowers "more pacific economic internationalists in China, while containment would likely weaken those forces and might bring to the fore more aggressive political and economic interests". Also, the risks of engagement are insignificant in the near term. "Because U.S. economic stakes in China are fairly small, they do not carry the danger of tying the hands of U.S. leaders should the Chinese pursue conflictual policies that require the United States to balance against China," they argue.[42] Wang Jisi notes the views of mainstream Chinese writers, who point out that "the growth of Chinese power today is integrated into economic globalization and therefore is vastly different from the emergence of the Soviet Union, whose development was separated from the industrialized world. Unlike Japan and Germany before and between the two world wars, they point out, China today is far from being militarized."[43]

In an era of transition in strategic perceptions if not in actual strategy, a final question is which power is revisionist and which is *status quo*. Each is tempted to see the other as revisionist. Thus, neo-conservatives and others in Washington see China as a revisionist power because it *can* challenge the Asia-Pacific power structure, notably through irredentism in the Strait of Taiwan and the South China Sea.[44] Meanwhile, Beijing views the unilateralist streak in American foreign policy — evident in the abrogation of the Anti-Ballistic Missiles Treaty, plans for Theatre Missile Defence, and the use of the doctrine of pre-emptive war in the invasion of Iraq — as proof that a revisionist power *is* challenging the *status quo* to create a firmer basis for its hegemony. Where the dominant power focuses on the capabilities of the rising power that can turn into threats, the rising power draws attention to the actions of the hegemonic power as existing threats. Where some Americans fear a reinvented Middle Kingdom preparing for a revival of the tributary system on its periphery, many Chinese baulk at the thought of the warships and aircraft of Manifest Destiny visiting the breached borders of their history.[45]

In common with other Southeast Asian countries, but insistently so given the extent of its investment in security relations with Washington, Singapore's nightmare is having to choose sides in a Sino-U.S. conflict. Indeed, there is no indication even that it would support American strategies aimed at containing China, Tim Huxley believes. "Despite its generally pro-Western stance, for domestic political reasons it is extremely unlikely that Singapore could ever overtly take the side of the United States and Taiwan in a future conflict with China," he writes. "While Washington may view defence relations with Singapore primarily in terms of their contribution to balancing China, Singapore's government sees their utility more in terms of maintaining regional stability in general terms, while also bolstering the island's security in the face of more local security concerns."[46]

How evolving perceptions, policies and plans on both sides affect Southeast Asia remains to be seen. U.S.-China relations have gone from a lover's pinch that hurts and is desired, to jilted strategic competition, which hurts and is not desired. Other countries have to live with the effect of Eros on the moods of Mars.

NOTES

1 Alan Boyd, "US reorganizes its military might", *Asia Times*, 21 November 2003.
2 Diplomat quoted in Ibid.
3 *New Straits Times*, 7 August 1989.
4 Ibid., 16 August 1989.
5 Commentary in the *Suara Pembaruan*, translated and published in *Straits Times*, 19 August 1989.

6 *Straits Times*, 18 August 1989.

7 *Straits Time*, 23 September 1989.

8 *Sunday Times*, Singapore, 8 October 1989.

9 *Straits Times*, 24 November 1989.

10 Bernama despatch, quoted in *Lianhe Zaobao*, Singapore, 6 January 1992, and cited in *Mirror of Opinion*, 6 January 1992, p. 1.

11 A. Nazri Abdullah, *Berita Harian*, 8 January 1992, cited in *Mirror of Opinion*, 9 January 1992, p. 10.

12 *New Straits Times*, 7 January 1992.

13 *Suara Pembaruan*, 9 January 1992, in *Mirror of Opinion*, 13 January 1992, pp. 5–6.

14 *Kompas*, 8 January 1992, in *Mirror of Opinion*, 11 January 1992, p. 6.

15 United States Navy, Commander, Seventh Fleet, <www.c7f.navy.mil/Pages/region.html>.

16 Dana Dillon and John J. Tkacik, Jr., "China's Quest for Asia", *Policy Review*, No. 134, December 2005 and January 2006 (Stanford: Hoover Institition), <www.policyreview.org/134/dillon.html>.

17 Trish Saywell, " 'Places not bases' puts Singapore on the line", *Far Eastern Economic Review*, 17 May 2001.

18 For Singapore's White Paper on the Jemaah Islamiyah arrests and the threat of terrorism, see <www.channelnewsasia.com/cna/arrests/>.

19 U.S. Ambassador to Singapore Patricia L. Herbold's remarks on terrorism in Southeast Asia, Singapore, 12 April 2006, <singapore.usembassy.gov/sp_terrorism041208.html>.

20 N. Ganesan, *Realism and Interdependence in Singapore's Foreign Policy*, op. cit., p. 122.

21 Eric Teo Chu Cheow, "Rising Sino-US Rivalry — A case in Point following the Recent Sino-Singaporean Row over Taiwan", *Taiwan Perspective e-Paper*, op. cit.

22 Evelyn Goh, *Meeting the China Challenge: The U.S. in Southeast Asian Regional Security Strategies* (Washington: East-West Center), Policy Studies 16, 2005, p. 25.

23 Evelyn Goh, "Singapore's Reaction to a Rising China: Deep Engagement and Strategic Adjustment", in Ho and Ku, eds., *China and Southeast Asia: Global Changes and Regional Challenges*, op. cit., p. 313.

24 Bruce Vaughn, *China-Southeast Asia Relations: Trends, Issues, and Implications for the United States*, op. cit., p. 4.
25 Ibid., pp. 7–8.
26 Robert S. Ross, "The Geography of the Peace: East Asia in the Twenty-first Century", in Michael E. Brown et al., eds., *The Rise of China*, an *International Security* Reader (Cambridge, Massachusetts, and London, England: The MIT Press, 2000), p. 185.
27 Ibid., pp. 186–88.
28 Ibid., p. 188.
29 Ibid., p. 189.
30 Charles Wolf, Jr., *Asian Economic Trends and Their Security Implications* (Santa Monica: Rand Corporation, 2000), <www.rand.org/pubs/monograph_reports/MR1143/index.html>.
31 *The National Security Strategy of the United States of America*, 17 September 2002 (Washington: The White House), p. 27. <www.whitehouse.gov/nsc/nss.pdf>.
32 *The Military Power of the People's Republic of China 2005*, Annual Report to Congress (Washington: Office of the Secretary of Defence).
33 Robert S. Ross, "A Realist Policy for Managing US-China Competition", Policy Analysis Brief, November 2005 (Muscatine, Iowa: The Stanley Foundation), p. 6.
34 Ibid, pp. 6–7.
35 "China issues white paper on national defense," *People's Daily Online*, <english.people.com.cn/200412/27/eng20041227_168787.html>.
36 Biwu Zhang, "Chinese Perceptions of American Power, 1991–2004", *Asian Survey* 45, issue 5: 667–86. In the same issue, Steve Chan argues that although China scores highly on most traditional measures of national power, it performs poorly in information technology and human capital: "Is There a Power Transition Between the U.S. and China? The Different Faces of National Power," pp. 687–701.
37 Da Wei Sun Ru, "Trend in Bush's China Strategy Adjustment", *Contemporary International Relations* 15, no. 11, November 2005: 3–4; 7–8.
38 Alastair Iain Johnston, "Is China a Status Quo Power?", *International Security* 27, no. 4 (Spring 2003): 38.

39 Ibid., p. 48.
40 Ibid., p. 39.
41 Ibid., p. 47.
42 Paul A. Papayoanou and Scott L. Kastner, *Assessing the Policy of Engagement with China*, Policy paper 40, July 1998 (San Diego: University of California, Institute on Global Conflict and Cooperation), p. 6.
43 Wang Jisi, "China's Changing Role in Asia", Asia Programs, January 2004 (Washington: The Atlantic Council of the United States), p. 4.
44 For a hawkish view of the implications of China's rise for the United States, see *Rebuilding America's Defences: Strategy, Forces and Resources for a New Century*, a Report of the Project for the New American Century, September 2000, <www.new americancentury.org/publicationsreports.htm>.
45 For an overview of conflicting perceptions and positions, see Evelyn Goh, "The Great Powers in the Asia-Pacific: Examining US-China Relations in the 'Post-Post-Cold War' Era", talking points prepared for the China Reform Forum-IDSS meeting on Asia-Pacific Security, Beijing, 19 July 2002, <www.ntu. edu.sg/home/ISCLGoh/US-China-talking-points.pdf>.
46 Tim Huxley, "Singapore's strategic outlook and defence policy", in Joseph Chinyong Liow and Ralf Emmers, eds., *Order and Security in Southeast Asia: Essays in Memory of Michael Leifer*, op. cit., pp. 146–47.

CHAPTER XI

ENGAGING INDIA

Singapore's attempt to engage India predates its engagement of China, but the divergence between the positions of Singapore and New Delhi on Cold War-generated issues, primarily the Vietnamese invasion of Cambodia, were accompanied by the city-state's growing closeness to Beijing. The end of the Cold War saw Sino-Singaporean relations continue to gain in depth, but it heralded a quieter and less-noticed change in the Republic's relations with India. "The end of bipolarity meant that these two states did not have to view mutual relations through the prism of their superpower preferences," Kripa Sridharan notes.[1] Hence, Singapore invested much energy in encouraging India's domestic economic reforms and inviting it to move beyond its central role in South Asia. This expansion of Indian influence began to take shape when, between 1992 and 1996, India first became a sectoral dialogue partner and then a full dialogue partner of ASEAN. India joined the ASEAN

Regional Forum in 1996 after Singapore lobbied hard to overcome ASEAN's reluctance to include New Delhi because of fears that its entry would import the sub-continent's political and military tensions into the ARF. It took nearly a decade, from 1987 to 1996, for India to become a stable participant in the ASEAN process, this effort culminating in the first India-ASEAN summit held in Phnom Penh in 2002.[2] "Singapore has accepted the role of India's 'sponsor' in Southeast Asia," Satu P. Limaye avers, in words reminiscent of the city-state's attempts to bring China into the economic and political orbit of Southeast Asian relationships.[3] Sridharan, too, believes that Singapore in particular among the ASEAN states has been "most alive and sensitive" to the changes underway in India.[4] Although India is not, unlike China, Japan and South Korea, a part of the ASEAN+3 process, its status as an ASEAN dialogue partner and its expanding economic, political and security engagement with Southeast Asia have broken the impasse once created by New Delhi's dismissive attitude towards the region's pro-capital, pro-America, "Coca Cola governments".[5]

Singapore's avowed sponsorship of India reflects a cardinal principle of its balance of power approach to international relations, which is that a regional order cannot be durable if it seeks to exclude an existing or an emerging power. In predicating its foreign policy on encouraging all great powers to participate in the affairs of Southeast Asia, Singapore worked on the basis that the powers must have a viable stake in the regional order for it to be sustainable. Its consistent approach was apparent in its attitude even to the two former binary opposites in the ordering of global affairs: the United States and the Soviet Union. Notwithstanding Singapore's ideological affinity to Washington and its opposition to communism as an ideology in the organization of national and international affairs, its disposition did not lead it to deny that Moscow was a legitimate player on the world stage. Its attitude to that country was conditioned by three fundamental factors. First, while Singapore was against communism, it felt that what ideology the Soviet Union — like any country, including Singapore — chose to follow was its own business; it was not up to others to dictate the complexion of the Soviet political system; and no matter what others did, Singapore would have normal relations with that country and trade with it. Secondly, the Soviet Union, like the other great powers, had a legitimate reason to be involved in Southeast Asia, and Singapore would not participate in any attempts to exclude it from the region. Thirdly, relations with Moscow would depend on Singapore's national interests, not on how communist Russia was viewed by others, including Singapore's friends.

The Republic's foreign policy stance, articulated early into independence — "Please do not expect us to make your enemies our enemies" — applied to the Soviet "enemy" of some as it did to the American "enemy" of others. Hence, Singapore signed an agreement with Moscow in 1968 enabling Soviet vessels to call for fuelling and minor repairs, and in 1971 Prime Minister Lee Kuan Yew said that he saw growing Soviet naval capacity as a useful balancing force in the region. Once Moscow developed its naval presence, Singapore could be a natural choice as a warm water port for the Indian Ocean fleet and the large Pacific fleet based in Vladivostok. Singapore did not foreclose its options *vis-à-vis* Moscow. Indeed, in one view, Singapore was left as the most pro-Soviet state in maritime Southeast Asia after the fall of Sukarno — quite by default, of course, given the antagonism towards Moscow in Jakarta and Kuala Lumpur — and this impression was reinforced when Lee called for a multilateral underpinning, with Russian participation, of the security of South and Southeast Asian states during a visit to the United States in 1967. The idea was received with delight in Moscow.[6] However, in keeping with its refusal to become a party to any attempt to exclude an external power from the region, the Republic was cool to the Soviet call for an Asian collective security system in 1969 since the plan's obvious target was China. It was only Soviet support for Vietnamese actions in Indochina that turned Singapore into one of Moscow's most vehement critics. Given the way Moscow was enabling Hanoi to threaten the rest of Southeast Asia, Singapore's unsentimental view of the Soviet Union as a great power with legitimate interests in the region changed rapidly into an extreme distrust of Moscow as the foreign patron of a local client-cum-hegemon. The reason for citing the Soviet Union in a discussion of India's Southeast Asian role today is not to imply that New Delhi will behave like Moscow, but to suggest that Singapore's approach to India is a part of a consistent foreign policy orientation towards the powers that even Cold War tussles over allegiances based on ideology did not destroy. Singapore's closeness to Washington did not translate into envisaging a regional order based on the absence of a key international player.

This having been said, Singapore's engagement of China, as the foregoing pages show, occurred in a regional context defined by America's political and strategic posture in the post-Cold War period. Singapore's engagement of India, too, began in the aftermath of the Cold War and is occurring in the unfolding context of what recently was named the Long

War in the *Quadrennial Defense Review Report* (QDR) released in early February 2006. The Long War is of broader scope than the War on Terror, in which it originated after the terror strikes in America on 11 September 2001. The Pentagon's new 20-year strategy envisions American troops being deployed in dozens of countries simultaneously to fight terrorism and other non-traditional threats. The strategy builds on the lessons learned by the U.S. military since 2001 in Iraq, Afghanistan and in counter-terrorism operations.[7] Although the report focuses on placing the war on terror in the larger perspective of the challenges facing the United States, that war is not its sole concern. It singles out China as the country that has "the greatest potential to compete militarily with the United States", and Washington's strategy in response calls for accelerating the fielding of a new Air Force long-range strike force, as well as for building undersea warfare capabilities.[8] Interestingly, under the 2001 QDR, the Pentagon had planned to be able swiftly to defeat two adversaries in overlapping military campaigns, with the option of overthrowing a hostile government in one. In the new strategy, one of those two campaigns can be a large-scale, prolonged " 'irregular' conflict, such as the counterinsurgency in Iraq".[9] Although this refinement of American objectives does not imply a direct targeting of China, it suggests that the war on terror does not detract from Washington's ability to address another contingency simultaneously, should it have to.

It is in this larger context that Singapore, which does not support the containment of China, engages India, a country that, like the city-state, is a partner of the United States in the war on terror. That engagement has not achieved as yet the economic and political depth of its engagement of China — although the Comprehensive Economic Cooperation Agreement signed in 2005 does not have a counterpart in the form of a Sino-Singapore free trade agreement — but it nevertheless is significant because, unlike the engagement of China, the engagement of India has strategic undertones. These undertones represent the possibility of a power shift as India expands its influence from South Asia to Southeast Asia, creating the basis of a common security domain that would overlap with China's straddling influence in Northeast Asia and Southeast Asia.

Singapore is situated at the heart of the region where the power of a rising India meets the power of a rising China and the city-state will be affected by the competition inherent in the simultaneous rise of the two Asian powers. "Their size, geographic proximity and contemporaneous rise to greater political and economic power ensure that competition will remain a feature of their relationship." Sino-Indian rivalry "is still felt more keenly in India than in China", and China increasingly "is a benchmark against which Indians judge their own economic performance and political status".[10] India has on its side the favour of an America whose relations with China noticeably have receded from the partnership achieved during the second phase of the Cold War and for some time thereafter. The current thaw in Sino-Indian relations — financed by expanding economic links between the two Asian achievers, and politically symbolized by Indian recognition of Tibet as a part of the territory of the People's Republic and by reciprocal Chinese acceptance of Indian sovereignty in the small Himalayan state of Sikkim — suggests that the two countries do not have to play a zero-sum game,[11] but the thaw does not detract from the possibility that the growth of Indian political and military power, occurring with American support and help, will introduce a degree of antagonistic competition between Beijing and New Delhi for influence in Southeast Asia. The city-state's ability to engage the two Asian powers, rising under the watchful eyes of America, could be tested should Chinese and Indian paths to security diverge in Southeast Asia.

INDIA ARRIVES

Indian Defence Minister Pranab Mukherjee summarized New Delhi's strategic perspectives in an introspective address in June 2005. He drew attention to a few salient facts. First, India is both a continental and maritime nation with a territory of more than three million square kilometres, a land frontier of 15,000 kilometres, a coastline of 7,500 kilometres, and a population of 1.1 billion, the second largest in the world. Secondly, he said, India's location at the base of continental Asia and at the top of the Indian Ocean gives it a "vantage point" with reference to West, Central, continental and Southeast Asia, and to the littoral states of the Indian Ocean from East Africa to Indonesia. Thirdly, India's peninsular projection into the Ocean "which bears its name, gives it a stake in the security and stability of these waters". Fourthly, it shares borders with 11 neighbours, most of whom do not share borders among themselves. Fifthly, it is an energy deficient country located close to some of the most important sources of oil and natural gas in the Gulf and Central Asia and adjacent to one of the most vital sea-lanes, through which 60,000 ships pass every year. Turning from geography to history, Mukherjee noted that developments from the 17th century onwards fundamentally had altered the traditional orientations and moorings of India's external relations. Thus, "European mercantilism grew into the maritime domination of the Indian Ocean, disrupting traditional trade and contacts between India and its regional maritime partners to the east and [the] west. Further north, in mainland Asia, it introduced relationships of domination and rivalry between imperial powers where earlier only local powers played out their dynastic destinies". In the 20th century, several developments with their roots in imperial history affected India's relationships with its historical neighbours in Asia. "Perhaps, the most fateful, was the Partition of India and the emergence of hard frontiers in the form of a hostile and revanchist Pakistan to the west and east of India. As a result, for the first time in its 4,000-year history, India found itself physically separated and shut out from its historical, cultural and commercial surroundings to the northwest of India and vice versa." Mukherjee concluded that the 20th century had been a "decided aberration" in the pattern of India's historical and traditional relationship with the outside world.

Speaking of economics, he noted that the historical experience of the British East India Company, and of imperialism in general, had left India suspicious of foreign trade. After independence, this attitude had found expression in "efforts to build a self-reliant economy wary of integration to the world economy. The model stood us in good stead for a while". The Cold War delayed the restoration of historical links broken by colonialism. "In retrospect, this was an era of shadow boxing; a hall of mirrors. The breakdown of the Berlin Wall and the end of the Cold War liberated India (and much of the developing world), from the false problematic of 'East' and 'West'. It provided an opportunity to recover our traditional, historical reflexes atrophied in the chilly theatre of [the] Cold War", he declared.[12] Mukherjee's speech contained the essentials of the retrospective self-perception that India brought to the table of the great powers after the pages of the Cold War had turned.

As a country that had invested much political capital in Moscow, India was marginalized in the international system when the end of the Cold War led to the implosion of the Soviet Union. India's balance-of-payments crisis at the start of the 1990s represented the economic equivalent of its political predicament of not finding a place in the post-Non-Aligned order. But within the end of the decade, India had re-emerged on the global scene, its economy rejuvenated by reforms and its political and military power transformed by the nuclear tests that it had carried out in May 1998.

The tests were crucial to the recasting of India on the world stage. Their immediate origins lay in New Delhi's national security concerns relating to the *de facto* military alliance between China and Pakistan. The tests did not allay Indian concerns entirely because they swiftly were followed by Pakistan's tests, which gave Islamabad a bite at the military parity with New Delhi that had eluded it since their parting of ways in 1947. "The government of India may deeply dislike any perception of parity with Pakistan, but did its best, in effect, to alter a favourable situation of acknowledged asymmetry into one of perceived parity," the Indian Nobel laureate Amartya Sen writes.[13] However, if the ultimate objective of India's tests, as is clear from the justifications that were made for them, was to achieve military parity with China, then the narrowing of Pakistan's military gap with India was a small price to be paid for India's nuclear breakthrough in its relations with China. The tests revealed the "enduring and deep-rooted aspiration of India for the role of a major power, and the related belief that the possession of an independent nuclear capability is an essential prerequisite for achieving that status".[14]

America did not intervene decisively against the Indian action. C. Raja Mohan speaks of New Delhi's nuclear defiance of Washington from 1996 to 1998 and the diplomatic reconciliation between the two capitals from 1998 to 2001 as "the most complex, daring and successful political manoeuvres the nation ever initiated".[15] Ironically, one reason for American benevolence might have been the record of China's nuclear diplomatic strategy in the 1960s. Raja Mohan relates how both China and India sought to break out of international constraints on their nuclear ambitions and adopt a moral posture to help legitimize their bid for membership of the nuclear club. Both settled for a minimum nuclear deterrent so as not to give the impression that they had embarked on an arms race, and both declared a no-first-use policy.[16] "Like China, India viewed nuclear weapons as political instruments. Both saw them more as strategic insurance against extreme threats and a symbol of their own aspirations in the international system rather than as weapons usable in a war."[17]

True, India's nuclear blasts had the effect temporarily of pushing the United States and China closer, as when, during his visit to the People's Republic in June 1998, President Clinton proclaimed Beijing a strategic partner and issued a strong joint statement with his Chinese hosts on preventing nuclear proliferation in the subcontinent.[18] However, Clinton himself visited India to initiate a political *rapprochement* in 2000. The same year, Indian President K.R. Narayanan visited China and a formal annual security dialogue began that enabled India to raise concerns about China's nuclear and missile cooperation with Pakistan and other issues of nuclear arms control.[19]

American and Chinese criticism of India's nuclear blasts proved shortlived. What was more significant than the passing criticism was that, as with China three decades earlier, the possession of nuclear weapons and the diplomatic ability to get the world's dominant power — the United States — to accept those weapons as a *fait accompli* transformed India's status on the international stage. China had done just that in 1964, when its nuclear tests announced the extent of the Sino-Soviet split and made China a valuable potential recruit to the American side of the Cold War — a possibility that was fulfilled in 1971 — in spite of Beijing remaining on the other side of the ideological divide between international capitalism and proletarian internationalism. In 1998, when India announced its arrival on the American-built world stage, it did not even have to devise an apology for its domestic system, which was a Westminster-style democracy moving towards capitalism. India found it easier to be a cartel-breaker in 1998 than China had found it possible to do so in 1964. The upshot was that India arrived as a peer power of China in 1998.

THE MANTRI, UNCLE SAM AND THE MANDARIN

Following on from New Delhi's success in replicating Beijing's entry into the ranks of nuclear weapons states, there is a view that India could be doing a "China" on China. Venu Rajamony, political counsellor in the Indian mission in Beijing from 1999 to 2002, cites Chinese concerns that, just as China and the United States put aside ideological and other differences in the early 1970s to forge a tacit alliance against the Soviet Union, India and the United States might find common ground by uniting against China. Was Washington trying to set off New Delhi against Beijing? And "is India emulating China's own example by displaying unprecedented pragmatism and diplomatic dexterity by aligning itself with the United States to obvious mutual benefit"?[20]

That an informal Indo-U.S. alignment is in progress hardly is in doubt. In an article written soon after the 1998 nuclear explosions, Mohammed Ayoob argued the case for a muscular partnership between Washington and New Delhi. "As the lone superpower and major provider of public goods in the international system, the United States has come to realize the importance of pivotal regional powers and the fact that international order can attain legitimacy and stability only if these same qualities are first achieved within regional orders."[21] Until recently, the United States had viewed India's nuclear ambitions primarily in the context of the India-Pakistan equation, in spite of New Delhi's insistence that China was the primary factor in India's nuclear policy — with the transfer to Pakistan of Chinese material and technology creating a Pakistani extension of the Chinese threat to India.[22] But given the potential for Sino-American discord over Taiwan, trade, human rights and China's place in the international order,[23] it made sense for Washington to help New Delhi become South Asia's "regional security manager, and to acquire the capabilities needed to counterbalance China in the wider Asian region".[24] Since the United States should build alliances with other Asian powers "in case of future clashes with China", India is "a logical choice" because its interests *vis-à-vis* China complement American interests, and because India has the military and economic potential and the political will to counter Chinese dominance. As for American worries of doing a China on India — facilitating the appearance of a challenger down the road to fend off the immediate rival, once the Soviet Union — Ayoob assured Washington that Indian aspirations were limited to managing the South Asian order, not the East Asian one. Yet, "because it shares America's objective of balancing China's power in Asia, India would willingly work with the United States toward this end outside of South Asia, especially in Southeast Asia and the Indian Ocean".[25]

The Mantri Greets Uncle Sam

Ayoob's succinct advocacy of Indian possibilities in an American-led order draws attention to the nub of Washington's Asia policy: its refusal to let any power or combination of powers seize control of the Asian mainland, push back America's forward naval presence, and gain the power to attack the American mainland. That logic was apparent in the Pacific war with Japan, in attempts to curb the growth of Soviet influence, and in the approach to a growing China. Undoubtedly, in the current phase of international relations, great and medium powers cannot afford a direct confrontation with the United States, making classical balancing alliances unlikely. "Since potential regional hegemons (France, Germany, Russia, India, China, and Japan) are all placed in Europe and Asia, an overtly anti-American and power politics-oriented alliance between two or more of these countries could easily scare neighbouring states, thus helping the U.S.

to build a counter-alliance."[26] Nevertheless, a Rand Corporation study by Zalmay Khalilzad and others urges the United States to utilize its current preponderance by adopting a new strategy towards Asia. The study suggests that augmenting Indian power is in America's interests because it permits Washington to pursue a balance-of-power strategy towards major rising powers and key regional states that are not members of the U.S. alliance structure, including China, India and Russia. Washington's strategy should be to circumvent these countries from threatening one another or the United States, while simultaneously preventing any combination of these powers from undercutting U.S. strategic interests in Asia.[27] Within that larger framework, Washington should include New Delhi actively in the management of the regional order, Ashley J. Tellis argues, because it is India that will be affected the most by state failures in southern and southeastern Asia — Myanmar constituting the link between Southeast Asia and an arc of insecurity running through Afghanistan, Pakistan, Nepal, Bangladesh and Sri Lanka.[28]

Even before the September 2001 terrorist attacks in the United States, there was some sympathy in Washington for India's demand that it recognize that Indian strategic interests spanned the extended strategic neighbourhood from the Suez Canal to the Strait of Malacca, a neighbourhood encompassing the Middle East, the Persian Gulf, South and Central Asia, and Southeast Asia. America's global obligations should factor in India's aspirations and autonomy in the area.[29] The possibilities of security convergence were apparent to Americans like Tellis, deputy to the ambassador in New Delhi from 2001 to 2003, who saw how Indian interests invariably dovetailed with American interests on many issues of great importance to Washington: the balance of power in Asia, the security of sea lanes in the Indian Ocean, WMD proliferation, terrorism, narcotics trafficking, and the rise of religious and secular extremism.[30] In the early months of 2001, the George W. Bush Administration rejected the Clintonian notion of China as a strategic partner and identified it as a potential competitor, "raising the prospect of a new American policy aimed at balancing China and placing some weight on India's strategic role in Asia".[31] In May 2001, Washington announced its national missile defence initiative, which was attacked by many countries as a recipe for an arms race and was seen by China as a means of eroding its deterrent *vis-à-vis* the United States, although the NMD's stated objective was to protect America and its friends from rogue states such as North Korea. India supported the controversial initiative, drawing attention to the NMD's ability to offset some of its own military imbalance with China.

Ayoob's advocacy of a robust Indo-American partnership, which began to take shape within three short years of India's nuclear explosions, was borne out by the change in Washington's imperatives and priorities following the terrorist attacks of 2001. From being a garrulous but minor irritant in American grand strategy, India was elevated to a primary if potential player in the post-9/11 world order. India seized the moment, breaking with its visceral opposition to foreign bases, not least on its own soil, as forward staging posts of unholy military alliances. The government of Indian Prime Minister Atal Behari Vajpayee communicated to the American mission in New Delhi that it would extend whatever support the United States desired, including military bases, in its global war on terror.[32] In spite of the fact that the war on terror became Washington's primary foreign concern — a war in which Beijing promised to help out, although not as enthusiastically as India — the "China factor" did not disappear from America's radar, although it receded somewhat as non-state actors carried out their non-negotiable hostility towards the United States. The *Quadrennial Defense Review Report,* issued by the U.S. Department of Defence on 30 September 2001, listed among America's "enduring national interests" the need to preclude "hostile domination of critical areas", including the "East Asian littoral" that stretched from the south of Japan through Australia into the Bay of Bengal. Maintaining a stable balance in that region would be particularly challenging, the report declared, because "the possibility exists that a military competitor with a formidable resource base will emerge in the region". "These carefully elliptical formulations referred to an increasingly powerful China that might, someday, dominate the 'East Asian littoral'."[33] In September 2002, the White House put India for the first time in the category of great powers, implying an Indian role in the Asian balance of power.

The Next Steps in Strategic Partnership agreement, announced in 2004, was a breakthrough that committed Washington and New Delhi to working together in the arenas of civilian nuclear energy, civilian space programmes, high-technology trade and missile defence "where India's possession of nuclear weaponry had previously made meaningful cooperation all but impossible".[34] Mukherjee, the Indian Defence Minister, and his American counterpart, Donald Rumsfeld, signed a 10-year defence agreement, the New Framework for the U.S.-Indian Defence Relationship, in June 2005; and the U.S.-India Joint Statement followed during Indian Prime Minister Manmohan Singh's visit to Washington in July 2005. "President Bush conveyed his appreciation to the Prime Minister over India's strong commitment to preventing WMD proliferation and stated that as a responsible state with advanced nuclear technology, India should acquire the same benefits and advantages as other such states. The President told the Prime Minister that he will work to achieve full civil nuclear energy cooperation with India as it realizes its goals of promoting nuclear power and achieving energy security. The President would also seek agreement from Congress to adjust U.S. laws and policies, and the United States will work with friends and allies to adjust international regimes to enable full civil nuclear energy cooperation and trade with India...", a joint statement declared. India agreed reciprocally that it "would be ready to assume the same responsibilities and practices and acquire the same benefits and advantages as other leading countries with advanced nuclear technology, such as the United States".[35]

The Indo-U.S. *entente cordiale* culminated in March 2006, when Bush and Singh announced in New Delhi an unprecedented agreement to provide American nuclear power assistance to energy-starved India while allowing it to step up its nuclear weapons production substantially. Under the agreement, India would separate its civilian and military nuclear programmes over the following eight years in order to gain access to U.S. expertise and nuclear fuel. India's civilian facilities would be subject to permanent international inspections for the first time. Of India's 22 nuclear plants, 14 classified for civilian use would be subject to new and permanent international inspections under the deal. India's eight other reactors, as well as future reactors designated for military use, would be off-limits.[36] According to the *Washington Post*, the pact would allow India to produce "vast quantities" of fissile material, and it would not require oversight of India's prototype fast-breeder reactors, which could produce significant amounts of super-grade plutonium when they operated fully. "The Bush administration originally sought a plan that would have allowed India to continue producing material for six to 10 weapons each year, but the new plan would allow India enough fissile material for as many as 50 weapons a year. Experts said this would far exceed what is believed to be its current capacity." American Under-Secretary of State for Political Affairs R. Nicholas Burns, who had been involved with working out the details of the pact, said that India, unlike Iran and North Korea, had earned special treatment from the United States because of its commitment to democracy and international inspections.[37]

Critics of the accord, which dealt a blow to the international non-proliferation regime, warned that the United States was using the negotiations to "emasculate India's nuclear-weapons capability and make its nuclear program dependent on US technology". "The US, under the Bush administration, has emerged as the most aggressive and reckless force in world geo-politics, as the American ruling elite seeks to use its military might to offset the decline in its world economic position. If it is willing to press for an exception to be made for India in the world nuclear regulatory regime, it is because it aims through the selective use of the carrot and stick to tie India to its geo-political strategy and ambitions."[38]

But the pact, which marked a significant break from decades of American nuclear policy, widely was read as an important part of a White House strategy to accelerate New Delhi's rise as a global power and as a regional counterweight to China.³⁹ Washington's aim was to take U.S.-Indo relations to a new level in keeping with the offer that U.S. Secretary of State Condoleezza Rice had made a year earlier of America helping India to become a world power. Strobe Talbott, who as Deputy Secretary of State in the Clinton Administration negotiated with India and Pakistan following their 1998 tests, writes that Washington wanted a compromise whereby it would "limit the extent to which the Indian bomb was an obstacle to better relations if India would, by explicit agreement, limit the development and deployment of its nuclear arsenal". India was disinclined to compromise and waited for the day when the United States would accept a nuclear-armed India as a fully-entitled member of the international community. "As one of the architects of the Indian strategy (Foreign Minister) Jaswant Singh came closer to achieving his objective in the dialogue than I did to achieving mine," Talbott writes unequivocally.⁴⁰

His conclusion was borne out by the 2006 pact between the two countries. Indian scholar Pratap Bhanu Mehta believes that the agreement is "an emphatic acknowledgment of India's transformation from a regional to a global power, an important step in transforming the rules of the world order to accommodate the aspirations of a rising power". Admittedly, India has agreed to safeguards for its civilian reactors in perpetuity, but it "artfully" has tied them to assurances on uninterrupted fuel supply. "It will be difficult to argue that this deal significantly caps India's nuclear capability," he argues, noting that, instead, it holds out the possibility of India transforming "the rules of the international order without sacrificing its military autonomy". On the political front, the fortunes of India's elites "comprehensively and intimately" are tied, for the first time in India's history, to America's fate. But Mehta recognizes a corresponding problem. "While the US has emphatically rejected equating India and Pakistan in any nuclear order, will China do the same?"[41] The accord obviously would not find favour in Pakistan. "Angered by the US insistence that any exception to the nuclear regulatory regime will be for India and India alone", Pakistani President Pervez Musharraf flew to Beijing the previous month to discuss increased Chinese assistance for his country's civilian nuclear programme.[42]

Both critics and supporters of the Indo-American nuclear agreement, which Bush signed into law in December 2006 after its tortuous progress through Congress, have a case. The deal does act as a potential constraint on India's strategic autonomy but, simultaneously, it allows India to legitimize its nuclear status, win recognition of this status, and produce more nuclear weapons, all with the tacit approval of the United States. It is a good example of the decision that New Delhi appears to have taken to rise in concert with U.S. expectations and not in opposition to them — in sharp contrast to Beijing's choice of peaceful development on terms that nevertheless have attracted American vigilance ranging from barely-concealed concern to outright hostility.

Of course, how long India would be prepared to adhere to a path in which its rise is secondary to American objectives remains to be seen. The United States would want an Indian nuclear force that has no intercontinental ballistic missiles (ICBMs), that grows slowly, and that has a low number of weapons. Amit Gupta argues that the no, slow and low framework "satisfies Washington because it does not give India a military capability to threaten the continental United States", but the framework condemns India to a third-tier nuclear status that makes it difficult for it to acquire a credible nuclear credibility and relegates it to being a state that cannot discuss seriously the future of the international nuclear order.[43] First-tier nuclear states — the United States and Russia — not only have far more nuclear weapons than their closest rivals, but they have global nuclear reach and can deter nuclear retaliation by other states. Second-tier nuclear states have smaller and less advanced nuclear forces, and they possess extra-regional but not global reach. They have a first-use, but not a first-strike, capability against more powerful states, and they do not have a credible deterrent capability against first-tier states. Third-tier nuclear states have small and technologically backward forces, are limited in range to their own regions, and are without a deterrent capability against the higher tiers.[44]

Not long after China went nuclear, the Indian analyst Sisir Gupta warned that becoming a third-tier nuclear state would not enhance India's security or its status. India would have to use its nuclear status to reshape the international system.[45] Amit Gupta concurs, arguing that India should develop a nuclear deterrent that is taken seriously by China and other nuclear states in the first and second tiers.[46] The testing of the Agni III missile, postponed repeatedly, would give India the ability to target China's eastern seaboard, a credible deterrent without which New Delhi would not be taken seriously in China's strategic calculations. A credible deterrent also would require the acquisition of a nuclear submarine fleet to provide India second-strike capability against China and Pakistan.[47] India needs fewer restrictions to be placed on its nuclear and conventional capabilities if it is to "play the role of stabilizer in Asia".[48]

Amit Gupta makes a maximalist argument for India's position in the nuclear hierarchy. How that position will square ultimately with the commonalities that C. Raja Mohan finds between India's and China's appropriate minimum nuclear deterrent only time will tell. But one factor ostensibly in India's favour is that it is, in common with the United States, Britain, France and Russia, a nuclear democracy, which arguably China and Pakistan are not (although Islamabad went nuclear under the democratically-elected government of Nawaz Sharif). Whether a repartitioning of world affairs takes place and is sustained — not between nuclear haves and nuclear have-nots, that being the old distinction, but now between nuclear democracies and nuclear non-democracies, with non-nuclear states in tow on each side — might well write the next chapter of international relations. For the time being, it is true to say that the call by Stephen Cohen, one of the most energetic proponents of Indo-U.S. *rapprochement*, for American policy to be adjusted to cope with a rising India is taking shape in the form of a relationship that does not amount to an alliance but that is significantly more intimate than in the past.[49]

The Mantri Meets the Mandarin

China's quarrels with India are not ancient. In the Chinese view, they originated in an imperial history that estranged India from its natural neighbours. Chinese analysts note how, using India as a springboard, the British expanded their empire to cover the territories of present-day India, Pakistan, Bangladesh and Myanmar, to administer Aden and some areas of the Persian Gulf, to exercise control over the Himalayan kingdoms of Bhutan, Nepal and Sikkim, to extend their sphere of influence to Afghanistan, and to "encroach" on Tibet. "While expanding the Indian empire, British colonialists deliberately fostered the ideology of great power chauvinism and national egoism among Indian politicians, administrative officials and intellectuals."[50] The Sino-Indian rift that came to a head in 1962 brought the colonial issue to the fore. The rift centred on the legality of the McMahon Line demarcated by the British at the Simla Convention of 1914. China refused to accept it as the border by arguing that historically "no treaty or agreement on the Sino-Indian boundary had ever been concluded between the Chinese central government and the Indian government".[51]

Frequent border clashes beginning in 1959 culminated in the war and the Indian military debacle of 1962 that Indian analysts have not forgotten. They castigate Chinese self-perceptions of centrality in the world and accuse Beijing of aggressively imperial behaviour and the self-serving use of revisionist history. They note that the Chinese and Indian military frontiers met for the first time in history in 1950, when China annexed Tibet, a buffer nearly the size of Western Europe. "Within 12 years of becoming India's neighbor, China invaded this country, with Mao Zedong cleverly timing the aggression with the Cuban missile crisis," Brahma Chellaney declares. However, had Beijing not set out to "teach India a lesson," in the words of then Premier Zhou Enlai, "this country probably would not have become the significant military and nuclear power that it is today. The invasion helped lay the foundation of

India's political rise".[52] The stakes were raised by China's nuclear explosion in 1964. A decade later, India tested a nuclear device. Although it called the event — known as Pokhran I after the site of the blast — a "peaceful nuclear explosion", India's security trajectory was clear and was confirmed by the 1998 blasts, Pokhran II. China featured prominently in Indian justifications of Pokhran II.

China's diplomatic campaign to isolate nuclear India, like the American campaign, proved shortlived. In the years since 1998, Sino-Indian relations have achieved an almost surreal dimension. There is the possibility of an economic *entente* based on the economic power of a combined population of more than two billion talented people, in which Indian excellence in software can join forces with China's advantages in hardware to replicate Silicon Valley across the world. ICs — Indians and Chinese — have been a driving force behind California's success with ICs, integrated circuits. If China is the world's factory, India can be its outsourced head office. Sino-Indian trade increased 14-fold over a decade, reaching US$13.6 billion by the end of 2004;[53] the restoration of their cross-border trade, three-quarters of which was carried on the Silk Road, alone could generate billions not being made now. Chinese and Indian companies have moved into each other's countries; Chinese consumer goods are flourishing on the Indian market; and whereas Indians once visited Chinese restaurants in Indian cities for Chinese food prepared with Indian tastes in mind, they now can go to Indian-run restaurants from Jalandhar to Kolkata to savour authentic Cantonese or Sichuan cuisine, which has entered mainstream Indian menus. So great has been the strategic partnership in culinary tastes that Maggi Mee, a brand of Chinese-style noodles, not only caught on in India but went so native in taste that Indian-style Maggi Mee now competes with the original brand on the shelves of supermarkets such as Mustafa in Singapore. Indeed, idols of Hindu deities made in atheist China are snapped up by devout Indians with a very secular eye on quality and price. An explosion of relations has occurred. Politically, many high-level bilateral visits have taken place since 1998, as have the first joint Indian-Chinese naval exercises and a symbolically-rich trip by the commander of an Indian Army's corps, a unit posted on the Indo-Tibetan border that bore the brunt of the 1962 war there, to People's Liberation Army bases in Tibet. There is talk of a Sino-Indian strategic partnership based on the idea, formulated neatly by former Indian Foreign Secretary Shyam Saran, that China and India "are too big to contain each other or be contained by any other country".[54]

Yet, Sino-Indian relations are marked by suspicion, hedging, counter-hedging and bloc-building that occasionally spill over into open rounds of diplomatic jousting. In the Shanghai Cooperation Organization, which brings together China, Russia, Kazakhstan, Kyrgyzstan, Tajikistan and Uzbekistan, Russians wary of Chinese intrusion into their backyard invited in India as an observer in July 2005. To counter the move, China brought Pakistan into the SCO as an observer. In a replay of that manoeuvring, this time in the opposite direction, China entered the South Asian Association for Regional Cooperation (SAARC) as an observer at the 13th SAARC summit in November 2005 (that tellingly met at the Bangladesh-China Friendship Centre in Dhaka). Bhutan sided with India to try and block China's entry, but a pro-China group including Nepal pushed for Beijing's entry as a condition for admitting Afghanistan into SAARC, which India sought. India responded by helping Japan to join the association as an observer. Japan's presence would help to provide some diplomatic balance to China's links with important South Asian countries — Pakistan, Bangladesh and Sri Lanka — that have defence and strategic cooperation agreements with Beijing. The impasse at SAARC rankled the Indian strategist K. Subrahmanyam so much that he suggested that New Delhi review its South Asian strategy and shift it away from the association.[55] His suggestion is a problematic one. Without Indian interest, SAARC would lose even the little regional relevance that it has, but without India and with China in, SAARC would represent an encirclement of India that New Delhi obviously would not desire.

The turf war between China and India reappeared at the inaugural East Asian Summit (EAS) in Kuala Lumpur in December 2005. With the exception of Malaysia, Southeast Asian countries supported India's participation in the EAS, viewing it as a counterweight to China, and they backed Australia's participation if it acceded to the ASEAN Treaty of Amity and Cooperation, which it did. Having failed to exclude India, Australia and New Zealand from the EAS, Beijing proposed on the eve of the summit that the existing ASEAN Plus Three (APT) group, and not the new 16-member East Asia Summit, "control the formation of any Asian community-building exercise".[56] "In other words, China insisted that EAC formation remain the responsibility of the core group, or APT. A proposal to divide EAS into two blocs — the core states with China as the dominant APT player, and the peripheral states with India, Australia and New Zealand, 'outsiders' according to a recent People's Daily editorial — led to a major rift."[57] What the EAS revealed was that China regards Japan and India with "substantial antipathy". Remaining leery of India's attempts to extend influence in China's backyard, Beijing regards New Delhi's Look East policy as part of a wider "congage China" strategy pursued by the Washington-Tokyo-New Delhi axis. Beijing seeks therefore to confine India to the periphery of a future East Asian Community.[58]

The turf war between China and India represents a sobering aspect of Asia's international relations. India sees Chinese intrusion into South Asia, a subcontinent that is defined by New Delhi's centrality, as a move to weaken it on home turf. China sees concessions to India's efforts to veto outcomes in its desired South Asian *cordon sanitaire* as a denial of Beijing's reach as an acknowledged great power. Recognizing an exclusive sphere of influence in the subcontinent — the heartland of Indian power — would limit China's access to its periphery — the periphery being that zone of a country's extended neighbourhood where classically the centre's claims to authority are tested most keenly.

Geography is not watertight, however. Chinese primacy in East Asia is contested in its immediate neighbourhood by Taiwan and Japan and by the global offshore balancer, the United States. Similarly, Indian primacy in South Asia is challenged by many of the smaller nations that ring it, notably Pakistan, which seeks to gain strategic depth from Central Asia and the Middle East (apart from its security relations with China) to balance India's preponderant power in South Asia. C. Raja Mohan declares bravely that imperial ideas of buffer states, spheres of influence, and insulated national spaces are anachronisms in an age of globalization.[59] He does not seem to have many takers. Notwithstanding the gaps in China's and India's spheres of influence, the trend is not towards relinquishing control over one's own sphere but towards asserting influence in the other's sphere. In the latest manifestation of their competition, India is moving into Southeast Asia, the immediate periphery of China's East Asian sphere of influence, even as China infiltrates the nation-sized gaps in South Asia and moves westwards towards the Middle East. The Indian Ocean is the new epicentre of Sino-Indian competition.

THE INDIAN OCEAN

The great Indian strategist Kovalam Madhava Panikkar once complained that most histories of India were written from the point of view of Delhi and its changing dynasties, not of India as a whole. The latter view would have revealed the country's vital interests in the Indian Ocean. This, Panikkar did in his concise but masterly *India and the Indian Ocean: An Essay on the Influence of Sea Power on Indian History*, the title declaring the book's intellectual gratitude to another masterpiece, Alfred Thayer Mahan's *The Influence of Sea Power upon History, 1660–1783*. Panikkar noted that over thousands of years, India had been conquered many times by overland invasions, but such conquests had ended with the conqueror's assimilation. Control exercised from the sea had been different. It had operated as a stranglehold, allowing the invader to monopolize India's trade, a factor of world importance because Indian ports practically were equidistant from the markets of Europe and East Asia, while Africa and the Pacific islands equally were accessible to India. As late as World War II, what had been proved was that the strategic area in Indian warfare was not so much the Myanmar frontier as Malaya, Singapore and the

Andamans. Japan's lightning conquest of Singapore and its control of the Bay of Bengal had shown that the threat to India could come more easily from the East than from the West. Japan's elimination as a naval power after the War had not resolved the problem because China could not be expected to neglect its naval interests in the future.[60]

Panikkar's words took time to imprint themselves on the strategic consciousness of independent India, which began life as a violently partitioned entity that had to integrate into its reduced domain such colonial curiosities as the princely states even as it sought to secure its land borders against estranged neighbours to the west and the north. Little attention was paid to naval potential in Asia, ignoring another historical analogy. This was that overlapping sea lanes of communication had been a significant factor in the evolution of Japanese-American rivalry in the Pacific in the first half of the 20th century. "By strengthening the defense of its own territories, each power ipso facto threatened the sea lanes of the other. A similar situation of overlapping and commingled sea lanes, though with a very different historical evolution, exists between China and India today in the Indian Ocean region (IOR)."[61]

The Indian Ocean remained Indian only in name. Great-power rivalry intensified there after Britain ceded the Diego Garcia islands to America in the 1960s and the Soviet Union occupied a vantage point in Cam Ranh Bay. At the Lusaka Non-Aligned Conference in 1970, India, Indonesia and Singapore were among the countries that pushed for the United Nations to adopt a declaration on the Indian Ocean as a Zone of Peace free of bases and military installations, and a UN resolution in 1972 put some diplomatic pressure on the great powers. But in reality, the Indian Ocean region remained anything but peaceful in the 1970s and the 1980s, when Iran had its Islamic revolution and the Soviet Union intervened in Afghanistan.[62] India itself received an unwelcome reminder of the strategic reality of the seas when Washington despatched the *USS Enterprise* to the Bay of Bengal as Pakistan's defeat loomed in the Bangladesh War of 1971. Although the ship's arrival did not alter the war's outcome, the Indians deemed it a nuclear threat.

In the years to come, Indian policy-makers and strategic thinkers would come to remember Curzon's emphasis on India's centrality in the Indian Ocean littoral, an essential ingredient of a forward policy in its extended neighbourhood — a point reiterated in Henry Kissinger's delineation of the Indian Ocean as India's natural strategic space.[63] Nations like Singapore and the Gulf states, which once had looked to India to provide security, had found it reluctant to do so. But the end of the Cold War "put India willy-nilly on the path of a new forward policy".[64] India's Look East policy, unveiled by Prime Minister Narasimha Rao in Singapore in 1994, is one of the most comprehensive and successive examples of that forward policy,[65] and Indian power in the Indian Ocean is central to the execution of that policy.

India's Maritime Doctrine was released in 2004. It outlined a shift from defending India's coastline to pursuing its interests throughout the IOR, the seas from the Persian Gulf to the Malacca Strait now being identified as India's legitimate area of interest. The long dream of excluding the great powers from the Indian Ocean was replaced by the realization that America was amenable to security arrangements involving India to secure common vital interests in the

IOR. Those interests included the security of sea lanes and the stability of markets, especially in energy resources. The congruence of Indo-American interests had been foreshadowed in the U.S. *National Security Strategy* unveiled in 2002. "We have a common interest in the free flow of commerce, including through the vital sea lanes of the Indian Ocean. Finally we share an interest in fighting terrorism and in creating a strategically stable Asia."[66] The Indian naval doctrine embraced the emerging possibilities of the American notion of littoral warfare and expressed a desire to guard the littoral region, match China and thwart its Indian Ocean aspirations.[67] Concretely, the maritime doctrine emphasized the need for a submarine-based credible minimum nuclear deterrence capability. "The authors of the maritime doctrine had the Look East policy in mind since it highlighted the need to build co-operative maritime security with the countries on the Indian Ocean littoral with regard to common tasks and challenges, including safe flows of trade and energy as well as threats of terrorism, piracy or transnational crime while expanding bilateral and multilateral interaction through joint exercises, joint patrolling and anti-terror operations."[68]

India's maritime doctrine is not, or is not yet, an effort to replicate a truly Curzonian strategy with sea power at its base, but the maritime component of India's forward policy is clear. The Indian Navy has carried out joint exercises with its East Asian counterparts for almost a decade, and has made port visits to the region as confidence-building measures.[69] As part of growing military cooperation with the United States, Indian missile boats patrolled the Malacca Strait alongside U.S. Navy vessels for a year after 9/11. Two Indian patrol craft provided security cover for a World

Economic Forum meeting in Mozambique in June 2004, following a July 2003 initiative when the Indian Navy provided protection to the African Union summit in Mozambique — the farthest that it had ventured. Commodore Uday Bhaskar of the Institute of Defence Studies and Analyses in New Delhi is reported to have said that the patrolling of the IOR is a subtle hint to China by ASEAN countries that India is a credible ally and long-term partner.[70] Whether or not ASEAN means to make the point to Beijing, it is apparent that Indian will not mind if China gets the hint.

The question is whether India possesses the capability to translate intention into reality. China's naval expansion is not a negligible feature of the Asian strategic landscape. In addition to being the only Asian state to possess a submarine-launched ballistic missile (SLBM) capability, there is China's desire to operate an aircraft carrier by 2015, as part of which it has acquired decommissioned carriers from Australia and Russia to study details of their construction. The People's Liberation Army Navy (PLAN) is seen as moving to project power well beyond China's shores.[71] Of particular interest to the Indians is China's naval cooperation with Myanmar. Beijing has been assisting it to construct five ports from Sittwe in the north to Victoria Point in the south, a radar station, an airstrip and a naval base in the Great Cocos, and an 800-mile Irrawady road-river link connecting China to the Bay of Bengal.[72] The Chinese also are believed to have established a Signals Intelligence facility on the Cocos islands, 30 nautical miles from the Andaman and Nicobar islands, enabling them to monitor India's missile tests off the eastern Orissa coast.[73]

While China's Indian Ocean foray is driven by the need to secure its energy lifelines, India's concerns stem from the possibility of China's nuclear submarines, missile-craft and strike aircraft using these bases/facilities to threaten India's eastern ports, sea-lines and even the Andaman and Nicobar Islands. The Irrawady route could provide China the necessary logistics "in case of a clash in the future".[74] To counter PLAN and to expand its own strategic reach, the Indian Navy sees itself as a force that, by 2012–15, comprises about 135 vessels and is centred around at least two, if not three, carrier battle groups. These would include boats with long-range precision-guided weapons capable of anti-ship, anti-submarine and decisive land-attack missions.[75]

In the meanwhile, India has expanded and upgraded its base on Andaman Island, called Fortress Andaman, from which "the entire stretch of the entrance to the Malacca Strait is easily reachable".[76] In an even more significant development, New Delhi has embarked on Project Seabird, an ambitious plan conceived of in the early 1980s but finally cleared in 1999, to help develop a genuinely blue-water navy. The exclusive naval harbour — visualized as an integrated defence facility incorporating a mega naval base, an air force station, a naval armaments depot and a missile silos naval base — is located in Karwar in the southern state of Karnataka. Project Seabird will be the first operational base with a port controlled exclusively by the Navy, thus permitting it to position and manoeuvre its operational fleet without having to worry about the movements of merchant vessels. The Navy's existing bases, including those in Mumbai and Vishakhapatnam, are located in enclaves within commercial ports, creating difficulties in times of war.[77] Also, Karwar is farther from Karachi than is than Mumbai, making Karwar safer as a node in India's naval calculations. Simultaneously, India is moving ahead with plans to dredge a deep-water canal in the Palk Strait between southern India and northern Sri Lanka. The aim of the Sethusamudram project, dubbed "India's Suez Canal", is not only to facilitate commercial shipping but to permit faster deployment of the Indian Navy.[78] When completed in 2008, it will stretch from Tuticorin port on India's southern coast to Adams Bridge in the Gulf of Mannar and northwards to the Bay of Bengal.

The idea was first mooted by the British Commander of the Indian Marines, A.D. Taylor, in 1860 and was floated again by Indian governments in 1955 and later. However, the project received the go-ahead only in 1995 "in line with India's developing economic and strategic interests".[79] The canal's strategic purpose is to enhance the Navy's ability to move warships between Indian's east and west coasts and to different parts of the Indian Ocean.

The Sethusamudram canal will be "an obvious complement" to the Karwar base, enabling warships to move more quickly to India's eastern coast and the Bay of Bengal. "The reduced sailing distance of 402 nautical miles is likely to be far more critical from a military standpoint than for commercial shipping. While the planned canal will only allow medium-sized ships through the Palk Strait, it could be readily dredged to allow larger vessels in the future."[80]

Up west, India's has invested in modernizing southeastern Iran's Chabahar port. In spite of India's vote against Iran's nuclear programme, Teheran seeks to go ahead with a groundbreaking gas pipeline project that will take natural gas from Iran's southern hydrocarbon-rich regions to energy-hungry India through Pakistan.[81]

Even as an East of Suez policy lurks on India's strategic horizon, bearing the legacy of Britain's policing role from Aden to Singapore, China has embarked on what might be called a West to Suez policy. Its "string-of-pearls" strategy connects the South China Sea to the Persian Gulf through military-related agreements with Thailand, Cambodia, Myanmar, Bangladesh, Sri Lanka, the Maldives and Pakistan, where the Chinese-assisted Gwadar port is located. Four months after the United States ordered its troops into Afghanistan to remove the Taliban, China and Pakistan joined hands to build the deep sea port on the Arabian Sea. In the context of American bases in Central and West Asia, which brought U.S. military forces virtually to China's doorstep, the American entry into Kabul alarmed Beijing as Washington extended its reach into Asian nations that ring western China. "Having no blue water navy to speak of, China feels defenseless in the Persian Gulf against any hostile action to choke off its energy supplies," Tarique Niazy writes.[82] That vulnerability made Beijing look to Gwadar as an alternative safe supply route for its energy shipments. Pakistan's interest lay in hosting a project that would give it strategic depth further to the southwest from its major naval base in Karachi, which long had been vulnerable to Indian naval action. Pakistan also built a naval base at Ormara to diversify its naval and commercial assets. Gwadar port will be complemented by an air defence unit, a garrison and an international airport.[83] The port, which provides China with a strategic foothold in the Arabian Sea and the Indian Ocean, demonstrates its strategic utility to South Asian nations such as Bangladesh, Nepal and Sri Lanka, which see China as a balancing factor in their relations with India. In the event that Gwadar becomes a

Chinese submarine base, pointed both at the Gulf and the western entrance to the Malacca Strait, it would transform China's unfolding Indian Ocean aspirations.

In this evolving maze of strategic sea routes, roads and gas pipelines, now reflecting the competitive quest for secure sources of energy to fuel the economies that finance military spending, one thing is clear. This is that India's East of Suez heritage intersects with China's West to Suez aspirations in places such as Singapore's maritime vicinity.

EASTERN SOUTH ASIA

A cautionary note is necessary here. While these aspects of Sino-India relations are incontrovertible, it would be a serious mistake to believe that those relations essentially are and ultimately must be conflictive. Consequently, it would be wrong to assume that their conflict mediates their relations with Southeast Asia, or that ASEAN is engaging India today primarily to balance China, let alone to contain China. This salutary warning is clear in retired Indian diplomat Sudhir Devare's book on security convergence between India and Southeast Asia, in which he insists that "India does not and should not seek closer military ties with Southeast Asia as a bulwark against China or Pakistan".[84] Any notion of security convergence based on that erroneous goal would be "flawed conceptually" and "disastrous practically".[85]

Devare makes the important point that, unlike as during the Cold War, India-Southeast Asia ties are driven by internal rather than external factors today.[86] Devare — a former Secretary in India's Ministry of External Affairs who was associated closely with the evolution of its Asia-Pacific policy — provides an exhaustive analysis of the entire range of economic, political, cultural relations between New Delhi and the capitals of Southeast Asia, including Yangon. Instead of being attempts to restrict China's role in Southeast Asia, many aspects of these flowering relations actually make the region a safer place for all powers, including Beijing. Multilateral cooperation on securing oil transport, along with shipping in general, from the threat of maritime terrorism and piracy is one such, pressing, aspect of India-Southeast Asia relations. Devare deals with the issue at length.[87]

Devare draws attention to underutilized fora of India-Southeast Asian cooperation. One is an envisaged Bay of Bengal Community emerging from BIMSTEC, the Bay of Bengal Initiative for Multi-Sectoral Technical and Economic Cooperation. Set up in June 1997 with Bangladesh, India, Sri Lanka and Thailand as members, the association — whose original acronym, retained in its current name, reflected the membership of Bangladesh, India, Myanmar, Sri Lanka and Thailand — admitted Myanmar as a full member in December 1997, and Bhutan and Nepal in 2004. The first organization of its kind to bring together ASEAN and South Asian states, it has identified communication, infrastructure, energy, trade investment, tourism and fisheries as being among areas of cooperation.

Although BIMSTEC's progress has been slow, Indian observers hope that New Delhi will use the initiative to begin a dialogue with Malaysia, Singapore and Indonesia to form a Bay of Bengal Community. "The concept of [a] Bay of Bengal community would become the common agenda of all littoral states. There is a mutuality of interests between India and these countries in promoting peace and stability in the region, as well as in maintaining a suitable environment for orderly all round development of these states."[88] Shehla Raza Hasan draws attention to the economic potential of "eastern South Asia", comprising the Indian states of West Bengal, Bihar, Orissa, Jharkhand, India's northeastern region, Nepal, Bhutan, Bangladesh and Myanmar: natural gas reserves of 190 billion cubic metres, coal reserves of 909 million tonnes, hydro-electric potential estimated at 49,000 MW, oil reserves pegged at 513 million tonnes, limestone reserves of 4,933 million tonnes and a forest cover that accounts for a fourth of India's entire forest area.[89]

The writer suggests that one way to integrate eastern South Asia is an Asian Highway built by reviving the historic Stillwell Road, a British-created link between India and Myanmar. The road begins in the Indian state of Assam, and passes through India's Arunachal Pradesh and upper Myanmar's Kachin state, before ending in China's Yunnan province. With road links existing between Myanmar and Thailand's Chiang Mai province, "it would not be impossible to actually drive from India through China to Singapore".[90]

Even less-important road links are important symbolically. Welcoming participants of the ASEAN-India car rally to Singapore in December 2004, then Prime Minister Goh Chok Tong commended them for having come a long way, "both physically and metaphorically". They had travelled 8,000 kilometres from Guwahati in Assam, through Myanmar, Thailand, Laos, Vietnam, Cambodia and Malaysia, before arriving in Singapore. In a metaphorical sense, they had come a long way because their journey had required not only skills but grit and determination. "In this, you reminded us of the ancient journeys undertaken by Indian voyagers to Southeast Asia. Looking back into history, one can see the changing interests shown by India in this part of the world." The drivers had made a political point as well. Goh declared: "This Rally has broken the psychological barrier that India is a distant land, separated from Southeast Asia by the Bay of Bengal and the Indian Ocean. By traversing the heartland of continental Southeast Asia, this Rally is a symbolic demonstration of what Prime Minister Dr Manmohan Singh has aptly called the 'essential oneness' of India and Southeast Asia."[91]

That concept has important uses. In an interesting article, C. Raja Mohan calls on the Government of India's eastern state of West Bengal to restore its capital, Kolkata's standing as the "hub of economic activity in a region that covers parts of the subcontinent, China, Myanmar and Southeast Asia". This effort, he recognizes, necessarily would involve "greater activism" by West Bengal in shaping India's foreign policy. "Purists will raise their eyebrows at the suggestion of a foreign policy for Kolkata," he writes. "But for all the claims to monopoly from national governments on foreign policy making, interests of states — especially those on the borders — have always shaped diplomacy over the centuries. In India, too, politics in Tamil Nadu has always coloured the national policy towards Sri Lanka. Similarly political classes in Uttar Pradesh and Bihar have long had influence on India's Nepal policy." In this context, Raja Mohan notes that West Bengal shares a long border with Bangladesh and provides key trade and transport links to Nepal and Bhutan, and once was the natural outlet for goods and people from western China, including Tibet. West Bengal today should take the initiative in economic and cultural diplomacy to advance India's Look East policy.[92] Here, again, Panikkar's warning against adopting a purely Delhi-centric view of the contours and the possibilities of India's neighbourhood comes to mind.

Another avenue of India's entry to Southeast Asia is the Mekong-Ganga Cooperation (MGC) initiative, launched in Vientiane in 2002 by India, Thailand, Vietnam, Laos, Cambodia and Myanmar to increase cooperation in tourism, culture and education. "The initiative was designed to define regions in the new global economy, while keeping their native identity and character intact."[93] It overlaps with China's Kunming Initiative, whose members include China, Myanmar, Bangladesh and India and which seeks to create direct commercial, economic and cultural links in the subregion.

One problem afflicting the MGC and the Kunming Initiative is that they are seen in competitive terms, "as parallel Indian and Chinese attempts to increase their respective influence in the Indo-China region", and the fear of changing the *status quo* prevents New Delhi and Beijing from "exploring possibilities for mutual economic development that can act as a confidence-building measure along the border".[94] However, Devare believes that an improvement in overall bilateral relations will reduce their apprehensions about each other's interests in the subregion.[95] Faizal Yahya, too, thinks that India's engagement of ASEAN's riparian states along the Mekong River — Cambodia, Laos, Myanmar, Thailand — serves to more than merely counteract China's influence on the region. New Delhi's presence in Southeast Asia provides a "balanced profile of engagement" with the region, with the major Asian powers having "a significant economic stake in its well-being".[96]

SINGAPORE

Goh Chok Tong has a neat metaphorical description of Singapore's position between China and India. "We see Singapore as being lifted by these two economies. I visualize ASEAN as a fuselage of a jumbo plane with China as one wing, and India the other wing. If both wings take off, ASEAN as the fuselage will also be lifted. Singapore is part of this fuselage."[97] He elaborates on the metaphor, drawing attention to Singapore's central location by noting that Northeast Asia, Southeast Asia and India all are within a seven-hour flight radius of Changi Airport.[98] Thus, as India looks eastwards, Singapore should be a "useful facility", the city-state's leaders such as George Yeo believe. "After all, Singapore was founded by the British East India Company for the China trade of an earlier era. From 1819 to 1867, Singapore was directly governed from Calcutta. Our legal and administrative systems are very much derived from the Raj in India. Our re-engagement of India is reviving all those earlier links."[99] Singapore does not want to be as close to India as Hong Kong is to China, but Beijing's FTA links with ASEAN countries do not mean that other countries should be excluded: "Strategically, Singapore is completely promiscuous. The Chinese understand that and so they have not asked for a special place."[100] Instead, the reality is that South Asia and East Asia are no longer two distinct strategic regions. According to Goh, "India's rise compels us to look at our environment in new ways. It will be increasingly less tenable to regard South Asia and East Asia as distinct strategic theatres interacting only at the margins." What this means also is that as China and India grow, "they will inevitably loom larger on each other's radar screens. Economic growth will give Beijing and New Delhi the resources to pursue wider strategic interests across the Asian continent". Goh asks: "How do we now fold a growing South Asia and East Asia into one equation?" He notes that, already, new experiments in regional organizations and processes — such as the Asia Cooperation Dialogue, the Indian Ocean Rim Initiative, the Bay of Bengal Community and BIMSTEC — are "challenging traditional notions of geography".[101]

Singapore's rejection of the notion that South Asia and East Asia are two distinct strategic regions and its desire to fold them into one equation signal a rejection as well of the idea that Southeast Asia, the region lying in between those regions, is a theatre that belongs exclusively to any sphere of influence, Sinic or Indic. However, given that India's engagement of Southeast Asia came after China's engagement, and trails it considerably, such assertions of the region's strategic autonomy could be read as a message to Beijing not to seek to exclude New Delhi from Southeast Asia's political and security calculi.

Singapore's links with India have grown, exemplified by the signing of the Comprehensive Economic Cooperation Agreement in 2005 against a backdrop of high-level political visits over the years. Singapore's Government-Linked Corporations and private-sector companies have invested in a wide variety of projects in India, such as logistics, electronics, software, health services, construction, industrial parks and other real-estate-linked projects. Several Multi-National Corporations are routing their investments in India through their Singapore subsidiaries. Moreover, international investment banks, and chartered accountancy and management consultancy firms have made Singapore their regional headquarters to service the Indian market. Task forces have been set up to facilitate general economic cooperation and cooperation in information technology. Seeing Singapore as a gateway to the Asia-Pacific, many Indian companies, mainly trading and software firms, have set up joint ventures and subsidiaries in the city-state to promote their activities in the region. Air India, Indian Airlines, public-sector banks and insurance companies have branches in Singapore.[102] Politically, New Delhi acknowledges that Singapore has played "a leading role" in ensuring India's inclusion in ASEAN, first as sectoral dialogue partner and then as full dialogue partner, which in turn has ensured India's membership of the ARF. Singapore also has supported India's participation in the APEC Working Groups and India's candidature in other multilateral fora, including UN organizations.[103]

To Mark Hong, "Singapore appreciates the balancing role that India can play with the other great Powers in Southeast Asia. India, on its part, appreciates the economic role that Singapore can play in its development". India is a nuclear-armed economic giant, an IT power that also is a regional power with legitimate interests in Southeast Asia.[104] Singapore's awareness of India's potential is apparent in the widening realm of security ties, as Manjeet Singh Pardesi shows.[105] Since 1991, naval ships from Singapore regularly have visited Port Blair in the Andamans and since 1996 also have visited Vishakhapatnam. As for the Indian Navy, it has conducted its largest number of joint naval exercises with Singapore, from search and rescue to anti-piracy and anti-submarine warfare. The two navies, which traditionally have exercised in the Indian Ocean Region, including the Arabian Sea and the Bay of Bengal, have extended their bilateral activities to the South China Sea as well. They have interacted in several multilateral exercises, too. These activities demonstrate the stakes that the city-state and India have in protecting their common commercial sea-lanes, combating piracy, choking off the narcotics trade, curbing gun-running, and preventing maritime terrorism. Then, in 2004, India granted Singapore's air force and army training facilities on its soil. "This was a significant step for India, which has traditionally avoided foreign military presence of any kind on its soil." In October 2004, Singapore and India held their inaugural bilateral exercise, named SINDEX 04, in central India. There is speculation that "India might seek access to naval logistics/access facilities in Singapore as a quid pro quo for granting Singapore training rights on its soil", Pardesi believes.

What is not hypothetical is that since 9/11, the two countries have shared intelligence on security and terrorism-related issues. "India's growing security cooperation with the US and the sheer number of joint Indo-US military exercises have been viewed positively by Singapore." Singapore is open to the idea of joint patrols with the Indian, American, and other regional navies in the Strait of Malacca.

K. Kesavapany, a distinguished Singapore diplomat, argues that one way in which Singapore could fit into rising India's plans would be strategic. "India has *de facto* inherited the British security role" stretching from Aden to Singapore. It makes sense, therefore, for India, Singapore and other littoral states to cooperate against piracy and possible maritime terrorism in Southeast Asia.[106]

Indeed, the American dimension of this cooperation cannot be discounted. Washington has identified Malaysia, the Philippines, Thailand and Indonesia as classic seam states, with Singapore and Vietnam "implicated by geographical proximity and circumstances". "The former four states have been specifically singled out for attention on the ostensible basis that they — some more than others — face daunting challenges managing cohesively fragile societies, separatism, and economic difficulties, and policing remote interiors and extensive maritime borders. The significance of the recent US military activism in this region should be viewed against this backdrop."[107] Of course, an India-Singapore-U.S. security triangle would be problematic if the seam states saw it as a threat to them, and it would not be in Singapore's interests to participate in that relationship. But nothing in that relationship threatens other countries inherently. After all, encouraged by the U.S. Administration, India reportedly was sounded out informally by the littoral states on the possibility of its help in patrolling the Malacca Strait during the ARF summit in 2004.[108] A formal request did not materialize, but the fact that an informal sounding was made indicates a degree of regional comfort with an Indian role in ensuring maritime security.

Kesavapany looks beyond purely strategic issues to argue that India's engagement with the region to its east could herald a new era for both South Asia's pre-eminent power and Southeast Asia. India, a "deeply *status quo* country" that needs international peace and stability for its domestic economic development, betted on three "losing horses" in the 1970s: the Soviet Union, autarchy and military might. Calling on New Delhi to keep faith with Nehru's belief that a Sino-Indian *détente* would help stabilize Asia, he says that the three horses that India is betting on now — China, integration with the rest of Asia under the Look East policy, and information technology — are candidates for victory.[109]

Singapore, positioned between China and India, has a
stake in that victory.

NOTES

1 Kripa Sridharan, "Transcending the Region: Singapore's India
   Policy", in N.N. Vohra, ed., *Emerging Asia: Challenges for India
   and Singapore* (New Delhi: India International Centre and
   Manohar 2003), p. 20.
2 J.N. Dixit, "Courting South East Asia", siliconindia.com,
   11 November 2002, <siliconindia.com/daily_byte/index.
   asp?bno=409>.
3 Satu P. Limaye, "2004: A Year of Living Actively", *Comparative
   Connections*, Pacific Forum CSIS, <www.csis.org/pacfor/cc/
   0404Qoa.html>.
4 Kripa Sridharan, "Regional Perceptions of India", in Frederic
   Grare and Amitabh Mattoo, eds., *India and ASEAN: The Politics
   of India's Look East Policy* (New Delhi and Singapore: Manohar,
   Centre De Sciences Humaines, Centre for the Study of National
   Security Policy and the Institute of Southeast Asian Studies,
   2001), p. 85.
5 J.N. Dixit, *Makers of India's Foreign Policy: Raja Ram Mohun
   Roy to Yashwant Sinha*, p. 12.
6 Bilveer Singh, *The Soviet Union in Singapore's Foreign Policy: An
   Analysis* (Kuala Lumpur: Institute of Strategic and International
   Studies, 1990), p. 20.
7 Ann Scott Tyson, "Ability to Wage 'Long War' Is Key To
   Pentagon Plan", *Washington Post*, 4 February 2006.
8 Ibid.
9 Ibid.
10 Teresita C. Schaffer and Pramit Mitra, "India as a global
   power?", *Deutsche Bank Research*, 16 December 2005, p. 9.
11 For a convincing account of this position, see B.M. Jain,
   India-China Relations: Issues, Trends and Emerging Scenarios
   (Hong Kong: University of Hong Kong, Centre of Asian
   Studies, China India Project, Occasional Paper No. 1, 2003),
   <www.hku.hk/cas/pub/Occasional1_bmjain.pdf>.
12 Address by Defence Minister Pranab Mukherjee at the
   Carnegie Endowment for International Peace, Washington
   DC, on India's strategic perspectives, 27 June 2005,

<www.carnegieendowment.org/files/Mukherjee_Speech_06-27-051.pdf>.

13 Amartya Sen, "India and the Bomb", in *The Argumentative Indian: Writings on Indian History, Culture and Identity* (London: Allen Lane, 2005), p. 264.

14 Baldev Raj Nayar and T.V. Paul, *India in the World Order: Searching for Major-Power Status* (Cambridge: Cambridge University Press, 2003), p. 3.

15 C. Raja Mohan, *Crossing the Rubicon: The Shaping of India's New Foreign Policy*, p. 89.

16 Ibid., pp. 150–51.

17 Ibid., p. 151.

18 Ibid., p. 146.

19 Ibid., p. 148.

20 Venu Rajamony, "India-China-U.S. Triangle: A 'Soft' Balance of Power System in the Making" (Washington: Centre for Strategic and International Studies, March 2002), <www.csis.org/saprog/venu.pdf>.

21 Mohammed Ayoob, "Potential Partners: India and the United States", *Asia Pacific Issues*, No. 42 (Honolulu: East-West Centre, December 1999), p. 5.

22 Ibid., p. 6.

23 Ibid.

24 Ibid., p. 9.

25 Ibid., p. 7.

26 Federico Bordonaro, "Great and Medium Powers in the Age of Unipolarity", *Power and Interest News Report*, 11 May 2005, <www.pinr.com/report.php?ac=view_report&report_id=297>.

27 Zalmay Khalilzad et al., *The United States and Asia: Toward a New U.S. Strategy and Force Posture* (Santa Monica, California: RAND, 2001), p. 47.

28 Ashley J. Tellis, *India As A New Global Power: An Action Agenda For The United States* (Washington: Carnegie Endowment for International Peace, 2005), pp. 40–43.

29 Stephen J. Blank, *Natural Allies? Regional Security in Asia and Prospects for Indo-American Strategic Cooperation* (Carlisle, PA: Strategic Studies Institute, U.S. Army War College, September 2005), p. 17.

30 Ibid., p. 15.

31 C. Raja Mohan, op. cit., p. 110.

32 Ibid., p. xi.
33 John W. Garver, *The China-India-U.S. Triangle: Strategic Relations in the Post-Cold War Era*, NBR Analysis 13, no. 5 (Seattle, Washington: The National Bureau of Asian Research, October 2002), p. 7.
34 Tellis, op. cit., p. 5.
35 "Joint Statement Between President George W. Bush and Prime Minister Manmohan Singh", (Washington, D.C.: The White House, 18 July 2005), <www.whitehouse.gov/news/releases/2005/07/print/20050718-6.html>.
36 Jim VandeHei and Dafna Linzer, "U.S., India Reach Deal On Nuclear Cooperation", *The Washington Post*, 3 March 2006, <www.washingtonpost.com/wp-dyn/content/article/2006/03/02/AR2006030200183_pf.html>.
37 Ibid.
38 Keith Jones, "Bush secures nuclear accord with India", World Socialist Web Site, 3 March 2006, <www.wsws.org/articles/2006/mar2006/indi-m03.shtml>.
39 VandeHei and Linzer, op. cit.
40 Strobe Talbott, *Engaging India: Diplomacy, Democracy, and the Bomb*, revised edition, (Washington: Brookings Institution Press, 2006), p. 5.
41 Pratap Bhanu Mehta, "Nuclear Pact Launches India Into Uncharted Waters", *YaleGlobal*, 7 March 2006, <yaleglobal.yale.edu/display.article?id=7085>.
42 Jones, op. cit.
43 Amit Gupta, *The U.S.-India Relationship: Strategic Partnership or Complementary Interests?* (Carlisle, PA: Strategic Studies Institute, U.S. Army War College, February 2005), p. 19.
44 Ibid., pp. 17–18.
45 Ibid., p. 18.
46 Ibid.
47 Ibid., pp. 18–19.
48 Ibid., p. 20.
49 Stephen P. Cohen, *India: Emerging Power*, op. cit.
50 Lin Liang Guang, "India's Role In South Asia: A Chinese Perspective", in Vernon L.B. Mendis, ed., *India's Role in South Asia* (Colombo: Bandaranaike Centre for International Studies, 1992), p. 45.
51 Quoted in G.V. Ambekar and V.D. Divekar, eds., *Documents on China's Relations with South and Southeast Asia, 1949–1962* (New Delhi: Oxford, 1964), cited in Jain, op. cit.

52 Brahma Chellaney, "Beijing's historical fantasies", *International Herald Tribune*, 12 December 2005.
53 Zhao Huanxin, "Historic Sino-Indian trade plan endorsed", *China Daily*, 12 April 2005.
54 Parwini Zora and Niall Green, "China and India manoeuvre to secure energy supplies", World Socialist Web Site, 31 January 2006, <www.wsws.org/articles/2006/jan2006/indi-j31_prn.shtml>.
55 Tarique Niazi, "Sino-Indian Rivalry", China Brief, 16 February 2006, <www.ocnus.net/artman/publish/article_22760.shtml#top>.
56 Mohan Malik, "The East Asia Summit: More Discord than Accord", *YaleGlobal*, 20 December 2005, <http://yaleglobal.yale.edu/article.print?id=6645>.
57 Ibid.
58 Ibid.
59 Raja Mohan, op. cit., p. 170.
60 K.M. Panikkar, *India and the Indian Ocean: An Essay on the Influence of Sea Power on Indian History*, second edition, 1961, first Indian reprint [Bombay: George Allen & Unwin (India), 1971], pp. 83–85.
61 John W. Garver, *Protracted Contest: Sino-Indian Rivalry in the Twentieth Century* (Seattle and London: University of Washington Press, 2001), p. 275.
62 Sudhir Devare, *India & Southeast Asia: Towards Security Convergence* (Singapore: Institute of Southeast Asian Studies, 2006), pp. 94–95.
63 Raja Mohan, op. cit., pp. 204–9.
64 Ibid., p. 209.
65 Ibid., p. 211.
66 <www.whitehouse.gov/nsc/nss8.html>.
67 "Indian Maritime Doctrine Revisited", India Defence Consultants, <www.indiadefence.com/indoctrine.htm>.
68 Devare, op. cit., pp. 117–18.
69 Ibid., pp. 114–15.
70 Rahul Bedi, "A new doctrine for the Navy", *Frontline* 21, issue 14, 3–16 July 2004, <www.hinduonnet.com/fline/fl2114/stories/20040716002104600.htm>.
71 Ibid.
72 Gurpreet S. Khurana, "Cooperation Among Maritime Security Forces: Imperatives for India and Southeast Asia", *Strategic Analysis* 29, no. 2 (April–June 2005): p. 305.
73 Bedi, op. cit.

74 Khurana, op. cit., p. 305.
75 Bedi, op. cit.
76 Devare, op. cit., p. 100.
77 Ravi Sharma, "A base for a blue-water navy", *Frontline* 22, issue 11, 21 May–3 June 2005, <www.hinduonnet.com/fline/fl2211/stories/20050603002809000.htm>.
78 Sarath Kumara, "New Delhi presses ahead with plans for an Indian 'Suez Canal'", World Socialist Web Site, <www.wsws.org/articles/2005/dec2005/inda-d14.shtml>.
79 Ibid.
80 Ibid.
81 "Iran: Chabahar port project will go on", *Persian Journal*, 21 February 2006, <www.iranian.ws/iran_news/publish/article_13457.shtml>.
82 Tarique Niazi, "Gwadar: China's Naval Outpost on the Indian Ocean", *China Brief* (The Jamestown Foundation, 28 February 2005), <www.asianresearch.org/articles/2528.html>.
83 Ibid.
84 Devare, op. cit., p. 72.
85 Ibid., p. 211.
86 Ibid., p. 210.
87 Ibid., pp. 99–112.
88 R.V.R. Murthy, "India's Security Concerns in the Bay of Bengal: With special reference to A&N Islands", *Dialogue* 7, no. 1 (July–September 2005), <http://www.asthabharati.org/Dia_July05/murthy%20.htm>.
89 Shehla Raza Hasan "The paradox of eastern South Asia", *Asia Times*, 19 March 2003, <www.atimes.com/atimes/South_Asia/EC19Df02.html>.
90 Ibid.
91 <www.embassyofindia.com/01_IndiaNewsJanuary2005/page2.html>.
92 C. Raja Mohan, "A foreign policy for Kolkata", *The Indian Express*, 23 August 2005.
93 Chandan Irom, "Whatever happened to India's Look East Policy? The Mekong-Ganga Cooperation", Manipur Online, 19 January 2002, <www.manipuronline.com/Features/January2002/mekongganga19.htm>.
94 Sonika Gupta, "India and China: Cooperative Border Development", *ORF Strategic Trends* II, issue 47 (New Delhi: Observer Research Foundation, 29 November 2004), <www.observerindia.com/strategic/st041129.htm>.
95 Devare, op. cit., p. 142.

96 Faizal Yahya, "India and Southeast Asia: Revisited", *Contemporary Southeast Asia* 25, no. 1 (April 2003), p. 99.
97 Timothy Ong, "No slowing down", *AsiaInc*, November 2004, <www.asia-inc.com/November04/QA_nov.htm>.
98 Address by Senior Minister Goh Chok Tong at the welcome reception of Meetings, Incentives, Conferences and Exhibitions (MICE) Asia, 24 July 2005, <app.stb.com.sg/asp/common/print.asp?id=3404&type=2>.
99 Speech by George Yeo, Minister for Trade and Industry, at the Economic Society of Singapore Dinner, 28 June 2004, <app.sprinter.gov.sg/data/pr/2004062804.htm>.
100 George Yeo at the World Economic Forum's India Economic Summit 2002, <www.weforum.org/site/knowledgenavigator.nsf/Content/_S7574?open&country_id=>.
101 Senor Minister Goh Chok Tong, "Reconceptualizing East Asia", Speech at the official launch of the Institute of South Asian Studies, 27 January 2005, <www.bridgesingapore.com/externalreports/SPEECH%20BY%20MR%20GOH%20CHOK%20TONG.pdf>.
102 "Relations between India and Singapore — A Brief Overview", The High Commission of India in Singapore," <www.embassyofindia.com/indsg_econ.htm>.
103 Ibid.
104 Mark Hong, "India-Singapore Relations: A Brief Overview", *Viewpoints* (Singapore: Institute of Southeast Asian Studies, October 2003), pp. 2–3, <www.iseas.edu.sg/viewpoint/mhoct03.pdf>.
105 Manjeet S. Pardesi, "Deepening Singapore-India Strategic Ties", *IDSS Commentaries*, 13/2005 (Singapore: Institute of Defence and Strategic Studies, 22 March 2005), pp. 2–3, <www.ntu.edu.sg/IDSS/publications/Perspective/IDSS132005.pdf>.
106 K. Kesavapany, *India's Tryst With Asia*, op. cit., p. 48.
107 Joey Long, "The Pentagon's Strategy Toward Southeast Asia: Bolstering the States along the Seams", *IDSS Commentaries*, 12/2005 (Singapore: Institute of Defence and Strategic Studies, 16 March 2005), p. 2, <www.ntu.edu.sg/idss/publications/Perspective/IDSS122005.pdf>.
108 Raakhee Suryaprakash, "Securing the Straits — Some New Moves", South Asia Analysis Group, Paper No. 1402, 3 June 2005, p. 3, <www.saag.org/papers15/paper1402.html>.
109 Kesavapany, op. cit., p. 77.

CHAPTER XII

CONCLUSION

Singapore is an "exceptional state" because its vulnerability — stemming from its miniscule size, its predominantly ethnic-Chinese population which traditionally has engaged in the economic activities of an *entrepôt*, and a geography that wedges it between two larger neighbours[1] — nevertheless is paired with an astounding degree of economic success.[2] It perhaps is this exceptional combination of vulnerability and excellence that also has made Singapore "the classic anticipatory state", the energies of whose leaders are aimed at "positioning Singapore to enable it to take advantage of future developments while avoiding dangerous currents".[3] Against the backdrop of a maritime history within which Raffles had created the essential economic features of contemporary Singapore, it reappeared as a trading state after World War II by drawing on the opportunities opened up by the San Francisco System that ensured the security of non-communist Pacific Asian states through economic growth. Singapore went on to engage India and China in the context of a Cold War in which its early closeness to India was replaced by a movement towards China that reflected the effect of the Vietnamese invasion and occupation of Cambodia on Singapore's security perceptions. After the end of the Cold War, Singapore engaged both Asian powers through a series of economic and political means, both bilateral and multilateral. As America's Long War on Terror begins, the least that can be said is that Singapore is entrenching its relations with India within a larger framework being established by the United States, but without giving up on its engagement of China, whose containment it remains opposed to.

Singapore's engagement of China reflects Randall L. Schweller's description of the term to mean the use of non-coercive means to blunt the non-*status quo* aspects of a rising power's behaviour so that it employs its growing power in ways that are consistent with peaceful change. To that end, soft-authoritarian Singapore has played an important interlocutory role for China in its relations with the West over crucial issues such as the Tiananmen Square killings and Hong Kong's return to the Chinese mainland. The Asian Values debate demonstrated the degree of congruence between the ideological outlook of Singapore and that of Beijing. Singapore's measured closeness to China has been apparent, too, in ASEAN, an essential platform for China's relations with Southeast Asia. Notwithstanding Singapore's inability to replicate its political and economic system in the Suzhou Industrial Park, it continued to engage China, and its relations with Taiwan, whose independence it does not support, did not detract from that endeavour.

Has Singapore's engagement of China been successful? It would be ridiculous to claim — and no such claim is made by the Singapore leadership — that a city-state could oblige a power of the size, history and potential of China to abide by the rules of the international order: No country could force Beijing to do so. However, it would not be immodest to claim that the Republic has facilitated the entry of the People's Republic into a global order presided over by the advanced capitalist democracies. China's entry has been complicated by a range of issues from trade disputes to human rights and Taiwan. At crucial points, Singapore's interlocutory role has offered the Chinese a partnership that they could trust, not because Singapore is a Chinese-majority state but because its experience of dealing with the realities of the international order, while retaining the essential features of its political and cultural autonomy, would be useful for China. That interlocutory role no longer is in evidence for the simple reason that Beijing does not need such a partner any more. An engagement policy could be said to be successful when it does not have to be termed that any more. So it is for Singapore's engagement of China.

Engaging India is at once simpler and full of possibilities. It is simpler because there is no need for Singapore to invest political energy in playing an interlocutory role for India in its relations with the West: India's political system makes such an effort unnecessary. It is full of possibilities because Singapore is an essential part of India's Look East policy, one in which economic, political and security considerations enmesh to create a new and powerful actor in Southeast Asian affairs. Singapore has stood out for its determination to ensure that New Delhi is not excluded from the evolving pattern of Southeast Asian relations. Relations never have been better between the city-state and the power that lends its name to the Indian Ocean. Whether and how India takes up the challenge of playing a new and definitive role from Aden to Singapore will have a strong bearing on Singapore's position in the new regional order that folds South Asia and East Asia into a single security region.

Looking ahead, Singapore's engagement of China can be expected to move on from interlocution to a multi-faceted partnership that is comparable to its evolving relations with India.[4] Sino-Indian relations themselves no doubt will have an impact on how Singapore's ties with the two Asian giants develop. If Sino-Indian political and strategic relations strengthen, building on the momentum generated by growing trade and investment, Singapore can hope to benefit from the improving climate that would be created in Asia at large. But if China and India draw apart in an era marked by their simultaneous rise as great powers, Singapore, like other nations in the neighbourhood, would be faced with difficult choices.

However, the classic anticipatory state no doubt would draw up its response to that eventuality well on time.

NOTES

1   Michael Leifer, *Singapore's Foreign Policy: Coping with Vulnerability*, op. cit., p. 1.
2   Ibid., p. 12.
3   Yuen Foong Khong, "Singapore: A time for economic and political engagement" in Alastair Iain Johnston and Robert S. Ross, eds., *Engaging China: The Management of an Emerging Power*, op. cit., p. 113.

4   China's and India's quest for energy security could see Singapore, an oil-refining and oil-storage hub that also is important to energy transport, continuing to matter vitally to the Asian giants.

BIBLIOGRAPHY

"Background Note: China". U.S. Department of State, Bureau of East Asian and Pacific Affairs, March 2005. <www.state.gov/ r/pa/ei/bgn/18902.htm>.

"China issues white paper on national defence". *People's Daily Online* <english.people.com.cn/200412/27/eng20041227_ 168787.html>.

"Indian Maritime Doctrine Revisited", India Defence Consultants, <www.indiadefence.com/indoctrine.htm>.

"Iran: Chabahar port project will go on". *Persian Journal*, 21 February 2006, <www.iranian.ws/iran_news/publish/ article_13457.shtml>.

"Joint Statement Between President George W. Bush and Prime Minister Manmohan Singh". Washington, D.C.: The White House, 18 July 2005. <www.whitehouse.gov/news/releases/ 2005/07/print/20050718-6.html>.

"Tiananmen Square, 1989: The Declassified History". <www.gwu.edu/~nsarchiv/NSAEBB/NSAEBB16/ documents/>.

"To what extent does the Suzhou Industrial Park project reflect both the potential and pitfalls of the Singapore-China connection?". <www.comp.nus.edu.sg/~malliped/SIP.pdf>.

Acharya, Amitav. *Constructing a Security Community in Southeast Asia.* Oxford: Routledge, 2001.

———. *Seeking Security in the Dragon's Shadow: China and Southeast Asia in the Emerging Asian Order.* Singapore: Institute of Defence and Strategic Studies, Working Paper No. 44, March 2003.

———. *The Quest for Identity: International Relations of Southeast Asia.* Singapore: Oxford University Press, 2000.

———. "Will Asia's Past Be Its Future?" *International Security* 28, no. 3 (Winter 2003/04): 149–64.

Alagappa, Muthiah. "Constructing Security Order in Asia: Conceptions and Issues". In *Asian Security Order: Instrumental and Normative Features,* edited by Muthiah Alagappa. Stanford: Stanford University Press, 2003.

Ayoob, Mohammed. "Potential Partners: India and the United States". *Asia Pacific Issues,* No. 42, Honolulu: East-West Centre, December 1999.

———. *India and Southeast Asia: Indian Perceptions and Policies.* London and New York: Routledge, published under the auspices of the Institute of Southeast Asian Studies, Singapore, 1990.

Baviera, Aileen S.P. "The South China Sea Disputes after the 2002 Declaration: Beyond Confidence-Building". In *ASEAN-China Relations: Realities and Prospects,* edited by Saw Swee-Hock, Sheng Lijun and Chin Kin Wah. Singapore: Institute of Southeast Asian Studies, 2005.

Bedi, Rahul. "A new doctrine for the Navy". *Frontline* 21, issue 14, 3–16 July 2004, <www.hinduonnet.com/fline/fl2114/stories/20040716002104600.htm>.

Blank, Stephen J. *Natural Allies? Regional Security in Asia and Prospects for Indo-American Strategic Cooperation.* Carlisle, PA: Strategic Studies Institute, U.S. Army War College, September 2005.

Bordonaro, Federico. "Great and Medium Powers in the Age of Unipolarity". *Power and Interest News Report,* 11 May 2005, <www.pinr.com/report.php?ac=view_report&report_id=297>.

Borschberg, Peter. "Hugo Grotius, East India Trade and the King of Johor". *Journal of Southeast Asian Studies* 30, no. 2 (September 1999): 225–48.

Boyd, Alan. "US reorganizes its military might". *Asia Times,* 21 November 2003.

Bozeman, Adda B. *Politics and Culture in International History.* Princeton: Princeton University Press, 1960.

Bull, Hedley. *The Anarchical Society: A Study of Order in World Politics.* Houndmills and London: Macmillan, 1977.

Burstein, Daniel and Arne De Keijzer. *Big Dragon China's Future: What It Means for Business, the Economy, and the Global Order.* New York: Simon & Schuster, 1998.

Calder, Kent E. "Securing security through prosperity: the San Francisco System in comparative perspective". *Pacific Review* 17, no. 1 (March 2004): 135–57.

Chan, Gerald. *Chinese Perspectives on International Relations: A Framework for Analysis.* Houndmills and New York: Macmillan Press and St. Martin's Press, 1999.

Chang Pao-min. *Kampuchea Between China and Vietnam.* Singapore: Singapore University Press, 1985.

Chang, Parris H. "Lessons From the 1996 Taiwan Strait Crisis for the U.S., Japan and Taiwan". Harvard Studies on Taiwan: Papers of the Taiwan Studies Workshop 3 (2000). <www.fas.harvard.edu/~fairbank/tsw/chang.html>.

Chang Yun-ping. "Upgrade defence abilities: Japanese expert". *Taipei Times*, 6 November 2005.

Chan Heng Chee, "Politics in an Administrative State: Where has the Politics Gone?" Singapore: University of Singapore, Department of Political Science, 1975.

———. "China and Asean: A Growing Relationship". A speech delivered at the Asia Society Texas Annual Ambassadors' Forum and Corporate Conference, Houston, 3 February 2006, <app.mfa.gov.sg/pr/read_content.asp?View,4416,>.

Chan, Steve. "Is There Power Transition Between the U.S. and China? The Different Faces of National Power". *Asian Survey* 45, issue 5: 687–701.

Chellaney, Brahma. "Beijing's historical fantasies". *International Herald Tribune*, 12 December 2005.

Chia Siow Yue. "Singapore: Advanced Production Base and Smart Hub of the Electronics Industry". In *Multinationals and East Asian Integration*, edited by W. Dobson and Chia Siow Yue. Ottawa and Singapore: International Development Research Centre and the Institute of Southeast Asian Studies, 1997.

China Daily. "Singapore says it opposes Taiwan independence", 12 July 2004.

Chin Kin Wah. "A New Phase in Singapore's Relations with China".

In *ASEAN and China: An Evolving Relationship*, edited by Joyce K. Kallgren et al. Berkeley: University of California, Institute of East Asian Studies, 1988.

Chiu Hungdah. *Hong Kong's Transition to 1997: Background, Problems and Prospects (With Documents)*. Occasional Papers/Reprint Series in Contemporary Asian Studies, Number 5 — 1993 (118). Baltimore: University of Maryland, School of Law.

Chi Wang. "Some Historical Reflections on Chinese Economic Reforms: From Wang Mang to Deng Xiaoping, 9 A.D. to the Present". In *Assessment of China into the 21st Century*, edited by A.M. Canyon. New York: Nova Science Publishers, Inc., 1997.

Chomsky, Noam. "From Central America to Iraq". *Khaleej Times*, 6 August 2004.

Chong, Alan. "Singaporean Foreign Policy and the Asian Values Debate, 1992–2000: Reflections on an Experiment in Soft Power". *Pacific Review* 17, no. 1 (March 2004): 95–133.

Christopher, Warren. "Democracy and Human Rights: Where America Stands". Remarks delivered by US Secretary of State Warren Christopher. World Conference on Human Rights, 14 June 1993, Vienna, Austria. Office of the Spokesman, US Department of State, <dosfan.lib.uic.edu/ERC/briefing/dossec/1993/9306/930614dossec.html>

Chua Beng-Huat. *Communitarian Ideology and Democracy in Singapore*. London and New York: Routledge, 1995.

Chung Kwong Yuen. "Leninism, Asian Culture and Singapore". *Asian Profile* 27, no. 3 (June 1999): 217–32.

Cienciala, Anna M. *The Rise and Fall of Communist Nations 1917–1994*. Lawrence, Kansas: University of Kansas, 1996), <http://raven.cc.ku.edu/~eceurope/communistnations since1917/ch10.html>.

Clark, Gregory. "The Tiananmen Square massacre myth". *Japan Times*, 15 September 2004.

Coedes, G. *The Indianized States of Southeast Asia*. Edited by Walter F. Vella and translated by Susan Brown Cowing. Honolulu: University Press of Hawaii, 1968.

Cohen, Stephen P. *India: Emerging Power*. Washington, D.C.: Brookings Institution Press, 2001.

Curzon, George. *The Place of India in the Empire: Being an Address before the Philosophical Institute of Edinburgh on October 19, 1909*. Elibron Classics, 2003, replica of 1909 edition by John Murray, London.

Da Wei Sun Ru. "Trend in Bush's China Strategy Adjustment". *Contemporary International Relations* 15, no. 11 (November 2005): 1–13.

Devare, Sudhir. *India & Southeast Asia: Towards Security Convergence.* Singapore: Institute of Southeast Asian Studies, 2006.

Dillon, Dana and John J. Tkacik, Jr. "China's Quest for Asia". *Policy Review*, No. 134 (December 2005 and January 2006). Stanford: Hoover Institution. <www.policyreview.org/134/dillon.html>.

———. "China's Quest for Asia". *Policy Review*, No. 134, December 2005 and January 2006 (Stanford: Hoover Institition), <www.policyreview.org/134/dillon.html>.

———. "China and ASEAN: Endangered American Primacy in Southeast Asia". *Backgrounder*, No. 1886, 19 October 2005. Washington, DC: The Heritage Foundation.

Dixit, J.N. "Courting South East Asia", siliconindia.com, 11 November 2002, <siliconindia.com/daily_byte/index.asp?bno=409>.

———. *Makers of India's Foreign Policy: Raja Ram Mohun Roy to Yashwant Sinha.* New Delhi: HarperCollins Publishers India and The India Today Group, 2004.

Draguhn, Werner . "The Indochina Conflict and the Positions of the Countries Involved". *Contemporary Southeast Asia* 5, no. 1 (June 1983): 95–116.

Elleman, Bruce. "Sino-Soviet Relations and the February 1979 Sino-Vietnamese Conflict". <www.vietnam.ttu.edu/vietnam center/events/1996_Symposium/96papers/elleviet.htm>.

Emmers, Ralf. *Maritime Disputes in the South China Sea: Strategic and Diplomatic Status Quo.* Singapore: Institute of Defence and Strategic Studies, Working Paper Series No. 87, September 2005.

Fairbank, John King, ed. *The Chinese World Order: Traditional China's Foreign Relations.* Cambridge: Harvard University Press, 1968.

Foo Choy Peng and Porter, Barry. "Suzhou: Sino-Singapore bid fails test". *South China Morning Post*, 30 June 1999.

Foot, Rosemary. "China in the ASEAN Regional Forum: Organizational Processes and Domestic Modes of Thought". *Asian Survey* 38, no. 5 (May 1998): 425–40.

Friedman, Thomas L. *The Lexus and the Olive Tree: Understanding Globalization.* New York: Farrar, Straus & Giroux, 1999.

Fukuyama, Francis. "The End of History". *The National Interest* 16 (Summer 1989): 3–18.

———. *The End of History and the Last Man.* New York: The Free Press, 1992.

Gabriel, Satya J. "Economic Liberalization in Post-Mao China: Crossing the River by Feeling for Stones", China Essay Series, Essay Number 7, October 1998, Mount Holyoke College, Department of Economics, <http://www.mtholyoke.edu/courses/sgabriel/economics/china-essays/7.html>.

Ganesan, N. *Realism and Interdependence in Singapore's Foreign Policy.* London and New York: Routledge, 2005.

Ganesan, Narayanan. "Singapore: Realist cum Trading State". In *Asian Security Practice: Material and Ideational Influences*, edited by Muthiah Alagappa. Stanford: Stanford University Press, 1998.

Garver, John W. *Protracted Contest: Sino-Indian Rivalry in the Twentieth Century.* Seattle and London: University of Washington Press, 2001.

———. *The China-India-U.S. Triangle: Strategic Relations in the Post-Cold War Era.* Seattle, Washington: National Bureau of Asian Research. *NBR Analysis* 13, no. 5, October 2002.

Gibson, William. "Disneyland with the Death Penalty". *Wired*, issue 1.04 (Sep/Oct 1993). <www.wired.com/wired/archive/1.04/gibson_pr.html>.

Goh Chok Tong. "Change and Stability in Asia". Speech at the US-ASEAN Business Council's Second Annual Leadership Dinner, Shangri-La Hotel, Singapore, 1 December 2004, <app.mfa.gov.sg/internet/press/view_press.asp?post_id=1152>.

———. "Cultural Values and Economic Performance". *Speeches '91: A Bimonthly Selection of Ministerial Speeches. Singapore:* Ministry of Information and the Arts.

———. "Reconceptualizing East Asia". Speech at the official launch of the Institute of South Asian Studies, 27 January 2005, <www.bridgesingapore.com/externalreports/SPEECH%20BY%20MR%20GOH%20CHOK%20TONG.pdf>.

———. Address at the welcome reception of Meetings, Incentives, Conferences and Exhibitions (MICE) Asia, 24 July 2005. <app.stb.com.sg/asp/common/print.asp?id=3404&type=2>.

Goh, Evelyn. "Singapore's Reaction to a Rising China: Deep Engagement and Strategic Adjustment". In *China and Southeast*

Asia: Global Changes and Regional Challenges, edited by Ho Khai Leong and Samuel C.Y. Ku. Singapore and Kaohsiung: Institute of Southeast Asian Studies and Centre for Southeast Asian Studies, National Sun Yat-sen University, Kaohsiung, Taiwan ROC, 2005.

———. "The ASEAN Regional Forum in United States East Asian strategy". *Pacific Review* 17, no. 1 (March 2004): 47–69.

———. "The Great Powers in the Asia-Pacific: Examining US-China Relations in the 'Post-Post-Cold War' Era". Talking points prepared for the China Reform Forum-IDSS meeting on Asia-Pacific Security, Beijing, 19 July 2002, <www.ntu. edu.sg/home/ISCLGoh/US-China-talking-points.pdf>.

———. *Great Powers and Southeast Asian Regional Security Strategies: Omni-Enmeshment, Balancing and Hierarchical Order*. Singapore, Institute of Defence and Strategic Studies, Working Paper No. 84, July 2005). <www.ntu.edu.sg/idss/publications/ WorkingPapers/WP84.pdf>.

———. *Meeting the China Challenge: The U.S. in Southeast Asian Regional Security Strategies*. Washington: East-West Centre, Policy Studies 16, 2005.

Goldstein, Avery. "Great Expectations: Interpreting China's Arrival". In *The Rise of China: An* International Security *Reader*, edited by Michael E. Brown et al. Cambridge, Massachusetts, and London, England: The MIT Press, 2000.

Grotius, Hugo. *De Jure Belli ac Pacis*, 1625, translated as *On the Law of War and Peace*. Available on <http://www.geocities.com/ Athens/Thebes/8098/?200524>.

———. *Mare Liberum*, translated with a revision of the Latin text of 1633 by Ralph Van Deman Magoffin, *The Freedom of the Seas, or the Right Which Belongs to the Dutch to Take Part in the East Indian Trade*. New York: Oxford University Press, 1916.

Gujral, I.K. "Aspects of India's Foreign Policy". A speech delivered at the Bandaranaike Centre for International Studies, Colombo, 20 January 1997, <www.stimson.org/southasia/?sn=sa 20020116302>.

Gupta, Amit. *The U.S.-India Relationship: Strategic Partnership or Complementary Interests?* Carlisle, PA: Strategic Studies Institute, U.S. Army War College, February 2005.

Gupta, Sonika. "India and China: Cooperative Border Development". New Delhi: Observer Research Foundation,

ORF Strategic Trends II, issue 47, 29 November 2004. <www.observerindia.com/strategic/st041129.htm>.

Haacke, Jurgen. "Michael Leifer and the balance of power". *Pacific Review* 18, no. 1 (March 2005): 43–69.

————. "Michael Leifer, the balance of power and international relations theory". In *Order and Security in Southeast Asia: Essays in Memory of Michael Leifer*, edited by Joseph Chinyong Liow and Ralf Emmers. London and New York: Routledge, 2006.

————. "The Significance of Beijing's Bilateral Relations: Looking 'Below' the Regional Level in China-ASEAN Ties". In *China and Southeast Asia: Global Changes and Regional Challenges*, edited by Ho Khai Leong and Samuel C.Y. Ku. Singapore and Kaohsiung: Institute of Southeast Asian Studies and Centre for Southeast Asian Studies, National Sun Yat-sen University, Kaohsiung, Taiwan ROC, 2005.

Han Minzhu, ed. *Cries for Democracy: Writings and Speeches from the 1989 Chinese Democracy Movement*. New Jersey: Princeton University Press, 1990.

Haq, Obaid Ul. "Foreign Policy". In *Government and Politics of Singapore*, revised edition, edited by Jon S.T. Quah et al. Singapore: Oxford University Press, 1987.

He Shengda and Sheng Lijun. "Yunnan's Greater Mekong Sub-Region Strategy". In *ASEAN-China Relations, Realities and Prospects*, edited by Saw Swee-Hock, Sheng Lijun and Chin Kin Wah. Singapore: Institute of Southeast Asian Studies, 2005.

High Commission of India in Singapore. "Relations between India and Singapore — A Brief Overview". <www.embassyof india.com/indsg_econ.htm>.

Hill, Michael. *'Asian Values' as Reverse Orientalism: The case of Singapore*. Singapore: National University of Singapore, Department of Sociology, Working Paper, No. 150, 2000.

Hong, Mark. "India-Singapore Relations: A Brief Overview". *Viewpoints*. Singapore: Institute of Southeast Asian Studies, October 2003. <www.iseas.edu.sg/viewpoint/mhoct03.pdf>.

Hore, Charlie. *The Road to Tiananmen Square*. London, Chicago and Melbourne: Bookmarks, 1991.

Huntington, Samuel. "The Clash of Civilizations?" *Foreign Affairs* 72, no. 3 (1993): 22–47.

————. *The Clash of Civilizations and the Remaking of World Order*. New York: Simon and Schuster, 1996.

Huxley, Tim. "Singapore's strategic outlook and defence policy". In *Order and Security in Southeast Asia: Essays in Memory of Michael Leifer*, edited by Joseph Chinyong Liow and Ralf Emmers. London and New York: Routledge, 2006.

Inoue Tatsuo. "Liberal Democracy and Asian Orientalism". In *The East Asian Challenge for Human Rights*, edited by Joanne R. Bauer and Daniel A. Bell. Cambridge: Cambridge University Press, 1999.

Irom, Chandan. "Whatever happened to India's Look East Policy? The Mekong-Ganga Cooperation". Manipur Online, 19 January 2002. <www.manipuronline.com/Features/January2002/mekongganga19.htm>.

Jain, B.M. *India-China Relations: Issues, Trends and Emerging Scenarios*. Hong Kong: University of Hong Kong, Centre of Asian Studies, China India Project, Occasional Paper No. 1, 2003. <www.hku.hk/cas/pub/Occasional1_bmjain.pdf>.

Jiang Zhuqing. "China: Lee's Taiwan visit damages relations". *China Daily*, 14 July 2004.

Johnston, Alastair Iain. "Is China a Status Quo Power?" *International Security* 27, no. 4 (Spring 2003): 5–56.

———. "Socialization in International Institutions: The ASEAN Way and International Relations Theory". In *International Relations Theory and the Asia-Pacific*, edited by G. John Ikenberry and Michael Mastanduno. New York: Columbia University Press, 2003.

———. *Cultural Realism: Strategic Culture and Grand Strategy in Chinese History*. Princeton: Princeton University Press, 1998.

Jones, Keith. "Bush secures nuclear accord with India". World Socialist Web Site, 3 March 2006, <www.wsws.org/articles/2006/mar2006/indi-m03.shtml>.

Kahn, Herman and Thomas Pepper. *The Japanese Challenge: The Success and Failure of Economic Success*. New York: Thomas Y. Crowell, 1979.

Kahn, Herman. *World Economic Development: 1979 and Beyond*. Boulder, Colorado: Westview, 1979.

Kang, David C. "Getting Asia Wrong: The Need for New Analytical Frameworks". *International Security* 27, no. 4 (Spring 2003): 57–85.

———. "Hierarchy and Stability in Asian International Relations". In *International Relations Theory and the Asia-Pacific*, edited by

G. John Ikenberry and Michael Mastanduno. New York: Columbia University Press, 2003.

Kao Kim Hourn and Sisowath Doung Chanto. "ASEAN-China Cooperation for Greater Mekong Sub-Region Development". In *ASEAN-China Relations, Realities and Prospects*, edited by Saw Swee-Hock, Sheng Lijun and Chin Kin Wah. Singapore: Institute of Southeast Asian Studies, 2005.

Kastner, Scott L. "Ambiguity, economic interdependence, and the U.S. strategic dilemma in the Taiwan Strait". <www.bsos.umd.edu/gvpt/kastner/Kastnerambiguity.pdf>.

Kausikan, Bilahari. "Asia's Different Standard". *Foreign Policy* 92 (Fall 1993): 24–41.

Keesing's Contemporary Archives. June 1993.

Kennedy, Paul. *The Rise and Fall of the Great Powers: Economic Change and Military Conflict from 1500 to 2000.* New York: Random House, 1987.

Kesavapany, K. *India's Tryst with Asia.* New Delhi: Asian Institute of Transport Development, 2006.

Khalilzad, Zalmay et al. *The United States and Asia: Toward a New U.S. Strategy and Force Posture.* Santa Monica, California: RAND, 2001.

Khong Yuen Foong. "Singapore: a time for economic and political engagement". In *Engaging China: The Management of an Emerging Power*, edited by Alastair Iain Johnston and Robert S. Ross. New York: Routledge, 1999.

Khoo, Nicholas and Smith, Michael L.R. "China Engages Asia? Caveat Lector". *International Security* 30, no. 1 (Summer 2005): 196–205.

Khurana, Gurpreet S. "Cooperation Among Maritime Security Forces: Imperatives for India and Southeast Asia", *Strategic Analysis* 29, no. 2 (April–June 2005):

Koh, Tommy. "The 10 Values That Undergrid East Asian Strength and Success". *International Herald Tribune,* 11 December 1993.

Korab-Karpowicz, W. Julian. *How Can International Relations Theorists Benefit from Reading Thucydides?* <www.da-vienna.ac.at/userfiles/KorabKarpowicz.pdf>.

Kristof, Nicholas D. "China Sees 'Market-Leninism' as Way to Future". *New York Times,* 6 September 1993.

Kumara, Sarath. "New Delhi presses ahead with plans for an Indian 'Suez Canal'". World Socialist Web Site, <www.wsws.org/articles/2005/dec2005/inda-d14.shtml>.

Kwok Kian-Woon et al., editors. *Our Place in Time: Exploring Heritage and Memory in Singapore*. Singapore: Singapore Heritage Society, 1999.

Latif, Asad-ul Iqbal. "India and the Emergence of Bangladesh: A Study in Diplomatic History". A thesis submitted to the University of Cambridge for the degree of Master of Philosophy in International Relations, 1988.

———. "The Security of New States, Pakistan and Singapore: A Study in Contrast and Compulsions". A thesis submitted to the University of Cambridge for the degree of Master of Letters in History, 1993.

Lawson, Stephanie. "Confucius in Singapore: Culture, Politics, and the PAP State". In *Weak and Strong States in Asia-Pacific Societies*, edited by Peter Dauvergne. St Leonards and Canberra ACT: Allen & Unwin in association with the Department of International Relations, Research School of Pacific and Asian Studies, Australian National University, 1998.

Lee Khoon Choy. "Foreign Policy". In *Socialism that Works… The Singapore Way*, edited by C.V. Devan Nair. Singapore: Federal Publications, 1976.

Lee Kuan Yew on China and Hongkong after Tiananmen, edited by Lianhe Zaobao. Singapore: Shing Lee Publishers, 1990.

Lee Kuan Yew. "Managing Globalization: Lessons from China and India". Keynote Speech at the official opening of the Lee Kuan Yew School of Public Policy, 4 April 2005 at Shangri-la Hotel.

———. "Developing a global guanxi". *Speeches* 17, no. 6, 1993.

———. "Peace and Progress in East Asia". Speech to a Joint Meeting of the United States Congress in Washington, D.C., on 9 October 1985. In *Speeches: A Bimonthly Selection of Ministerial Speeches*, September–October '85, vol. 9, no. 5.

———. *From Third World to First: The Singapore Story, 1965–2000*. Singapore: Singapore Press Holdings and Times Editions, 2000.

———. Speech at the ceremony to mark the achievements of the Suzhou Industrial Park's 10th anniversary, Suzhou, 10 June 2004. <stars.nhb.gov.sg/data/pdfdoc/2004061102.htm>.

Lee Lai To. *China and the South China Sea Dialogues*. Westport and London: Praeger, 1999.

———. "The Lion and the Dragon: A View on Singapore-China Relations". *Journal of Contemporary China* 10, no. 28 (August 2001): 415–25.

————. *China's Changing Attitude Towards Singapore, 1965–1975.* Singapore: University of Singapore, Department of Political Science, November 1975.

Leifer, Michael. "China in Southeast Asia: Interdependence and Accommodation". In *China Rising: Nationalism and Interdependence*, edited by David S.G. Goodman and Gerald Segal. London and New York: Routledge, 1996.

————. *Singapore's Foreign Policy: Coping with Vulnerability.* London: Routledge, 2000.

————. "Truth about the Balance of Power". In *Michael Leifer: Selected Works on Southeast Asia*, compiled and edited by Chin Kin Wah and Leo Suryadinata. Singapore: Institute of Southeast Asian Studies, 2005.

Lele, Amod. "State Hindutva and Singapore Confucianism as Responses to the Decline of the Welfare State". *Asian Studies Review* 28 (September 2004): 267–82.

Leys, Simon. Foreword to the translation of *The Analects of Confucius.* New York: W.W. Norton, 1997.

Lim, Y.C. Linda. "The Foreign Policy of Singapore". In *The Political Economy of Foreign Policy in Southeast Asia*, edited by David Wurfel and Bruce Burton. Houndmills and London: Macmillan, 1990.

Limaye, Satu P. "2004: A Year of Living Actively". *Comparative Connections*, Pacific Forum CSIS, <www.csis.org/pacfor/cc/0404Qoa.html>.

Lin Liang Guang. "India's Role In South Asia: A Chinese Perspective". In *India's Role in South Asia*, edited by Vernon L.B. Mendis. Colombo: Bandaranaike Centre for International Studies, 1992.

Liu, Dana M. *The China-Singapore Suzhou Industrial Park: Singapore's Role in China's Development.* Baltimore: The Johns Hopkins University, The Paul H. Nitze School of Advanced International Studies, no date.

Long, Joey. "The Pentagon's Strategy Toward Southeast Asia: Bolstering the States along the Seams". Singapore: Institute of Defence and Strategic Studies. *IDSS Commentaries*, 12/2005, 16 March 2005. <www.ntu.edu.sg/idss/publications/Perspective/IDSS122005.pdf>.

Lydon, Christopher. "My Singapore Sling". *Transom Review* 2, no. 5 (June 2002):

Lynn-Jones, Sean M. "Why the United States Should Spread

Democracy". International Security Programme, Belfer Centre for Science and International Affairs, John F. Kennedy School of Government, March 1998, <www.ciaonet.org/wps/ lys02/>.

Maddison, Angus. *The World Economy: A Millennial Perspective.* Paris: Development Centre of the Organisation for Economic Co-operation and Development, 2001.

Mahbubani, Kishore. "The West and the Rest". *The National Interest* 28 (Summer 1992). Reprinted in Kishore Mahbubani, *Can Asians Think?* Singapore and Kuala Lumpur: Times Books International, 1998.

——. "Understanding China". *Foreign Affairs* 84, no. 5 (September/October 2005): 49–60.

Majumdar, R.C. *India and South East Asia*, edited by K.S. Ramachandran and S.P. Gupta. Delhi: B.R. Publishing Corporation, 1979.

Malik, Mohan. "The East Asia Summit: More Discord than Accord". *YaleGlobal*, 20 December 2005, <http://yaleglobal.yale.edu/ article.print?id=6645>.

Mehta, Pratap Bhanu. "Nuclear Pact Launches India Into Uncharted Waters". *YaleGlobal*, 7 March 2006, <yaleglobal. yale.edu/display.article?id=7085>.

Mendes, Errol P. *Asian Values and Human Rights: Letting the Tigers Free.* Human Rights Research and Education Centre, University of Ottawa, 1996. <www.cdp-hrc.uottawa.ca/publicat/ asian_values.html>.

Miksic, John. "Between Two Mandalas: Singapore, Siam, and Java". The Benjamin Batson Memorial Lecture 2005, Asia Research Institute, Working Paper Series No. 51, September 2005.

Ministry of Foreign Affairs, Singapore. *From Phnom Penh to Kabul.* Singapore: Ministry of Foreign Affairs, September 1980.

——. "Questions and Answers with DPM Lee Hsien Loong on his visit to Taiwan", 19 July 2004. <app.mfa.gov.sg/internet/ press/view_press.asp?post_id=1098>.

Morris, Stephen J. *Why Vietnam Invaded Cambodia: Political Culture and the Causes of War.* Stanford: Stanford University Press, 1999.

Mukherjee, Pranab. Address at the Carnegie Endowment for International Peace, Washington D.C., on India's strategic perspectives, 27 June 2005. <www.carnegieendowment.org/ files/Mukherjee_Speech_06-27-051.pdf>.

Murthy, R.V.R. "India's Security Concerns in the Bay of Bengal:

With special reference to A&N Islands". *Dialogue* 7, no. 1 (July–September 2005). <http://www.asthabharati.org/ Dia_July05/murthy%20.htm>.

Myrdal, Gunnar. *The Asian Drama: An Inquiry into the Poverty of Nations*. New York: Twentieth Century Fund, 1968.

Nathan, Andrew J. and Perry Link, eds. *The Tiananmen Papers*, compiled by Zhang Liang. New York: Public Affairs, 2001.

Nayar, Baldev Raj and T.V. Paul. *India in the World Order: Searching for Major-Power Status*. Cambridge: Cambridge University Press, 2003.

Neier, Aryeh. "Asia's Unacceptable Standard". *Foreign Policy* 92 (Fall 1993): 42–51.

Nguyen-vo, Thu-huong. *Khmer-Viet Relations and the Third Indochina Conflict*. Jefferson, North Carolina, and London: McFarland & Company, 1992.

Niazi, Tarique. "Gwadar: China's Naval Outpost on the Indian Ocean". *China Brief*. The Jamestown Foundation, 28 February 2005. <www.asianresearch.org/articles/2528.html>.

———. "Sino-Indian Rivalry". *China Brief*, 16 February 2006, <www.ocnus.net/artman/publish/article_22760.shtml#top>.

Nixon, Richard. *Beyond Peace*. New York: Random House, 1994.

Ong, Timothy. "No slowing down". *AsiaInc*, November 2004. <www.asia-inc.com/November04/QA_nov.htm>.

Onwimon, Somkiat. "India's Relations with the ASEAN Countries, 1966–1975: A Transaction Analysis". A dissertation presented to the Graduate Faculties of the University of Pennsylvania in partial fulfillment of the requirements for the degree of Doctor of Philosophy, 1981.

Panikkar, K.M. *India and the Indian Ocean: An Essay on the Influence of Sea Power on Indian History*. Second edition, 1961, first Indian reprint, 1971. Bombay: George Allen & Unwin (India).

Papayoanou, Paul A. and Scott L. Kastner. *Assessing the Policy of Engagement with China*. San Diego: University of California, Institute on Global Conflict and Cooperation. Policy paper 40, July 1998.

Pardesi, Manjeet S. "Deepening Singapore-India Strategic Ties". Singapore: Institute of Defence and Strategic Studies, *IDSS Commentaries*, 13/2005, 22 March 2005. <www.ntu.edu.sg/ IDSS/publications/Perspective/IDSS132005.pdf>.

Pardesi, Manjeet Singh. "Deducing India's Grand Strategy of Regional Hegemony from Historical and Conceptual Perspectives". Institute of Defence and Strategic Studies, Singapore, Working Paper No. 76, April 2005.

Patra, Benudhar. "Kalinga in South East Asia". *Orissa Reference Annual 2004.*

Patten, Chris. *East and West.* London and Basingstoke: Macmillan, 1998.

Paul, Eric Charles. "The Viability of Singapore: An Aspect of Modern Political Geography". Unpublished Ph.D. dissertation submitted to the University of California. Berkeley, 1973.

Pepper, Suzanne. "Hong Kong on the Eve of Reunification with China". In *China Briefing: The Contradictions of Change*, edited by William A. Joseph. Armonk, New York, and London, England: M.E. Sharpe, published in cooperation with the Asia Society, 1997.

Pereira, Alexius A. *State Collaboration and Development Strategies in China: The Case of the China-Singapore Suzhou Industrial Park (1992–2002).* London and New York: RoutledgeCurzon, 2003.

Pereira, Derwin. "China Rising: Conflict or Cooperation with the United States?". Research Paper for the Master in Public Administration, Harvard University, 2006.

———. "Congress, the Presidency and US-China policy: A comparison of the Bush and Clinton Presidencies". Research Paper for the Master in Public Administration, Harvard University, 2006.

Rahman, Chris. "Defending Taiwan, and why it matters". *Naval War College Review* LIV, no. 4 (Autumn 2001): 69–93.

Raja Mohan, C. "A foreign policy for Kolkata". *The Indian Express*, 23 August 2005.

———. *Crossing the Rubicon: The Shaping of India's New Foreign Policy.* New Delhi: Penguin Books, 2005.

Rajamony, Venu. "India-China-U.S. Triangle: A 'Soft' Balance of Power System in the Making". Washington: Centre for Strategic and International Studies, March 2002. <www.csis.org/saprog/venu.pdf>.

Rasheed, Zainul Abidin. Singapore Minister of State for Foreign Affairs. Speech at the opening of the Second Japan-ASEAN

Security Symposium, Shangri-La Hotel, 27 October 2004, <www.mfa.gov.sg/internet>.

Raza Hasan, Shehla . "The paradox of eastern South Asia". *Asia Times*, 19 March 2003, <www.atimes.com/atimes/South_Asia/EC19Df02.html>.

Rebuilding America's Defences: Strategy, Forces and Resources for a New Century. A Report of the Project for the New American Century, September 2000, <www.newamericancentury.org/publicationsreports.htm>.

Regnier, Philippe. *Singapore: City-State in South-East Asia*. London and Honolulu: C. Hurst & Company and University of Hawaii Press, 1991.

Republic of Singapore Parliamentary Debates: Official Report. Vol. 24, 16 December 1965, cols. 257-8.

Rosecrance, Richard. *The Rise of the Trading State: Commerce and Conquest in the Modern World*. New York: BasicBooks, 1986.

Ross, Robert S. "The Geography of the Peace: East Asia in the Twenty-first Century". In *The Rise of China: an International Security* Reader, edited by Michael E. Brown et al. Cambridge, Massachusetts, and London, England: The MIT Press, 2000.

———. "A Realist Policy for Managing US-China Competition". Muscatine, Iowa: The Stanley Foundation. Policy Analysis Brief, November 2005.

Roy, Arundhati. "The Loneliness of Noam Chomsky". *The Hindu*, 24 August 2003.

Roy, Denny. "Singapore, China, and the 'Soft Authoritarian' Challenge". *Asian Survey* 34, no. 3 (March 1994): 231–43.

Saywell, Trish. " 'Places not bases' puts Singapore on the line". *Far Eastern Economic Review*, 17 May 2001.

Schaffer, Teresita C. and Mitra, Pramit. "India as a global power?" *Deutsche Bank Research*, 16 December 2005.

Schell, Orville. *Mandate of Heaven: A New Generation of Entrepreneurs, Dissidents, Bohemians, and Technocrats Lays Claim to China's Future*. New York: Simon & Schuster, 1994.

Schier, Peter. "The Indochina Conflict from the Perspective of Singapore". *Contemporary Southeast Asia* 4, no. 2 (September 1982): 226–35.

Schwartzberg, Joseph E. *A Historical Atlas of South Asia*. Second imprint. Oxford: Oxford University Press, 1992.

Schweller, Randall L. "Managing the Rise of Great Powers: History and Theory". In *Engaging China: The Management of an Emerging Power*, edited by Alastair Iain Johnston and Robert S. Ross. New York: Routledge, 1999.

Security Implications of Conflict in the South China Sea: Exploring Potential Triggers of Conflict. A Pacific Forum CSIS Special Report prepared by Ralph A. Cossa. Honolulu, Hawaii, March 1998.

Sen, Amartya. "Culture and Human Rights". In Amartya Sen, *Development as Freedom*. New York: Anchor Books, 2000.

———. "Democracy as a Universal Value". *Journal of Democracy* 10.3 (1999): 3–17.

———. "India and the Bomb". In Amartya Sen, *The Argumentative Indian: Writings on Indian History, Culture and Identity*. London: Allen Lane, 2005.

Shambaugh, David. "China Engages Asia: Reshaping the Regional Order". *International Security* 29, no. 3 (Winter 2004/05): 64–99.

Sharma, Ravi. "A base for a blue-water navy". *Frontline* 22, issue 11, 21 May–3 June 2005, <www.hinduonnet.com/fline/fl2211/stories/20050603002809000.htm>.

Shen Baoxiang, Wang Chengquan and Li Zerui. "Human Rights in the World Arena". *Hongqi*, 8 (1982). Republished in *China & the World* (3), edited by Zhou Guo. Beijing: *Beijing Review*, Foreign Affairs Series, 1983.

Singh, Bilveer. *The Soviet Union in Singapore's Foreign Policy: An Analysis*. Kuala Lumpur: Institute of Strategic and International Studies, 1990.

———. *The Vulnerability of Small States Revisited: A Study of Singapore's Post-Cold War Foreign Policy*. Yogyakarta: Gadjah Mada University Press, 1999.

Sisson, Richard and Leo E. Rose. *War and Secession: Pakistan, India, and the Creation of Bangladesh*. Berkeley, Los Angeles and Oxford: University of California Press, 1990.

Skidmore, David and William Gates. "After Tiananmen: The Struggle Over U.S. Policy Toward China in the Bush Administration". <www.drake.edu/artsci/PolSci/personal webpage/tiananmen.html>.

Sridharan, Kripa. "Transcending the Region: Singapore's India Policy". In *Emerging Asia: Challenges for India and Singapore*, edited by N.N. Vohra. New Delhi: India International Centre and Manohar, 2003.

———. "Regional Perceptions of India". In *India and ASEAN: The Politics of India's Look East Policy*, edited by Frederic Grare and Amitabh Mattoo. New Delhi and Singapore: Manohar, Centre De Sciences Humaines, Centre for the Study of National Security Policy and the Institute of Southeast Asian Studies, 2001.

———. *The ASEAN Region in India's Foreign Policy*. Aldershot and Brookfield: Dartmouth, 1996.

———. "The Evolution and Growth of India-Singapore Relations". In *Singapore-India Relations: A Primer*, edited by Yong Mun Cheong and V.V. Bhanoji Rao. Singapore: Singapore University Press, 1995.

Steinglass, Matt. "Whose Asian Values?" *Boston Globe*, 20 November 2005.

Storey, Ian. "Singapore and the Rise of China: Perceptions and Policy". In *The China Threat: Perceptions, Myths and Reality*, edited by Herbert Yee and Ian Storey. London and New York: RoutledgeCurzon, 2004.

Stuart-Fox, Martin. "Southeast Asia and China: The Role of History and Culture in Shaping Future Relations". *Contemporary Southeast Asia* 26, no. 1 (2004): 116–39.

———. *A Short History of China and Southeast Asia: Tribute, Trade and Influence*. Crows Nest, NSW: Allen & Unwin.

Subrahmanyam, K. "Indochina — Strategic Perspectives". In *India and Indochina: Perspectives of Cooperation*, edited by T.N. Kaul. New Delhi: Patriot Publishers, on behalf of the Indian Centre for Studies on Indochina, 1987.

———. "The Aden-Singapore illusion". *The Indian Express*, 11 December 2004.

Sueo Sudo. *The International Relations of Japan and Southeast Asia*. London and New York: Routledge, 2002.

Suryaprakash, Raakhee. "Securing the Straits — Some New Moves". South Asia Analysis Group. Paper No. 1402, 3 June 2005, <www.saag.org/papers15/paper1402.html>.

Sutter, Robert G. "Seeking Integration and Deterrence — The U.S. Role in Shaping China's Future". In *China's Economic Future: Challenges to U.S. Policy*, edited by the Joint Economic Committee, Congress of the United States, Studies on Contemporary China. Armonk, New York, and London, England: M.E. Sharpe, 1997.

Talbott, Strobe. *Engaging India: Diplomacy, Democracy, and the Bomb*, revised edition. Washington: Brookings Institution Press, 2006.

Tamney, Joseph B. *The Struggle Over Singapore's Soul: Western Modernization and Asian Culture*. Berlin and New York: Walter de Gruyter, 1996.

Tan Ta Sen. "Did Zheng He Set Out to Colonize Southeast Asia?" In *Admiral Zheng He & Southeast Asia*, edited by Leo Suryadinata. Singapore: Institute of Southeast Asian Studies and International Zheng He Society, 2005.

Tan, Terence. "Admiral Zheng He 'Set out to Colonise Southeast Asia'". *Straits Times*, 11 November 2004.

Tay, Alice Erh-Soon. "'Asian Values' and the Rule of Law". Jura Gentium, Centre for Philosophy of International Law and Global Politics. <www.tsd.unifi.it/jg/en/index.htm?surveys/rol/tay.htm>.

Tay, Simon S.C. "Human Rights, Culture, and the Singapore Example". *McGill Law Journal*, 41 (1996): 743–80.

Tellis, Ashley J. *India as a New Global Power: An Action Agenda for the United States*. Washington: Carnegie Endowment for International Peace, 2005.

———. "Indo-US Relations Headed for a Grand Transformation?", *YaleGlobal Online*, 14 July 2005, <http://yaleglobal.yale.edu/article.print?id=5999>.

Teo Chu Cheow Eric. "Rising Sino-US Rivalry — A Case in Point Following the Recent Sino-Singaporean Row over Taiwan". *Taiwan Perspective e-Paper*, Issue No. 41, Institute for National Policy Research, Taipei, 30 September 2004.

The Military Power of the People's Republic of China 2005. Annual Report to Congress. Washington: Office of the Secretary of Defence.

The National Security Strategy of the United States of America. Washington: The White House, 17 September 2002. <www.whitehouse.gov/nsc/nss.pdf>.

Thompson, Mark R. "'Asian Values' as '*Zivilisationskritik*'?", <www.essex.ac.uk/ecpr/events/jointsessions/paperarchive/mannheim/w4/thompson.pdf>.

———. "Pacific Asia after 'Asian values': authoritarianism, democracy, and 'good governance'". *Third World Quarterly* 25, no. 6 (2004): 1079–95.

Tregonning, K.G. "Lee Kuan Yew and the Americans". *The Bulletin*, 25 September 1965.

Tripathi, Salil. "Innocents Abroad". *Asiaweek*, 19 January 2001.

Tyson, Ann Scott. "Ability to Wage 'Long War' Is Key To Pentagon Plan", *The Washington Post*, 4 February 2006.

United States Navy, Commander, Seventh Fleet, <www.c7f.navy.mil/Pages/region.html>.

VandeHei, Jim and Linzer, Dafna. "U.S., India Reach Deal On Nuclear Cooperation". *The Washington Post*, 3 March 2006, <www.washingtonpost.com/wp-dyn/content/article/2006/03/02/AR2006030200183_pf.html>.

Vandenborre, Alain. *The Little Door to the New World: China-Singapore-India*. Singapore: SNP Editions, 2005.

Vasil, Raj. *Asianising Singapore: The PAP's Management of Ethnicity*. Singapore: Heinemann Asia, 1995.

Vaughn, Bruce. *China-Southeast Asia Relations: Trends, Issues, and Implications for the United States*. Washington, D.C.: Congressional Research Service, The Library of Congress, 8 February 2005.

Vogel, Ezra F. *Japan as Number One: Lessons for America*. Cambridge, Massachusetts: Harvard University Press, 1979.

Wade, Geoff. "Ming China and Southeast Asia in the 15th Century: A Reappraisal". Asia Research Institute, National University of Singapore, Working Paper Series Number 28 (July 2004).

———. "The *Ming Shi-Lu* as a source for Southeast Asian History", <http://epress.nus.edu.sg/msl>.

———. "The Zheng He Voyages: A Reassessment". Asia Research Institute, Working Paper Series Number 31 (October 2004).

Wade, Robert. *Governing the Market: A Decade Later*. LSE Development Studies Institute, Working Paper Series, No. 00-03 (March 2000).

Wang Gungwu. "Ming Foreign Relations: Southeast Asia". In *China and the Chinese Overseas*. Singapore: Times Academic Press, 1991.

———. "Early Ming Relations with Southeast Asia: A Background Essay", and "China and Southeast Asia 1402–1424". In *Community and Nation: China, Southeast Asia and Australia*. St Leonards, NSW: Asian Studies Association of Australia in association with Allen & Unwin, 1992.

———. *The Chinese Way: China's Position in International Relations*.

Oslo: Scandinavian University Press, Norwegian Nobel Institute Lecture Series, 1995.

Wang Jisi. "China's Changing Role in Asia". Washington: The Atlantic Council of the United States, Asia Programs, January 2004.

———. "International Relations Theory and the Study of Chinese Foreign Policy: a Chinese Perspective". In *Chinese Foreign Policy: Theory and Practice*, edited by Thomas W. Robinson and David Shambaugh. Oxford: Clarendon Press, 1994.

Wang Mengkui (chief editor). *China's Economic Transformation Over 20 Years*. Organized and sponsored by the China (Hainan) Institute of Reform and Development. Beijing: Foreign Languages Press, 2000.

Wang Wei-cheng Vincent. "The Logic of China-ASEAN FTA: Economic Statecraft of 'Peaceful Ascendancy' ". In *China and Southeast Asia: Global Changes and Regional Challenges*, edited by Ho Khai Leong and Samuel C.Y. Ku. Singapore and Kaohsiung: Institute of Southeast Asian Studies and Center for Southeast Asian Studies, National Sun Yat-sen University, Kaohsiung, Taiwan ROC, 2005.

Weisberg, Jacob. "DOS Capitalism: Thomas Friedman embraces the forces of globalization", 18 April 1999, <www.slate.com/id/25365/>.

Wight, Martin. *International Theory: The Three Traditions*, 1996 reprint, compiled and edited by Gabriele Wight and Brian Porter. London: Leicester University Press, for the Royal Institute of International Affairs, London, 1991.

Wolf, Jr., Charles. *Asian Economic Trends and Their Security Implications*. Santa Monica: Rand Corporation, 2000), <www.rand.org/pubs/monograph_reports/MR1143/index.html>.

Wolters, O.W. *History, Culture, and Region in Southeast Asian Perspectives*. Revised edition. Ithaca, New York: Cornell University, Southeast Asia Program Publications, in cooperation with the Institute of Southeast Asian Studies, Singapore, 1999.

Wong Kan Seng. "The Real World of Human Rights". Singapore Government Press Release, 09-1/93/06/16.

Wong Lin Ken. "The Strategic Significance of Singapore". In *A History of Singapore*, edited by Ernest C.T. Chew and Edwin

Lee. Singapore, Oxford and New York: Oxford University Press, 1991.

World Bank. *The East Asian Miracle: Economic Growth and Public Policy.* Oxford: Oxford University Press, 1993.

Wu Yuan-li. *Strategic Significance of Singapore: A Study in Balance of Power.* Washington, D.C.: American Enterprise Institute for Public Policy Research, 1972.

——. *Tiananmen to Tiananmen: China Under Communism 1947–1996.* Occasional Papers/Reprint Series in Contemporary Asian Studies, Number 1 — 1997 (138). Baltimore: University of Maryland, School of Law.

Yahya, Faizal. "India and Southeast Asia: Revisited". *Contemporary Southeast Asia* 25, no. 1 (April 2003): 79–103.

Yeo, George. The World Economic Forum's India Economic Summit 2002. <www.weforum.org/site/knowledgenavigator.nsf/Content/_S7574?open&country_id=>.

——. Speech at the Economic Society of Singapore Dinner, 28 June 2004, <app.sprinter.gov.sg/data/pr/2004062804.htm>.

Yeo, Yong-Boon George. "An East Asian Renaissance". *Speeches* 16, no. 6, 1992.

——. "Promoting Chinese culture in a multi-racial Singapore". *Speeches* 16, no. 3, 1992.

Zakaria, Fareed. "Culture is Destiny; A Conversation with Lee Kuan Yew". *Foreign Affairs* (March/April 1994). <www.fareedzakaria.com/articles/other/culture.html#top>.

——. "The Rise of Illiberal Democracy". *Foreign Affairs* (November 1997), <www.fareedzakaria.com/ARTICLES/other/democracy.html>.

Zhang Biwu. "Chinese Perceptions of American Power, 1991–2004". *Asian Survey* 45, issue 5: 667–86.

Zhang Tiejun. "Chinese Strategic Culture: Traditional and Present Features". *Comparative Strategy* 21 (2002): 73–90.

Zhao Huanxin, "Historic Sino-Indian trade plan endorsed". *China Daily*, 12 April 2005.

Zheng Yongnian and Tok Sow Keat. *How China Views Singapore.* Singapore: East Asian Institute, Background Brief No. 184, 19 March 2004.

Zheng Yongnian. "Nationalism, Globalism, and China's International Relations". In Weixing Hu et al., *China's International Relations in the 21st Century: Dynamics of Paradigm*

Shifts. Lanham, New York and Oxford: University Press of America, 2000.

———. *Discovering Chinese Nationalism in China: Modernization, Identity, and International Relations*. Cambridge: Cambridge University Press, 1999.

Zora, Parwini and Niall Green. "China and India manoeuvre to secure energy supplies". World Socialist Web Site, 31 January 2006, <www.wsws.org/articles/2006/jan2006/indi-j31_prn.shtml>.

INDEX

International Zheng Ho
    Society, Singapore, 6
internationalist tradition, 26
investors
    drawn to Singapore, 88
Iran
    Chabahar port, 267
    nuclear programme, 267
Iraq, 238
    ejection from Kuwait, 213
    invasion of, 229
iron and steel
    exports to Singapore, 56
Irrawady road-river link, 265
Islam, 148

J
Janata Party, 75
Japan, 186
    dissatisfaction with current
        distribution of power,
        41
    elimination as naval power,
        262
    military cooperation with
        United States, 225
    modernization after WWII,
        140
    possibility of military
        intervention, 186
    post-war economic rise, 20
    power of, 221
Japanese Defense Agency, 225
Japanese Occupation, 19
Jemaah Islamiyah, 219
Johnston, Alastair Iain, 3, 227
Johore sultanate, 18
Joint Declaration, 116, 121, 122
    political shape of Hong
        Kong, 117

joint maritime seismic studies,
    196

K
Kampuchea Krom, 60
Kang, David C., 8
Kalinga War, 147
Kampelman, Max, 106
Kant, Immanuel, 26
Kahn, Herman, 140
Kastner, Scott L., 188, 228
Kausikan, Bilahari, 141, 142
Kazakhstan, 223
Kennedy, Paul, 129
Kesavapany, K., 277, 278
Khalilzad, Zalmay, 247
Khmer Rouge 61, 63
Khruschev, Nikita, 48
Kissinger, Henry, 15, 16, 50,
    62, 96, 263
    trip to Beijing, 58
Koh, Tommy, 139
Korean peninsula, 208
Kripa Sridharan, 77
Kulke, H., 17
Kuomintang (KMT), 183, 185
Kuwait
    ejection of Iraq, 213
Kwa Chong Guan, 18
Kyrgyzstan, 223

L
Laos
    installation of Vietnamese
        client regimes in, 60
Lang Son, 64
Le Duc Tho, 62
Lee Hsien Loong, 32, 174, 189
    visit to Taiwan, 1
Lee Koon Choy, 32